SENSORDEVICES 2016

The Seventh International Conference on Sensor Device Technologies and Applications

July 24 - 28, 2016

Nice, France

SENSORDEVICES 2016 Editors

Sergey Yurish, IFSA, Spain

Winfried Vonau, Kurt-Schwabe-Institut, Germany

Irinela Chilibon, National Institute of Research and Development for Optoelectronics - Bucharest, Romania

Printed from e-media with permission by:

Curran Associates, Inc.
57 Morehouse Lane
Red Hook, NY 12571

CURRAN ASSOCIATES INC.
proceedings
.com

Some format issues inherent in the e-media version may also appear in this print version.

Printed by Curran Associates, Inc. (2016)

International Academy, Research, and Industry Association (IARIA)
412 Derby Way
Wilmington, DE 19810

Phone: (408) 893-6407
Fax: (408) 527-6351

petre@iaria.org

Additional copies of this publication are available from:

Curran Associates, Inc.
57 Morehouse Lane
Red Hook, NY 12571 USA
Phone: 845-758-0400
Fax: 845-758-2633
Email: curran@proceedings.com
Web: www.proceedings.com

Table of Contents

Colorimetric Sensor Array based on Ink-jet Printing Method for Gas Detection System 1
Jeong Ho An, Dami Kim, Sanghyo Kim, Do Young Lee, and Inkyun Jeon

Identification and Discrimination of Herbicide Residues Using a Conducting Polymer Electronic Nose 4
Alphus Dan Wilson

Mobile Sensor System for Alcohol Control and Numerical Signal Analysis 10
Rolf Seifert, Hubert Keller, Thorsten Conrad, and Jens Peter

Surface Acoustic Wave Sensors for Fine Particle Detection 15
Lyes Djoumi, Virginie Blondeau-Patissier, Meddy Vanotti, Etienne Quivet, and Daphne Buiron

Gasoline Sensor Based on Piezoelectric Lateral Electric Field Resonator 17
Boris Zaitsev, Andrey Teplykh, Irina Borodina, and Iren Kuznetsova

Coating Process for MEMS Based 3-axis Force Sensors 22
Andres Felipe Ospina Trivino, Saifeddine Aloui, Mathieu Grossard, and Alain Micaelli

Influence of Structure Configuration on Strained Devices: A Piezoelectric-oriented Survey 29
Irinela Chilibon

PLD as Possible Tool for the Fabrication of Chemosensors Based on Amorphous Membranes 35
Winfried Vonau, Frank Gerlach, and Kristina Ahlborn

Capillary Sensor with Fluorescence Reading of Effects of Diesel and Biodiesel Fuel Degradation in Storage 41
Michal Borecki, Michael L. Korwin-Pawlowski, Mateusz Geca, and Przemyslaw Prus

Development of Methanol Sensors: Carbon Nanotubes Blended Hydroxyapatite Nano-Ceramics 48
Shaikh Reshma Anjum and Rajendra Khairnar

Development of a Mechanical Sleeve Diagnosis Test 53
Andre Borges and Vitor Carvalho

Measurement of Water in Oil for Active Bearing Performance Monitoring Using Optical Fiber Sensor System 59
Florin Tatar, Elfed Lewis, and Gerard Dooly

SAW Based Phononic Crystal Liquid Sensor with Integrated Periodic Microfluidic Channels 63
Aleksandr Oseev, Ralf Lucklum, Mikhail Zubtsov, Marc-Peter Schmidt, and Soeren Hirsch

High Speed Magneto–Optical Sensor for Magnetic Stripe Readout 68

Johannes Egger and Bernhard Zagar

Progress in Design and Fabrication of Resonator Quantum Well Infrared Photodetectors (R-QWIP) 72
Jason Sun, Kwong K Choi, Kimberley Olver, and Richard Fu

A Device for Self-monitoring Breath Analysis 77
Danila Germanese, Marco Righi, Massimo Guidi, Massimo Magrini, Mario D'Acunto, and Ovidio Salvetti

SAT406M. Physiological Status Determination of a Wrist-Worn Personal Locator Beacon User: Preliminary Results 83
Alejandro de Miquel, Pere Molina, Ismael Colomina, Marta Blazquez, Daniel Katz, Ohad Barak, Michel Monnerat, and Thibaud Calmettes

Rehabilitation Robot Based on Three-axis Force/Torque Sensor 88
Gab-Soon Kim, Han-Sol Kim, and Jae-Hyun Jung

White Light Interferometry: Correlogram Correlation for Surface Height Gauging 91
Ilia Kiselev and Michael Drexel

Crude Oil Detection using CMOS Image Sensor and UV LED 95
Sangwoo Oh, Moonjin Lee, Dongmin Seo, Kiyoung Ann, and Sungkyu Seo

Response Time Investigation Based on GaAs Position Sensitive Detector 97
Tzu-Hsuan Huang, Meng-Chi Wu, Chieh Lo, Hao Lo, and Wen-Shiung Lour

SENSORDEVICES 2016

Forward

The Seventh International Conference on Sensor Device Technologies and Applications (SENSORDEVICES 2016), held between July 24-28, 2016 in Nice, France, continued a series of events focusing on sensor devices themselves, the technology-capturing style of sensors, special technologies, signal control and interfaces, and, particularly, sensors-oriented applications.

Most of the sensor-oriented research and industry initiatives are focusing on sensor networks, data security, exchange protocols, energy optimization, and features related to intermittent connections. Recently, the concept of Internet-of-things gathers attention, especially when integrating IPv4 and IIPv6 networks.

We welcomed technical papers presenting research and practical results, position papers addressing the pros and cons of specific proposals, such as those being discussed in the standard fora or in industry consortia, survey papers addressing the key problems and solutions on any of the above topics short papers on work in progress, and panel proposals.

The conference had the following tracks:

- Gas sensors
- Ultrasonic and piezosensors
- Sensor devices
- Medical devices and sensors applications
- Sensor device technologies

We take here the opportunity to warmly thank all the members of the SENSORDEVICES 2016 technical program committee, as well as all the reviewers. The creation of such a high quality conference program would not have been possible without their involvement. We also kindly thank all the authors that dedicated much of their time and effort to contribute to SENSORDEVICES 2016. We truly believe that, thanks to all these efforts, the final conference program consisted of top quality contributions.

Also, this event could not have been a reality without the support of many individuals, organizations and sponsors. We also gratefully thank the members of the SENSORDEVICES 2016 organizing committee for their help in handling the logistics and for their work that made this professional meeting a success.

We hope SENSORDEVICES 2016 was a successful international forum for the exchange of ideas and results between academia and industry and to promote further progress related to sensor devices themselves as well as their applications. We also hope that Nice, France provided a pleasant environment during the conference and everyone saved some time enjoy the beautiful French Riviera.

SENSORDEVICES 2016 Advisory Committee

Sergey Y. Yurish, International Frequency Sensor Association (IFSA), Spain
Petre Dini, Concordia University, Canada / China Space Agency Center, China
Elena Gaura, Coventry University, UK
Vittorio Ferrari, Università di Brescia, Italy

SENSORDEVICES 2016 Research/Industry Chairs

Raluca - Ioana Stefan-van Staden, National Institute of Research for Electrochemistry and Condensed Matter, Bucharest, Romania
Alberto Yúfera, Centro Nacional de Microelectronica (CNM-CSIC) - Sevilla, Spain

SENSORDEVICES Special Area Chairs

Ultrasonic and piezoelectric sensors
Thomas Herzog, Fraunhofer Institute for Non-Destructive Testing IZFP - Dresden, Germany
Henning Heuer, Fraunhofer Institute for Non-Destructive Testing IZFP - Dresden, Germany
Optical sensors
Vítor Carvalho, IPCA / Minho University-Algoritmi R&D, Portugal
Irinela Chilibon, National Institute of Research and Development for Optoelectronics - Bucharest, Romania
Testing and validation
Ksenia V. Sapozshnikova D.I. Mendeleyev Institute for Metrology - St. Petersburg, Russia
Vibration sensors
Subodh Kumar Singhal, National Physical Laboratory, New Delhi, India

SENSORDEVICES 2016

Committee

SENSORDEVICES Advisory Committee

Sergey Y. Yurish, International Frequency Sensor Association (IFSA), Spain
Petre Dini, Concordia University, Canada / China Space Agency Center, China
Elena Gaura, Coventry University, UK
Vittorio Ferrari, Università di Brescia, Italy

SENSORDEVICES 2016 Research/Industry Chairs

Raluca - Ioana Stefan-van Staden, National Institute of Research for Electrochemistry and Condensed Matter, Bucharest, Romania
Alberto Yúfera, Centro Nacional de Microelectronica (CNM-CSIC) - Sevilla, Spain

SENSORDEVICES Special Area Chairs

Ultrasonic and piezoelectric sensors
Thomas Herzog, Fraunhofer Institute for Non-Destructive Testing IZFP - Dresden, Germany
Henning Heuer, Fraunhofer Institute for Non-Destructive Testing IZFP - Dresden, Germany

Optical sensors
Vítor Carvalho, IPCA / Minho University-Algoritmi R&D, Portugal
Irinela Chilibon, National Institute of Research and Development for Optoelectronics - Bucharest, Romania

Nanosensors
TBA

Testing and validation
Ksenia V. Sapozshnikova D.I. Mendeleyev Institute for Metrology - St. Petersburg, Russia

Vibration sensors
Subodh Kumar Singhal, National Physical Laboratory, New Delhi, India

SENSORDEVICES 2016 Technical Program Committee

Iyad Abuhadrous, Palestine Technical College, Palestine
Jesús B. Alonso Hernández, University of Las Palmas de Gran Canaria, Spain
Farid Amirouche, University of Illinois at Chicago, USA
Fabrice Andrieux, Lancaster University, UK
Ammar Aryan, Université de Caen Basse-Normandie, France

Copyright Information

For your reference, this is the text governing the copyright release for material published by IARIA.

The copyright release is a transfer of publication rights, which allows IARIA and its partners to drive the dissemination of the published material. This allows IARIA to give articles increased visibility via distribution, inclusion in libraries, and arrangements for submission to indexes.

I, the undersigned, declare that the article is original, and that I represent the authors of this article in the copyright release matters. If this work has been done as work-for-hire, I have obtained all necessary clearances to execute a copyright release. I hereby irrevocably transfer exclusive copyright for this material to IARIA. I give IARIA permission or reproduce the work in any media format such as, but not limited to, print, digital, or electronic. I give IARIA permission to distribute the materials without restriction to any institutions or individuals. I give IARIA permission to submit the work for inclusion in article repositories as IARIA sees fit.

I, the undersigned, declare that to the best of my knowledge, the article is does not contain libelous or otherwise unlawful contents or invading the right of privacy or infringing on a proprietary right.

Following the copyright release, any circulated version of the article must bear the copyright notice and any header and footer information that IARIA applies to the published article.

IARIA grants royalty-free permission to the authors to disseminate the work, under the above provisions, for any academic, commercial, or industrial use. IARIA grants royalty-free permission to any individuals or institutions to make the article available electronically, online, or in print.

IARIA acknowledges that rights to any algorithm, process, procedure, apparatus, or articles of manufacture remain with the authors and their employers.

I, the undersigned, understand that IARIA will not be liable, in contract, tort (including, without limitation, negligence), pre-contract or other representations (other than fraudulent misrepresentations) or otherwise in connection with the publication of my work.

Exception to the above is made for work-for-hire performed while employed by the government. In that case, copyright to the material remains with the said government. The rightful owners (authors and government entity) grant unlimited and unrestricted permission to IARIA, IARIA's contractors, and IARIA's partners to further distribute the work.

Colorimetric Sensor Array based on Ink-jet Printing Method for Gas Detection System

Jeong Ho An
Department of Polymer Science & Engineering
Sungkyunkwan University
Suwon-Si, Republic of Korea
jhahn1us@skku.edu

Dami Kim and Sanghyo Kim
Department of Bionanotechnology
Gachon University
Seongnam-Si, Republic of Korea
rlaeka41@gmail.com and samkim@gachon.ac.kr

Do Young Lee and Inkyun Jeon
Optolane Inc.,
Seongnam-Si, Republic of Korea
doyoung@optolane.com and andyjeon@optolane.com

Abstract—**Hazardous gas detection is one of the important issues in the industry dealing with the toxic chemicals. The colorimetric sensor array has been developed for detection of the Toxic Industrial Chemicals (TICs). This study describes a colorimetric sensor array by using printing method and Complementary Metal Oxide Semiconductor (CMOS) image sensor for highly sensitive gas detection system. The sensor array is produced by the piezo inkjet-printer in order to achieve array uniformity, cost efficiency and ability to adjust the array thickness. The initial colors of sensor array are changed by chemical gases within 10 seconds of exposure to Time Weighted Average (TWA) concentration. Detection of the color change was performed before and after a gas exposure. This printing method of sensor array demonstrates the potential for sensing application of sensitivity, rapidity and it is a simple method to use.**

Keywords - *Hazardous Gas sensing, Inkjet printing, CMOS Image sensor, Colorimetric sensor.*

I. INTRODUCTION

Gas detection system is the most important one in industries and recently colorimetric array of gas detection is identified as the dominant method of application. Usually, chemical and pH indicators are applied to configure the array. But the array composed of a variety of dyes in a tool can selectively determine the hazardous gas. A colorimetric method of detecting a hazardous gas by color change has the advantage of low cost, simplicity and can be made as a portable device [1]. The printing method of making array is an effective way to create the array spot on gas detection chip and to create an accurately depositing spot with a small amount of dye on the surface of a wide range of substrate. Piezo inkjet technology is a versatile tool for various fabrication processes of the substrate [2] and has advantages of no risk of substrate damage, low cost and ease for parallel mass production. Furthermore, printing method can take place as an alternative method to the application of analytical chemistry, biological sample array and the various fabrication areas. Chip array is analyzed by the CMOS image sensor and various chemical indicators for specific detection of toxic gases are used to make the sensor array. That array shows the colors that composed of red, green and blue (RGB) and the CMOS image sensor can absorb RGB value. The RGB value can be converted to various color spaces that allow for quantification of color change of the gas concentration on the linear relationship of the component consisting of various color spaces. The hazardous gas detection system for performing chip fabrication with printing method, detection using CMOS image sensor and analysis can provide great application for gas sensors in the industry.

II. EXPERIMENTAL

A. *Inkjet-printed sensor arrays*

An Epson Stylus T10 is used as an inkjet printer. All array spots are fabricated by printing method on the polyethylene terephthalate (PET) film with four types of chemicals or pH indicator dyes which are Methyl Red (MR), Nitrazine Yellow (NY), Bromo Phenol Blue (BPB), and Bromo Cresol Green (BCG). Printing of dyes prepared to use water and ethanol based solvent for inkjet-print. Dissolved dyes were filtered by syringe filter with 0.1 ㎛ pore size of PVDF membrane. Each array is printed as spots of 2.4mm diameter with 800nm thickness and then dried at room temperature for 3 days to make them stable of initial color of the array.

B. *CMOS image sensor*

A CMOS image sensor is a device that can absorb photons which constitute a color or image. CMOS image sensor converts the color to a digital value of RGB by using analog to digital converter (ADC). The experiment was carried out using CMOS image sensor that contains 376 x

314 pixel array of 10 bit ADC [3]. Color detection based on the CMOS image sensor was performed before and after gas exposure. The overall test scheme is shown in Fig. 1.

C. *Gas exposure test*

Hydrochloric acid and ammonia gas were used in this experiment and the standard of exposure limits is given as the TWA concentration of each gas. TWA concentration of hydrochloric acid was 5ppm and that of ammonia was 20ppm. The gas concentrations of the exposure test were allowable to the level of TWA. Each of the gases used in this study was prepared in 1 liter hermetic chamber and vaporized from liquid phase of chemical at 60°C. After complete vaporization, a gas was exposed to the array chips for 10 seconds.

D. *Data processing and converting of color space*

The color value of RGB was measured by CMOS image sensor after the exposure and compared with the initial color. The average color value of 120 pixels in the center of a 2.4mm spot is converted into a digital RGB value. RGB value is directly converted using CIELAB-CIEXYZ conversions which allow all components of that color space to have full 8-bit range of RGB.

III. Result

The sensor arrays produced by printing method were exposed to ammonia and hydrochloric acid gases at three different concentrations (ammonia; 5ppm, 10ppm, and 20ppm, hydrochloric acid; 1.25ppm, 2.5ppm, and 5ppm). The color changes of an array under hydrochloric acid show a significant change in MR and NY spots whereas BPB and BCG spots are more sensitive to ammonia gas as shown in Fig 2. The color changes were detected using CMOS image sensor after gas exposure and RGB value were directly converted to the CIE-Lab color space to calculate the color differentiation value, as shown in Fig. 3. The color differentiation values depend on the concentration of each gas. Fig. 4 shows the luminance values of BCG and BPB. Luminance values are gradually reduced as the concentration of ammonia gas increases. This suggests that it is possible to quantify the gas concentration based on the color change comparison. The uniform spot array of chemical indicator is manageable by using printing method. It is possible to quantify a gas concentration by optimizing dye array state, including uniformity, a suitable concentration condition, and the thickness.

IV. Conclusion

Various industries, factories, and laboratories are amongst the major places requiring the use of toxic gases that may lead to serious problems if released, and can be dangerous to human life. We have carried out a series of trials to standardize the colorimetric toxic gas detection system. In addition, further studies are underway regarding the use of the same technology to detect 10 toxic gases and to test the detection system under various conditions. We believe that the toxic gas detection system will be a suitable and sensitive device.

Acknowledgment

This research was supported by the R&D Program for Society of the National Research Foundation (NRF) funded by the Ministry of Science, ICT & Future Planning (2013M3C8A3078806 and 2015M3A9E2031372).

References

[1] Abe K, Suzuki K, Citterio D., Inkjet-printed microfluidic multianalyte chemical sensing paper, *Anal. Chem. 13*, 80(Aug. 2008)

[2] Soga T, Jimbo Y, Suzuki K, Citterio D,. Inkjet-printed paper-based colorimetric sensor array for the discrimination of volatile primary amines. *Anal. Chem. 17*, 85(Sep. 2013)

[3] Devadhasan JP, Shao M, Kim S., CMOS Image Sensor for Rapid Chemical Detection. *JOLST* **2**, 1(June 2014).

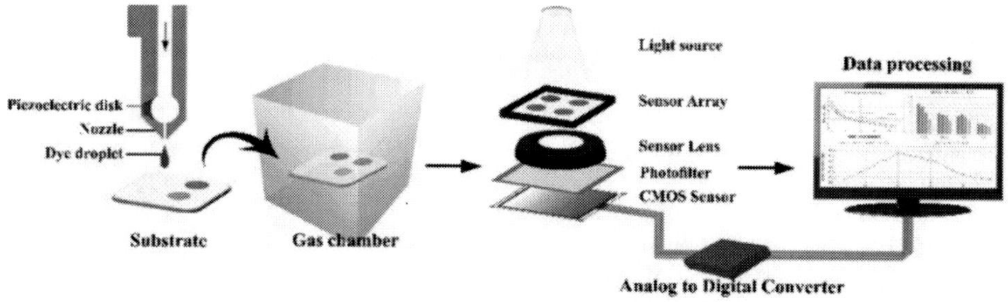

Figure 1. Gas detection system based on the piezo inkjet printing method.

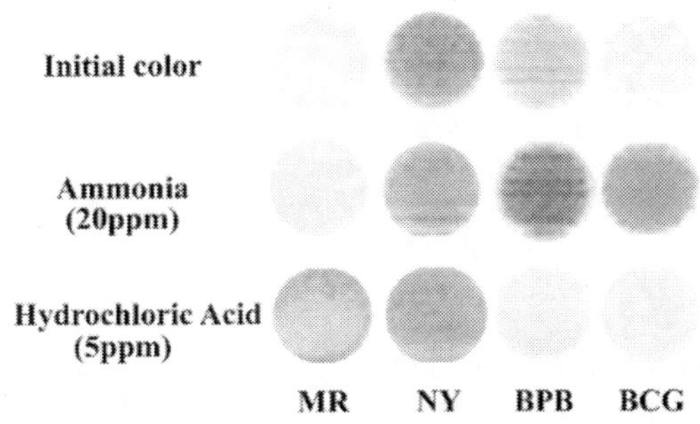

Figure 2. The colorimetric sensor array and color difference of dyes.

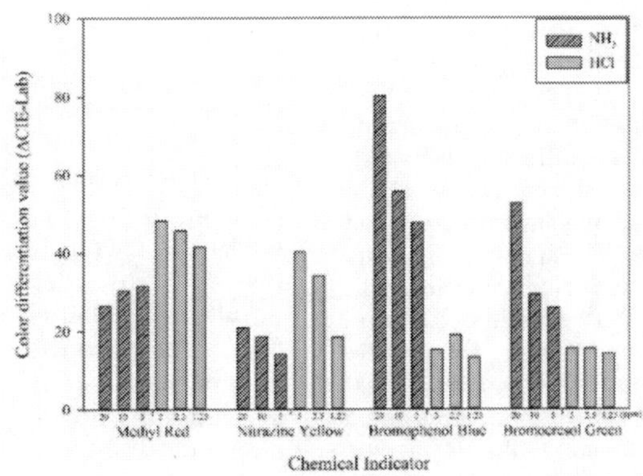

Figure 3. Color differentiation value of CIE-Lab color space.

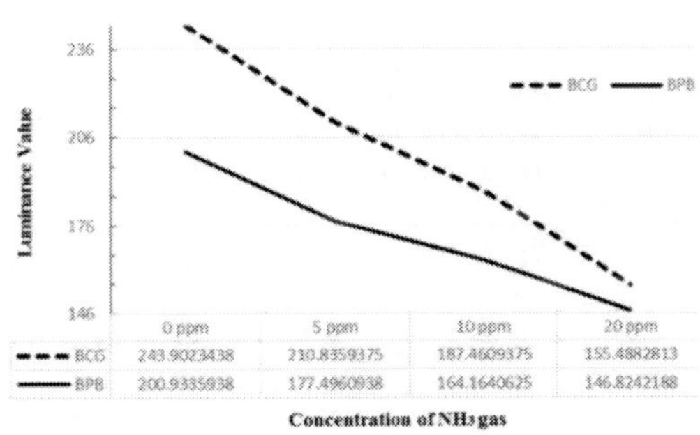

Figure 4. Luminance value gradient of BCG and BPB at ammonia gas.

Identification and Discrimination of Herbicide Residues Using a Conducting Polymer Electronic nose

Alphus Dan Wilson
Forest Insect and Disease Research
USDA Forest Service, Southern Hardwoods Laboratory
Stoneville, MS, USA
e-mail: dwilson02@fs.fed.us

***Abstract*— The identification of herbicide residues on crop foliage is necessary to make crop-management decisions for weed pest control and to monitor pesticide residue levels on food crops. Electronic-nose (e-nose) methods were tested as a cheaper, alternative means of discriminating between herbicide residue types (compared with conventional chromatography methods), by detection of headspace volatiles released from inert surfaces. Detection methods were developed for a conducting polymer (CP)-type electronic nose device, the Aromascan A32S, to identify and discriminate among eight herbicide types from five different herbicide organic chemical classes including: chlorophenoxy acids, cyclohexenones, dinitroanilines, organoarsenics, and phosphonoglycines. A herbicide-specific aroma signature library was developed from known herbicide residues. The A32S e-nose effectively distinguished between eight different herbicide residues, correctly identifying them at frequencies ranging from 81-98%. The distribution of aroma class components, based on artificial neural net (ANN) training and analysis, indicated the percentage membership of aroma classes shared by herbicide types. Principal component analysis (PCA) provided indications of the relatedness of herbicide types based on sensor array response patterns (aroma profiles) of individual herbicides. PCA generated precise statistical values (quality factors of significance) as numerical indications of chemical relatedness between herbicides based on pairwise comparisons of headspace volatiles from individual herbicide types. The potential applications, advantages and disadvantages of e-nose methods (compared to current chromatographic methods) for the detection and identification of herbicide residues on crop surfaces in agronomic fields are discussed.**

Keywords- artifician olfaction; electronic aroma detection; e-nose; pesticide residue detection; volatile organic compounds.

I. INTRODUCTION

The presence of pesticide residues on food crops is a major health concern especially on fresh fruits and leafy vegetables. Environmental regulations specify pesticide residue levels that are allowed on food products in commercial markets. Consequently, there is a strong need to determine pre-harvest and postharvest pesticide residue levels on the surfaces of plant products using rapid chemical-detection methods to effectively monitor and enforce pesticide residue regulatory requirements for plant products prior to fresh food introductions into commercial markets.

Electronic chemical-detection methods are well suited for rapid detections of pesticide residue levels needed for making pesticide-management decisions and for monitoring pesticide levels on food crops and produce [1]. Portable electronic-nose (e-nose) devices are useful for these applications due to rapid detections, high reproducibility, accurate determinations, and high sensitivity to volatile organic compounds (VOCs), such as commercial pesticides. E-nose sensors produce unique electronic signature patterns in response to VOCs released from chemical sources [2]-[4]. Electronic noses, unlike other analytical instruments, are capable of identifying VOCs without having to identify individual chemical compounds present in volatile mixtures [5]-[7]. Many different types of e-nose sensors have been developed including optical sensors [8], metal oxides [9] [10], semi-conducting polymers [11]-[13], and conducting polymers [14]-[16] for different applications. The broad agricultural and food industries have utilized electronic aroma detection (EAD) technologies to evaluate food quality and freshness [17]-[21], detect industrial wastes [22][23], diagnose plant diseases [24], and many other applications [25][26], including the detection of environmentally hazardous agricultural chemicals [27]-[29].

The Aromascan A32S e-nose, selected for efficacy testing in this pilot study, currently is commercially available only for specialized applications following a recent instrument redesign after the current study was completed. This instrument contains 32 conducting polymer (CP) sensors in the sensor array that respond to changes in electrical resistance (ER) when pesticide molecules adsorb to the surface of each sensor. The resulting combined-sensor output from the sensor array generates a unique aroma signature pattern that is specific to the gaseous volatile organic compounds (VOCs) present in the headspace above the sample analyte. Alternative e-nose technologies, such as carbon nanofiber (CN) and metal oxide semiconductor (MOS) types, also operate by measuring ER, but other e-nose types such as quartz crystal microbalance (QCM) and surface acoustic wave (SAW) operate by measuring mass changes or frequency shifts associated with gas-analyte adsorption to sensors [30].

The objectives of this study were to 1) determine the capability and effectiveness of the Aromascan A32S e-nose to discriminate between eight different herbicide residue types in vitro based on analysis of headspace volatiles, 2) assess the potential usefulness of these methods for making crop-management decisions involving detections of herbicide types on crop foliage for pest-control applications, and 3) a minor objective to determine whether principal component analysis (PCA) of herbicide e-nose aroma patterns (from the sensor array) can provide indications of chemical relatedness between herbicide types based on aroma characteristics and interactions with the sensor array. Six herbicide chemical classes were tested with representatives of each class including organoarsenics (cacodylic acid and MSMA), dinitroanilines (pendimethalin and trifluralin), a phosphoglycine (glyphosate), a cyclohexenone derivative (sethoxydim), a chlorophenoxy acid (2,4-D), and a chlorinated pyridine oxamic acid (triclopyr).

This paper is composed of an introduction to pesticide residue detection on crops in Section 1, followed by e-nose experimental methods used in Section 2, describing the specific materials and methods used in associated with e-nose run and analytical procedures, followed by results in Section 3 that provide details of experimental research results and findings for CP e-nose analyses of herbicide residues, including sensor outputs, aroma map, and QF analysis of PCA data. Discussion and conclusions (Section 4) are based on e-nose experimental results, summarizing significant findings and efficacy compared with conventional chromatographic methods of pesticide residue identification.

II. MATERIALS AND METHODS

A. *Herbicide residue samples collected for analysis*

Eight herbicides, having different chemical (pesticide) classes and modes of actions, were selected for this study. The herbicides analyzed via conductive polymer analysis (CPA) using an electronic-nose (e-nose), a type of electronic aroma detection (EAD) technology [24], included cacodylic acid (CA), dichlorophenoxy acetic acid (2,4-D), glyphosate (GL), pendimethalin (PM), sethoxydim (SE), monosodium acid methane arsonate (MA), triclopyr (TC), and trifluralin (TF). All herbicides were obtained in formulations that were commercially available from manufacturers, rather than from technical grade preparations to facilitate practical efficacy testing of formulations actually used in weed-control applications for agronomic crop production.

B. *Sample preparation and prerun procedures*

Small aliquots (10 µl) of each herbicide were analyzed separately at a standard concentration of 20 ppm by placing them into 14.8 cm3 uncapped glass vials inserted into a 500 ml Pyrex glass sampling bottle no. 1395 (Corning Inc., Corning, NY) fitted with reference air, sampling, and exhaust ports on a polypropylene bottle cap. The sensitivity of CP e-noses range from 0.1 to 100 ppm [30]. Reference air entered the sampling bottle through a 3 mm polypropylene tube extending to just above the bottom of the sampling bottle. The sampling bottle was held in the sampling chamber at a constant air temperature of 25 °C and purged with moisture-conditioned reference air for 2 min prior to building headspace. The sampling bottle was sealed and volatiles from each herbicide analyte were allowed to build headspace and equilibrate for 30 min prior to each run. Prerun tests were performed as needed to determine sample air relative humidity compared with that of reference air. Reference air was set at 4% relative humidity at 25 °C. The sampling bottle cap and exhaust port were opened between runs to purge the previous sample with conditioned reference air. A reference library (recognition file) for pesticide types was constructed using artificial neural net training by defining aroma classes using reference databases of known pesticides. This recognition file was used to identify unknown samples.

C. *Instrument configuration and run parameters*

Electronic-nose analyses of herbicides were conducted with an Aromascan A32S (Osmetech Inc., Wobum, MA) intrinsically conducting polymer (ICP) e-nose instrument with 32 sensors in the sensor array consisting of polypyrrole, polyanaline, and polythiophene sensor types with 15 volts across sensor paths. Eight sensors, (including sensors 11, 12, 21-24, 31 and 32) that did not respond or did not contribute to the discrimination of pesticide volatiles, were turned off. The response sensitivities of individual sensors, measured as percent changes in electrical resistance response across sensor paths relative to base resistance (%ΔR/Rbase), varied with the type of polymer used in the sensor matrix coating, the type of proprietary ring substitutions used to modify its conductive properties, and the type of metal ions used to dope the matrix to improve and modulate sensor response. Detailed analyses indicating relative analyte sensitivities for individual sensors in the array to various analyte types (representative of different chemical classes) were reported previously [24]. The block temperature of the sensor array was maintained at 30 °C. Reference air was preconditioned by passing it sequentially through a carbon filter, silica gel beads, inline filter, and Hepa filter to remove organic compounds, moisture, solid particulates, and microbes, respectively (to prevent interference of these factors), prior to humidity control and introduction into the sampling bottle. The flow rate of sampled reference air was maintained at 702 cm3 min-1 with a calibrated ADM 3000 flow meter (Agilent Technologies, Wilmington, DE). Sensor surfaces were purged between runs using a 2% isopropanol wash. The instrument was interfaced with a personal computer via an RS232 cable and controlled with Aromascan Version 3.51 software. The instrument plumbing (reference air flow route through the instrument) was altered for static sampling of the headspace by allowing air flow, maintained at 605 cm^3 min-1 flow rate, to release out of the external vent port of the instrument during analytical runs, closing the exhaust port on the sampling bottle so that headspace volatiles were taken by vacuum suction from a homogeneous static air mass within the sampling bottle to minimize headspace-dilution effects.

D. *Data acquisition parameters and run schedules*

Data from the sensor array were collected at 1 s intervals using a 0.2 detection threshold (y-units), a 15–20 y-max graph scale, and with a pattern average of five data samples taken per run during data acquisition. A uniform run schedule was used consisting of reference air 20 s, sampling time 90 s, and wash 20 s, followed by 90 s of reference air for a total run time of 220 s. A 2 min reference air purge was completed between runs after each sample was removed from the sampling bottle.

E. Construction of reference libraries and validation

An e-nose aroma reference library was constructed from the eight herbicides included in this study. Database files were linked to specific aroma classes defining each herbicide type. All databases were constructed from sensor output data collected during a 20 s interval, 85-105 s into the run cycle, immediately prior to closing of the reference air valve at the end of each run. The recognition network options (neural net training parameters) used for each training session were: training threshold = 0.60, recognition threshold = 0.60, number of elements allowed in error = 5, learning rate = 0.10, momentum = 0.60, error goal = 0.010 ($P = 0.01$), hidden nodes = 5, maximum iterations (epochs) = 10,000, using normalized input data, not actual intensity data. A typical neural net training required 2–35 min, depending on database size, using an IBM-compatible personal computer with a minimum of 64 mb of RAM and 350 MHz run speed. Neural net trainings were validated by examining training results to compare individual database files for similarity matches to each specific aroma class by test-assigned aroma class distributions among related aroma classes included in each library. The specific detailed analytical methods used for identification of unknowns, data processing, and statistical determinations followed the procedures and specifications indicated by Wilson et al. [24].

F. Principal component analysis

Detailed pairwise comparisons of herbicide types (aroma classes) were determined using principal component analysis (PCA) algorithms provided by the Aromascan 3.51 software. Three-dimensional PCA was used to distinguish between herbicide headspace volatiles. PCA mapping parameters were: iterations = 30, units in Eigen values (%), and use of normalized input data. PCA generated a quality factor (statistical significance value) for each aroma comparison. The relatedness (distance between data clusters) of mapped aroma profiles between herbicide types provided indications of similarity in aroma elements and chemical characteristics as well as interactions with the sensor array.

III. RESULTS

A. Identification of herbicide analytes

The Aromascan A32S electronic nose provided consistent correct identifications for all eight herbicide residue types analyzed based on differences in sensor-array responses to headspace volatiles (Table 1). Individual sensor responses to each herbicide varied widely within the 3 to 8 percent sensor-intensity range (% change in sensor response relative to base resistance) with good precision as indicated by low standard deviations (SD) of mean normalized values. Sensors 25, 26, and 30 had no responses to some herbicides. In particular, sensor 26 could not detect any of the herbicides, whereas sensors 25 and 30 were unable to detect four herbicides including sethoxydim, monosodium acid methane arsonate , triclopyr and trifluralin.

TABLE I. SENSOR OUTPUT RESPONSE PATTERNS FROM THE A32S E-NOSE SENSOR ARRAY DERIVED FROM EIGHT HERBICIDE RESIDUE TYPES

E-nose	Herbicide residue sensor responses[a]							
Sensor	CA	2,4-D	GL	PM	SE	MS	TC	TF
1	4.76	4.22	5.16	5.05	3.54	4.75	6.87	3.97
2	4.31	3.87	4.70	4.60	3.15	4.32	6.20	3.59
3	4.92	4.49	5.35	5.21	3.74	5.02	7.08	4.22
4	2.34	2.46	2.53	2.84	2.96	2.60	3.57	4.27
5	2.34	2.39	2.53	2.86	2.93	2.59	3.56	4.21
6	2.34	2.45	2.53	2.84	2.98	2.61	3.58	4.30
7	5.19	5.34	5.31	4.88	4.83	5.83	6.84	4.64
8	5.25	5.12	5.40	5.11	4.74	5.61	6.65	4.33
9	4.47	4.83	4.42	4.07	4.75	4.79	5.33	3.86
10	3.84	4.60	3.80	3.38	5.39	5.04	5.19	4.30
13	3.54	3.66	3.43	3.37	4.67	3.89	3.77	4.67
14	3.30	3.26	3.23	3.15	4.21	3.44	3.79	4.38
15	3.61	3.98	3.57	3.33	4.65	4.14	4.27	4.52
16	3.36	3.49	3.34	3.28	4.50	3.65	3.80	4.64
17	4.59	4.49	4.06	4.36	5.65	5.27	0.42	5.15
18	4.74	4.57	4.30	4.58	5.70	5.30	0.88	5.17
19	4.45	4.32	4.08	4.37	5.31	5.09	0.94	4.91
20	3.49	4.21	2.53	3.50	6.55	3.71	-2.51	5.40
25	5.38	5.16	5.63	5.78	NR	NR	NR	NR
26	NR	NR	NR	NR	NR	NR	NR	NR
27	6.45	6.71	6.75	5.85	6.82	8.11	8.47	6.98
28	6.38	6.21	6.58	6.01	6.63	7.49	8.27	6.60
29	6.21	5.78	6.47	6.50	6.31	6.76	8.00	5.91
30	4.76	4.40	4.32	5.08	NR	NR	NR	NR

a. Values are mean sensor response intensities; herbicide type abbreviations: cacodylic acid (CA), dichlorophenoxy acetic acid (2,4-D), glyphosate (GL), pendimethalin (PM), sethoxydim (SE), monosodium acid methane arsonate (MA), triclopyr (TC), and trifluralin (TF).

Normalized output values from individual sensors were significantly different between herbicides types at the $P < 0.001$ level of significance. The resulting electronic aroma signature patterns (EASPs) or aroma profiles for individual herbicides, composed of the collective outputs of all the sensors in the sensor array, were different and unique for each herbicide type. The high level of significant differences between sensor outputs for all of the sensors (in each aroma profile) provided a highly unique electronic signature to identify and discriminate herbicide residue types on inert surfaces (in vitro) without the presence of plant volatiles when on crop surfaces of the same plant species.

The instrument correctly identified individual herbicide residues at frequencies ranging from 81-98% among all herbicide residue types tested. None of the herbicides from any of the six chemical classes was incorrectly identified. Also, no herbicide from the five chemical classes was unsuccessfully identified or classified as unknown due to variations in aroma signature patterns. All of the herbicides were clearly assigned an aroma profile with a majority aroma class present in the reference library. None of the herbicides determinations were found to be incorrect or ambiguous, defined as determinations that resulted in a herbicide residue type being assigned to a different majority aroma class from separate analyses of sample replications.

B. *Discrimination between herbicide residues*

The discrimination of herbicide residue types was further evaluated by determining the aroma class distributions of principal components of VOCs in headspace volatiles of the herbicide types (Table 2). Aroma class distributions indicate percentage components in common between herbicides residue types.

The occurrence of secondary aroma elements within the aroma class distribution provided some indications of chemical relatedness between herbicides. Cacodylic acid residues had a relatively large proportion of secondary aroma elements in common with pendimethalin (16.6%) and sethoxydim (11.5%). Similarly, glyphosate shared secondary elements of 12.5% with MSMA, while pendimethalin shared secondary elements of 11.9% with trifluralin. The proportion of secondary aroma elements attributed to aroma classes besides the principal aroma elements ranged from <1% for MSMA to highs of >16% for cacodylic acid.

TABLE II. DISTRIBUTION OF ELECTRONIC-NOSE AROMA CLASS COMPONENTS AMONG EIGHT HERBICIDE RESIDUE TYPES

	Aroma class distribution (%)[a]							
	Herbicide residues types							
Herbicide	**CA**	**2,4-D**	**GL**	**PM**	**SE**	**MS**	**TC**	**TF**
CA	**88.5**	9.4	4.2	16.6	11.5	—	—	—
2,4-D	9.6	**92.8**	—	—	2.9	12.5	—	—
GL	4.7	3.4	**87.9**	—	—	5.2	—	—
PM	2.6	—	6.5	**94.4**	2.3	—	—	11.0
SE	7.2	—	—	—	**95.0**	—	—	2.9
MS	—	0.7	2.2	—	6.1	**94.3**	2.8	0.6
TC	2.9	—	2.5	1.5	—	1.4	**98.4**	—
TF	—	3.3	—	5.9	—	4.6	—	**98.7**

a. Values indicate mean percent aroma class distributions indicated for each herbicide type; read from left to right (by row), not top to bottom. Herbicide abbreviations correspond to those given in the materials and methods section (herbicide residue sample types) and in Table I.

The number of principal and secondary aroma elements present in the aroma profiles of individual herbicide residues ranged from three in sethoxydim to six in MSMA, with the majority having four to five total aroma elements in common between herbicide residues. The total percentage of secondary aroma elements in common between herbicide residues contributed to ≤ 25.0% of the aroma class distribution for most herbicide types with cacodylic acid being the exception (41.7%). The lowest total secondary elements in common with other herbicides occurred for trichlopyr (8.3%); while intermediate totals were recorded for sethoxydim (10.1%), MSMA (12.4%), glyphosate (13.3%), trifluralin (13.8%) and higher totals for pendimethalin (22.4%) and 2,4-D (25.0%).

C. *Principal component analysis*

Analysis of eight herbicide residues using PCA by pairwise comparisons of headspace volatiles (in all possible combinations) provided greater details of possible chemical relatedness and differences between individual herbicide types based on sensor response patterns (aroma profiles). The relatedness among the eight herbicide types varied greatly based on Euclidean distance as indicated in Table 3. The larger the QF value, the greater the significant differences for pairwise herbicide comparisons.

TABLE III. PAIRWISE-COMPARISONS BETWEEN AROMA PROFILES OF EIGHT HERBICIDE RESIDUE TYPES BASED ON 3-DIMENSIONAL PCA

Aroma class	*Aroma class*	*QF value*[a]	*Aroma class*	*Aroma class*	*QF value*[a]
CA	2,4-D	1.4	2,4-D	GL	1.6
	GL	9.5*		PM	1.8
	PM	7.1*		SE	11.5*
	SE	35.6**		MS	69.2***
	MS	95.5***		TC	17.7*
	TC	88.2***		TF	15.0*
	TF	34.4**	GL	PM	11.2*
GL	SE	3.8*	PM	SE	22.0**
	MS	>300****		MS	231.6****
	TC	62.3***		TC	>300****
	TF	15.1**		TF	>300****
MS	TC	15.3**	SE	MS	43.3**
	TF	3.3*		TC	42.2**
TC	TF	31.2**		TF	7.1*

a. Statistical analysis symbols for quality factor (QF) significant difference levels between aroma classes were as follows: * = $P < 0.05$; ** = $P < 0.01$; *** = $P < 0.001$; **** = $P < 0.0001$. The percentages of the total variance, accounting for the variability explained by each orthogonal principal component (PC), were as follows: PC 1 = 91.3%; PC 2 = 7.7%.

QF values ranged from 1.4 between cacodylic acid and 2,4-D (indicating close relatedness) to >300 between glyphosate and MSMA, and between pendimethalin and both triclopyr and trifluralin, indicating low relatedness between pairs. The small QF values for 2,4-D compared with glyphosate (1.6) and pendimethalin (1.8) indicated close relationships based on aroma characteristics even though these herbicides are from different chemical classes. Cacodylic acid vs. MSMA (both organoarsenics), had a high QF value (95.5) suggesting low relatedness in aroma profiles. The comparison of the two dinitroanilines, pendimethalin and trifluralin, also resulted in a high QF value (>300) despite their chemical relatedness. Significant differences in R-groups may account for aroma profile differences between herbicides in the same chemical class. The relatedness between the aroma profiles of eight herbicide residue types, based on 3-dimensional PCA, was graphed as an aroma map (Figure 1).

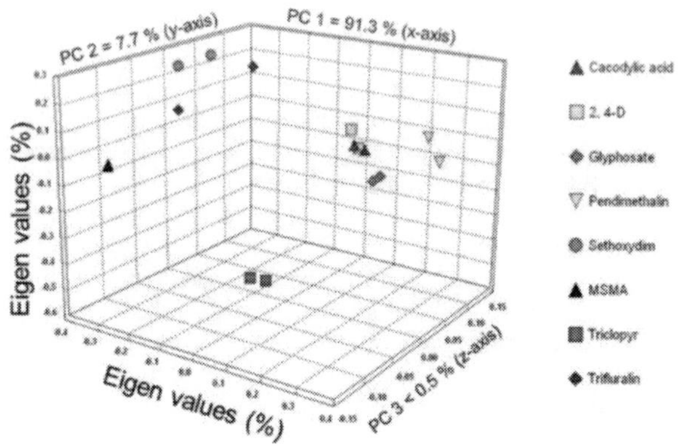

Figure 1. E-nose aroma map showing the chemical relatedness between eight herbicide residue types using Principal Component Analysis (PCA).

The percentages of the total variance for this analysis, accounting for the variability explained by each orthogonal principal component (PC), are as follows: PC 1 = 91.3%; PC 2 = 7.7%; and PC 3 < 0.5%, representing the x-, y-, and z-axis of the aroma map, respectively. A high proportion (99.0%) of the variation was explained by the first two principal components (PC 1 and PC 2). Data points of each herbicide type clustered closely on the aroma map with the exception of trifluralin. As expected, data points of 2,4-D were closely clustered with those of cacodylic acid, indicating a very close relationship based on aroma characteristics.

IV. DISCUSSION AND CONCLUSIONS

Electronic-nose devices previously have been used to detect pesticides including fungicides, insecticides, and miticides [1][31]. Déjous et al. [32] used a surface acoustic wave (SAW) e-nose to detect organophosphates in ambient air. Literature on e-nose detection of pesticides residues on fruits, crops, and other plant surfaces is quite limited [33]. E-nose aroma signature libraries developed for detection of pesticides on crop and plant surfaces for field use must necessarily include the specific types of VOCs that are characteristic of those released from the types of plant and parts upon which pesticide residues are being detected. Previous research has demonstrated the capability of e-noses to discriminate between VOCs from different plant species and various tissue types from woody plants [34]-[36], and in the crop environment [37]-[39].

Further research on the e-nose detection of pesticides residues on plant surfaces, following efficacy testing in vitro in the present pilot study, will be required to determine efficacy for field crops and fresh produce subject to Environmental Protection Agency (EPA) pesticide residue regulations. E-nose data of crop pesticide residues are primarily qualitative and only semi-quantitative, a possible limitation for EPA residue testing. The detection limit for CP-type e-nose devices is approximately 0.1 ppm, which is low enough for pesticide residue testing in most countries. Pesticide residue concentrations do not affect aroma signature patterns, but only intensity of sensor responses. Analyses of data indicating unique aroma signature patterns, based on output results from the sensor array of the A32S CP electronic-nose, provided effective discriminations between headspace volatiles from herbicide residues. Discriminations and correct identification of herbicide sample types in vitro were determined at high levels of statistical confidence.

The discrimination of pesticide residues on crop plants is an important function in crop management to assure that the appropriate active ingredient has been applied to a crop for pest control and harvesting operations. Herbicides are used for weed control and as chemical defoliants to facilitate crop harvesting operations. Thus, detection of herbicide residues is necessary to confirm application of appropriate chemicals to achieve desired results for specific crops.

The use of e-nose devices for pesticide residue detection has several advantages over conventional methods such as gas chromatography (GC), liquid chromatography (LC), and mass spectrometry (MS). These expensive chemical analysis methods require laborious and time-consuming sample preparations, solvent extractions, reference standards of each pesticide, and costly analytical equipment. By comparison, electronic-nose methods do not require expensive sample preparations, chemical solvents, or pesticide standards and may potentially consist of relatively cheap instruments such as handheld portable e-nose devices for field use.

ACKNOWLEDGMENT

The author thanks Mrs. Charisse Oberle for her help in running CP e-nose analyses of herbicide residue samples, reviewing the manuscript, and assembling references.

REFERENCES

[1] A.D. Wilson, "Identification of insecticide residues with a conducting-polymer electronic nose," Chem. Sens., vol. 4, 2014, pp 1-10.

[2] A. Rizzolo, et al., "Electronic nose to detect volatile compound profile and quality changes in 'Spring Belle' peach (Prunus persica L.) during cold storage," J. Agric. Food Chem., vol. 61, 2013, pp 1671–1685.

[3] B. Zhou, J. Wang, and J. Qi, "Identification of different wheat seeds by electronic nose," Int. Agrophys., vol. 26, 2012, pp 413-418.

[4] J. Lan, B. Liu, Z. Chen, Z. Song, and J. Lin, "Discriminate model of electronic nose for distinguishing volatiles of microbial fermentation bed in swine house," Fujian J. Agric. Sci., vol. 1, 2012, pp 1–4.

[5] J.P. Santos, M. Alexandrea, and C. Cruz, "Hand held electronic nose for VOC detection," Chem. Eng. Trans., vol. 30, 2012, pp 181–186.

[6] O.O. Oladipupo, and O.A. Eletta, "Neuro-identification of some commonly used volatile organic compounds using electronic nose," Chem. Process Eng. Res., vol. 2, 2012, pp 43–53.

[7] D. Gao, J. Ji, J. Gong, and C. Cai, "Quantitative analysis of different volatile organic compounds using an improved electronic nose," Meas. Sci. Technol., vol. 23, 2012, pp 205-210.

[8] J. White, J.S. Kauer, T.A. Dickinson, and D.R. Walt, "Rapid analyte recognition in a device based on optical sensors and the olfactory system," Anal. Chem., vol. 68, 1996, pp 2191–2202.

[9] K. Brudzewskia, S. Osowskia, and W. Pawlowskia, "Metal oxide sensor arrays for detection of explosives at sub-parts-per million concentration levels by the differential electronic nose," Sens. Actuators B Chem., vol. 161, 2012, pp 528–533.

[10] M. Baietto, L. Pozzi, A.D. Wilson, and D. Bassi, "Evaluation of a portable MOS electronic nose to detect root rots in shade tree species," Comput. Electron. Agric., vol. 96, 2013, pp 117–125.

[11] M. Egashira, and Y. Shimizu, "Odor sensing by semiconductor metal oxides," Sens. Actuators, vol. 13, 1993, pp 443–446.

[12] M.E. Meyerhoff, "Polymer membrane electrode based potentiometric ammonia gas sensor," Anal. Chem., Vol. 52, 1980, pp 1532–1534.

[13] H.S. Yim, et al., "Polymer membrane-based ion-, gas- and bio-selective potentiometric sensors," Biosens. Bioelectron., vol. 8, 1993, pp 1–38.

[14] V. Parra, et al., "E-tongue based on a hybrid array of voltammetric sensors based on phthalocyanines, perylene derivatives and conducting polymers: Discrimination capability towards red wines elaborated with different varieties of grapes," Sens. Actuator, vol. 115, 2006, pp 54–61.

[15] J.V. Hatfield, P. Neaves, P.J. Hicks, K.C. Persaud, and P. Tavers, "Toward an integrated electronic nose using conducting polymer sensors," Sens. Actuators, vol. 18, 1994, pp 221–228.

[16] B. Bai, C. Li, F. Chen, and G. Shi, "Aligned three-dimensional microstructures of conducting polymer composites," Polymer, vol. 48, 2007, pp 5259-5267.

[17] E.A. Baldwin, et al., "Effect of Liberibacter infection (Huanglongbing disease) of citrus on orange fruit physiology and fruit/fruit juice quality: chemical and physical analyses," J. Agric. Food Chem., vol. 58, 2010, pp 1247–1262.

[18] H. Zhang, and J. Wang, "Detection of age and insect damage incurred by wheat with an electronic nose," J. Stored Prod. Res., vol. 43, 2007, pp 489–495.

[19] E.A. Baldwin, J. Bai, A. Plotto, and S. Dea, "Electronic noses and tongues: Application for the food and pharmaceutical industries," Sensors, vol. 11, 2011, pp 4744–4766.

[20] C. Dighavkar, A. Patil, S. Patil, and R. Borse, "Al-doped TiO2 thick film resistors as H2S gas sensor," Sci. Technol., vol. 9, 2010, pp 39–47.

[21] M. Zhang, X. Wang, Y. Liu, X. Xu, and G. Zhou, "Species discrimination among three kinds of puffer fish using an electronic nose combined with olfactory sensory evaluation," Sensors, vol. 12, 2012, pp 12562–12571.

[22] A.H. Abdullah, et al., "Chicken farm malodour monitoring using portable electronic nose system," Chem. Eng. Trans., vol. 30, 2012, pp 55–60.

[23] L. Dentoni, et al., "Development of an electronic nose for environmental odour monitoring," Sensors, vol. 12, 2012, pp 14363–14381.

[24] A.D. Wilson, D.G. Lester, and C.S. Oberle, "Development of conductive polymer analysis for the rapid detection and identification of phytopathogenic microbes," Phytopathology, vol. 94, 2004, pp 419–431.

[25] H. Zhang, and J. Wang, "Evaluation of peach quality attributes using an electronic nose," Sens. Mater., vol. 21, 2009, pp 419–431.

[26] R. Labrador, J. Soto, R. Martinez-Manez, and L. Gil, "An electronic tongue for qualitative analyses of anions in natural water," J. Appl. Electrochem., vol 39, 2009, pp 2505–2511.

[27] S. Li, A. Simonian, and B.A. Chin, "Sensors for agriculture and the food industry," Electrochem. Soc. Interfac., vol. 19, 2010, pp 41–46.

[28] L. Dentoni, et al., "Development of an electronic nose for environmental odour monitoring," Sensors, vol. 12, 2012, pp 14363–14381.

[29] H. Kim, et al., "Electronic-nose for detecting environmental pollutants: Signal processing and analog front-end design," Analog Integr. Circ. Signal Process., vol. 70, 2012, pp 15–32.

[30] A.D. Wilson, "Recent progress in the design and clinical development of electronic nose technologies," Nanobiosens. Dis. Diagn., 2016, vol. 5, pp. 15-27.

[31] A.D. Wilson, "Fungicide residue identification and discrimination using a conducting polymer electronic-nose," Proceedings of the Fourth International Conference on Sensor Device Technologies and Applications, Barcelona, Spain, Xpert Publishing Services, Wilmington, DE, USA, 2013, pp. 116-121.

[32] C. Déjous, D. Rebiére, J. Pistré, C. Tiret, and R.A. Planade, "A surface acoustic wave gas sensor: Detection of organophosphorus compounds," Sens. Actuators B, vol. 24, 1995, pp 58–61.

[33] A.D. Wilson, "Diverse applications of electronic-nose technologies in agriculture and forestry," Sensors, vol. 13, 2013, pp 2295–2348.

[34] A.D. Wilson, D.G. Lester, and C.S. Oberle, "Application of conductive polymer analysis for wood and woody plant identifications," For. Ecol. & Managem., vol. 209, 2005, pp. 207-224.

[35] A.D. Wilson, "Application of a conductive polymer electronic-nose device to identify aged woody samples," in Proceedings of The 3rd International IARIA Conference on Sensor Device Technologies and Applications, S. Yurish, I. Chilibon, V. Carvalho, S. Gervais-Ducouret, Eds. DE: Wilmington, Xpert Publishing Services, 2012, pp. 77–82.

[36] M. Baietto, A.D. Wilson, D. Bassi, and F. Ferrini, "Evaluation of three electronic noses for detecting incipient wood decay," Sensors, vol. 10, pp. 1062-1092.

[37] A.D. Wilson, and M. Baietto, "Applications and advances in electronic-nose technologies," Sensors, vol. 9, 2009, pp. 5099-5148.

[38] A.D. Wilson, "Review of electronic-nose technologies and algorithms to detect hazardous chemicals in the environment," Proc. Technol., vol. 1, 2012, pp. 453-463.

[39] L. Capelli, S. Sironi, and R. Del Ross, "Electronic noses for environmental monitoring applications," Sensors, vol. 14, 2014, pp. 19979-20007.

Mobile Sensor System for Alcohol Control and Numerical Signal Analysis

Rolf Seifert and Hubert B. Keller
Institute of Applied Informatics (IAI)
Karlsruhe Institute of Technology
D-76344 Eggenstein-Leopoldshafen, Germany
e-mail: rolf.seifert@kit.edu, hubert.keller@kit.edu

Thorsten Conrad and Jens Peter
3S GmbH
D-66121 Saarbrücken
e-mail: conrad@3S-ing.de, peter@3S-ing.de

Abstract—**An innovative mobile sensor system for alcohol control in the respiratory air is introduced. The gas sensor included in the sensor system is thermo-cyclically operated. Ethanol is the leading component in this context. However, other components occur in the breathing air which can influence the concentration determination of ethanol. Therefore, mono-ethanol samples and binary gas mixtures are measured by the sensor system and analyzed with a new calibration and evaluation procedure which is also incorporated in the system. The applications demonstrate a good substance identification capability of the sensor system and a very good concentration determination of the components.**

Keywords-alcohol control; mobile sensor system; thermo-cyclic operation; data analysis; substance identification; concentration determination.

I. INTRODUCTION

There is a broad field of applications for chemical analysis of gases and volatile organic compounds (VOCs) like discriminated monitoring of toxic gas leakages, online monitoring of volatile components in chemical and biochemical processes, quality monitoring in food processing, etc. In this context, metal oxide gas sensors (MOGs) are well introduced as gas sensing devices. This is due to the fact that they are very sensitive, have good long-term stability and are low in price. But on the other hand, when these sensor devices are operated isothermally, they are not at all selective. That means that they cannot be used for sophisticated analysis of gas mixtures. Therefore, other approaches are necessary like a gas sensor array of MOGs [1] [2] or by thermos-cyclic operation of the MOG and simultaneous sampling of the conductance which leads to so-called "conduction over time profiles" (CTPs) [3] [4] [5]. These profiles give a fingerprint of the surface processes with the gas and represent the gas mixture under consideration. The gas specific features of the CTPs can be used for component identification and concentration determination. At the Karlsruhe Institute of Technology (KIT), many procedures were established to evaluate such signal patterns [6] and also for source localization [7].

In this report, we will introduce an innovative mobile sensor system for alcohol control in the respiratory air. In this context, ethanol is the leading component. But because also other components like acetone can occur in the breathing air, we consider not only mono-ethanol samples, but also binary gas mixtures. The analysis of these samples is performed with the calibration and evaluation program ProSens2, which is an integral component of the sensor system.

In Section 2, the mobile sensor system is described. A short outline of the calibration and evaluation procedure ProSens2 is given in Section 3. In Section 4, the data analysis is performed, including the ethanol investigation and the investigation of binary ethanol-acetone mixtures as well. Section 5 summarizes the results of this report.

II. MOBILE SENSOR SYSTEM

A. *Sensor System Platform And Adapter*

For breath control in the respiratory air, especially for alcohol control, an innovative sensor system platform was developed. Based on this platform, an adapter for smartphones was developed for mobile monitoring of the breathing air.

This adapter consists of a combined and modular hardware- and software system, which runs an embedded metal oxide gas sensor in a thermos-cyclic mode and which determines the alcohol content on the basis of the measurement results via an innovative calibration- and evaluation procedure ProSens2 in real time. The analysis results will then be displayed on the smartphone.

B. *Electronics for Heater Control And Data Acquisition*

In order to characterize and operate semiconducting gas sensor elements with respect to the application, a sensor platform was developed which ensures a robust functioning of hard- and firmware. This platform supports a variety of commercially available metal oxide gas sensors. In this investigation, the sensor MLV from Applied Sensors [8] was used. Via its graphical user interface different parametrizable temperature cycles can be configured.

The core unit of the platform is a base-board with a powerful micro-controller communicating with external modules in a master-slave-configuration. The base-board is able to manage up to four gas sensor modules and features ambient condition monitoring.

The platform outputs the sensor raw data (basically the measured voltages), which can easily be transformed into resistances or conductances or pre-calculated values for a reduced data stream. Via USB, the platform is connected to a standard PC where the data live visualization and the storage is carried out. Via Bluetooth the platform can be connected to mobile applications running on smart phones.

For the measurements in this paper, a platform with the following specifications was used:

- The temperature control allows a set-point accuracy of 2°C within an overall temperature range of 100 to 500 °C. The set-point can be updated every 10ms.
- The read-out circuit features a sampling time of better than 1ms.
- Measurement voltage accuracy is around of 5 mV (by using a 10-bit-ADC).
- The dynamic range of the read-out circuit is between 1k and 100M.

C. *Temperature Cycle*

Based on the above-explained electronics, several temperature cycles have been applied to the sensors while being exposed to the gas mixtures.

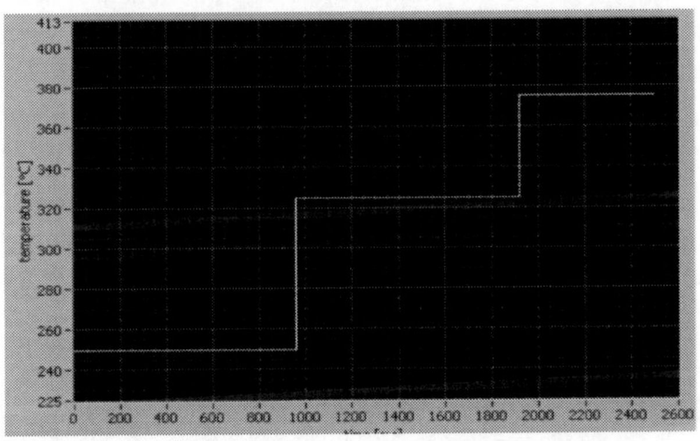

Figure 1. Thermo-cyclic (step-wise) temperature cycle.

For the experiments carried out in the scope of the publication, the temperature cycle in the following Figure 1 has been considered.

III. Calibration- and Evaluation Procedure ProSens2

As mentioned above, the calibration- and evaluation procedure ProSens2 is included in the mobile sensor system. ProSens2 is an updated version of ProSens [9] to meet the requirements of this sensor system. ProSens2 consists like ProSens of a calibration part and an evaluation part.

Using the calibration part of ProSens2, the mathematical calibration model is calculated based on calibration measurements. The mathematical calibration model is a parametric model and only the parameters will be transferred to the evaluation part of ProSens2.

If an unknown gas sample is measured, the evaluation part of ProSens2 performs a substance identification and concentration determination of the sample, based on the calibration parameters. For substance identification, ProSens2 calculates a so-called theoretical CTP and compares this CTP with the real measured CTP. Only if the distance of theoretical CTP and measured CTP is smaller than a pre-determined decision threshold, ProSens2 recognizes the unknown sample with the gas sample under consideration. In this case, the concentration determination will be performed.

Substance identification is very important to avoid misleading analysis results like false alarms.

IV. Data Analysis

Ethanol is the leading component for alcohol control in the respiratory air. To investigate the performance of the sensor system, pure ethanol samples were analyzed in a first application.

But there can be also further components in the respiratory air which have to be considered to avoid misleading results. One of these components is the acetone in the breathing air. Acetone is an indicator for diabetes. Therefore, binary ethanol-acetone gas samples were investigated in a second application.

The measurements were performed with the above described sensor system using the cyclic variation of the working temperature in Figure 1. The determination of the mathematical calibration models and the data analysis were performed with the included program ProSens2.

A. *Application 1: Ethanol Investigation*

To establish the mathematical calibration model with the calibration part of ProSens2, three gas samples of ethanol gas with concentrations 50ppm, 100ppm and 175ppm were measured.

To investigate the performance of the sensor system and the embedded evaluation procedure, three further gas samples were measured: ethanol with 135ppm, acetone with 2ppm and H2 with 10ppm.

As mentioned above, ProSens2 calculates the so-called theoretical CTP and compares this CTP with the real measured CTP. In Figure 2, the theoretical CTP and measured CTP of the ethanol sample is plotted. It can be clearly seen, that the difference between the two curves is very small. This means that ProSens2 recognizes that this sample is an ethanol gas.

Theoretical CTP and measured CTP for acetone rsp. H2 are shown in Figure 3 rsp. Figure 4. In both cases, the difference between the two curves is very large. So ProSens2 recognizes that in both cases the measured sample is not an ethanol gas.

Of course, the decision for substance identification is not based on the visual impression. Therefore, a "difference value" is calculated from the sum of quadratic differences of every sample point of the measured CTP and the theoretical CTP. Only if this difference value is smaller than a predetermined decision value, ProSens2 identifies the unknown gas sample with the related calibrated gas mixture. Table I shows the difference value for the gas samples.

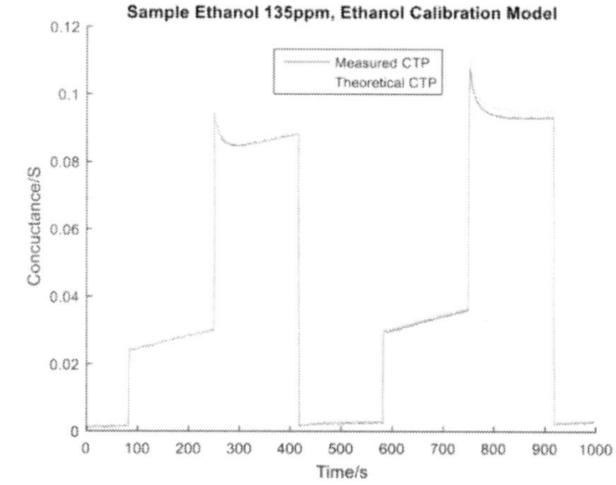

Figure 2. Comparison of measured CTP and theoretical CTP based on the ethanol calibration model for sample ethanol 135ppm.

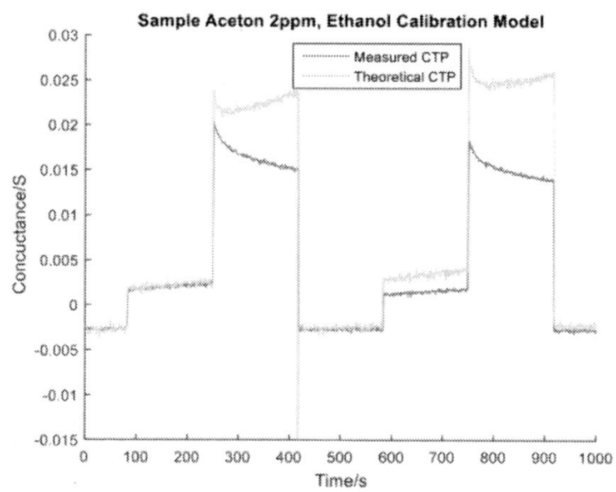

Figure 3. Comparison of measured CTP and theoretical CTP based on the ethanol calibration model for sample aceton 2ppm.

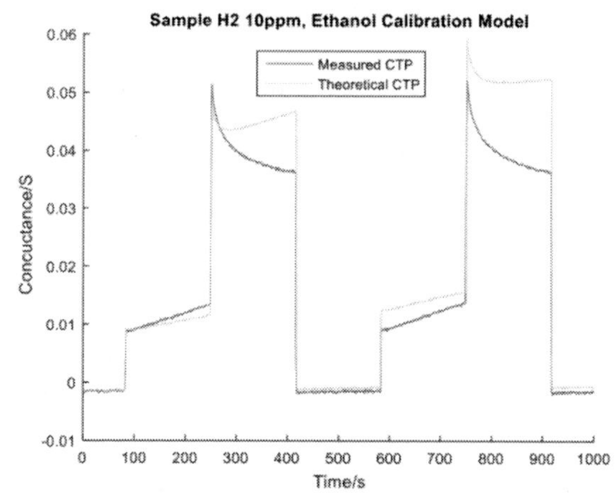

Figure 4. Comparison of measured CTP and theoretical CTP based on the ethanol calibration model for sample H2 10ppm.

It can be clearly seen that the difference values in the blue marked fields of Table I, which correspond not to an ethanol gas, are significantly larger than the difference value in the other field which corresponds to an ethanol gas. This means that ProSens2 is able to perform very good substance identification.

TABLE I. DIFFERENCE VALUES FOR THE GAS SAMPLES

Ethanol 135ppm	Acetone 2ppm	H2 20ppm
2.1e-05	7.8e-04	5.9e-04

After substance identification, ProSens2 calculates the concentration of the ethanol sample. Table II demonstrates the very good analysis result.

TABLE II. ANALYSIS RESULTS OF THE ETHANOL INVESTIGATION

Dosed Concentration	Analyzed Concentration	Relative Analysis Error
135ppm	140,2ppm	5,3%

B. *Application 2:Binary Ethanol-Acetone Mixture*

In a second application, binary ethanol-acetone mixtures were considered because additional components in the respiratory air can influence the ethanol concentration determination.

To establish the mathematical calibration model with the calibration part of ProSens2, the gas samples of an ethanol-acetone gas mixture given in Table III were again measured using thermo-cyclic operation of the sensor system.

TABLE III. ANALYSIS RESULTS OF THE ETHANOL INVESTIGATION

Ethanol-Acetone in ppm	Ethanol-Acetone in ppm	Ethanol-Acetone in ppm
50-0,5	50-1	50-2
100-0,5	100-1	100-2
175-0,5	175-1	175-2

This means that only 9 samples were required for the establishing of the calibration model. This is a very good aspect because calibration measurements are very time consuming and expensive.

To investigate the performance of the sensor system with the evaluation procedure ProSens2, three further binary ethanol-acetone gas mixtures and two non-binary ethanol-acetone gas mixtures were measured in the same manner as the samples for calibration and analyzed together with the samples of the calibration process. The samples are given in Table IV.

The blue marked lines in this table refer to non-binary ethanol-acetone gas mixtures based on the calibration model of the binary ethanol-acetone mixture.

TABLE IV. GAS SAMPLES FOR EVALUATION

Ethanol-Acetone in ppm	Ethanol-Acetone in ppm	Ethanol-Acetone in ppm
50-0,5	50-1	50-2
100-0,5	100-1	100-2
135-0,5	135-1	135-2
175-0,5	175-1	175-2
Acetone in ppm	1	
H2 in ppm	20	

The following figures show again the comparison of theoretical CTP and measured CTP on the basis of the ethanol-acetone calibration model. In Figure 5, the two curves are quite together. This means that the sample is identified as a binary ethanol-acetone mixture. In Figures 6 and 7, the difference between the two curves is very large. That means they are not identified as the binary gas mixture under consideration.

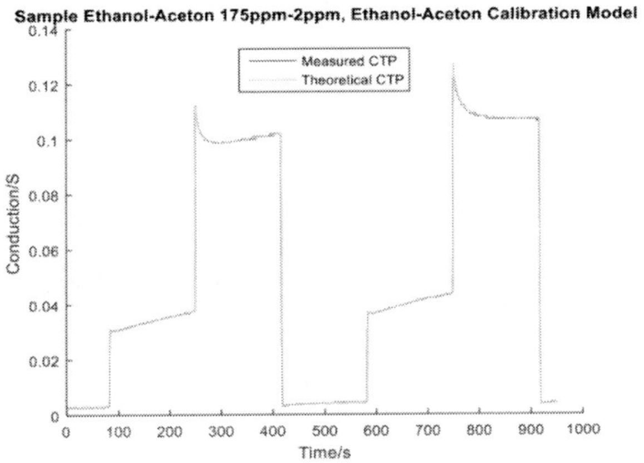

Figure 5. Comparison of measured CTP and theoretical CTP based on the ethanol-acetone calibration model for sample ethanol 175ppm acetone 2ppm.

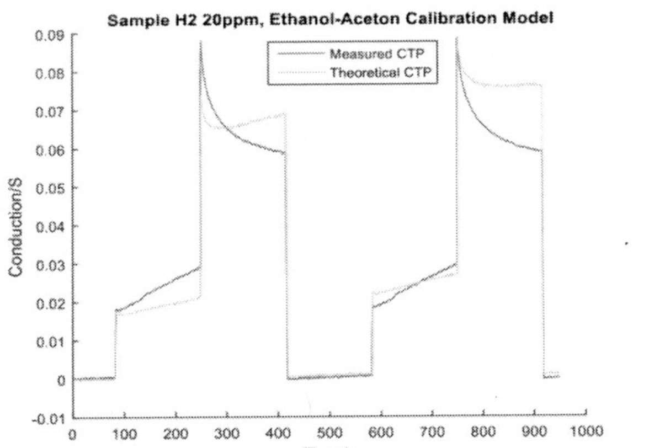

Figure 6. Comparison of measured CTP and theoretical CTP based on the ethanol-acetone calibration model for sample H2 20ppm.

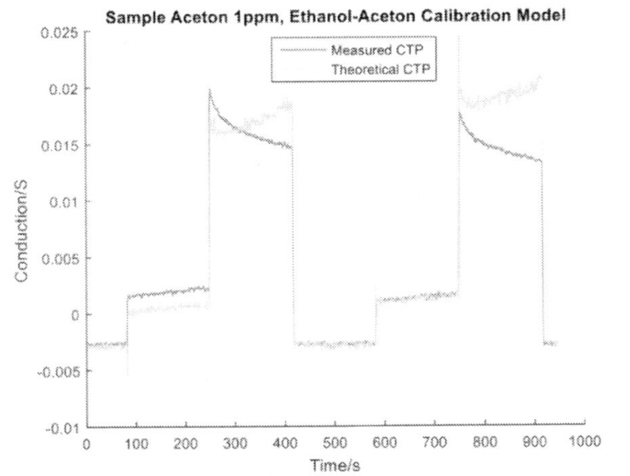

Figure 7. Comparison of measured CTP and theoretical CTP based on the ethanol-acetone calibration model for sample acetone 1ppm.

The following Table V shows the difference values between measured CTP and theoretical CTP.

TABLE V. DIFFERENCE VALUES FOR THE GAS SAMPLES

Ethanol/Aceton	0,5ppm	1ppm	2ppm
50ppm	0.0001	0.0004	0.0007
100ppm	0.0007	0.0006	0.0023
135ppm	0.0044	0.0018	0.0013
175ppm	0.0002	0.0007	0.0007
Acetone 1 ppm	0.2508		
H2 20 ppm	0.2955		

It can be clearly seen that the difference values in the blue marked fields of Table V, which do not correspond to ethanol-acetone gas mixtures, are significantly larger than the difference values in the other fields which correspond to ethanol-acetone samples. This means that ProSens2 is able to perform also in this application very good substance identification.

TABLE VI. ANALYZED CONCENTRATION VALUES OF THE ETHANNOL COMPONENTS IN PPM

Ethanol/Acetone (dosed values)	0,5ppm	1ppm	2 ppm
50ppm	49,5	50,5	50,0
100ppm	101,0	100,0	99,2
135ppm	141.6	140,0	140,1
175ppm	175,5	175,4	174,1

After substance identification, ProSens2 calculates the ethanol concentration of the ethanol-acetone sample. Table

VI demonstrates the very good analysis results even in the case of a binary gas mixture with relative analysis errors smaller than 4%.

V. Conclusion and Future Work

In this report, a test platform for alcohol control as a pre-release of the later mobile electronics was developed which ensures a robust functioning of hard- und firmware. This platform supports a sariety of commercially available metal oxide gas sensors. A specific aspect of the targeted application of breath alcohol detection is the reproducible generation of ethanol at nearly condensing gas atmosphere like it is assumed for breath monitoring. Operating the sensor system in a special thermo cyclic operation mode leads to CTPs which can be used for substance identification and concentration determination of the components of the gas mixture. Therefore, a calibration and evaluation procedure called ProSens2 was established. As shown in the application, ProSens2 is able to identify pure ethanol samples as well as binary ethanol-acetone mixtures in a very good manner and is also capable to determine the concentration of the ethanol samples and of the components of the ethanol-acetone mixtures with relative errors lower than 5%.

In future work, the influence of further interfering components in the breathing air will be checked, including the interference of moisture in the respiratory air. Furthermore, the capability of the mobile sensor system for other applications will be investigated. Areas of research could be monitoring of diabetes, where acetone is the leading component, or the supervision of asthma with NO as the leading component.

Acknowledgment

This work is financially supported by the Central Innovation Program for small and medium-sized enterprises (SME) of the German Bundesministerium für Wirtschaft und Technologie (BMWi).

References

[1] P. Althainz, J. Goschnick, S. Ehrmann, and H. J. Ache, "Multisensor Microsystem for Contaminants in Air", Sens. Actuators, B33, 1996, pp. 72-76.

[2] V. V. Sysoev, I. Kiselev, M. Frietsch, and J. Goschnick, "Temperature Gradient Effect on Gas Discrimination Power of a Metal- Oxide Thin-Film Sensor Microarray", Sensors 4, 2004, pp. 37-46.

[3] K. Frank et al., "Metal oxide gas sensors for field analysis: Novel SnO2/La2O3 sensor element for analysis of dissolved toluene/ethanol binary mixtures", Sensor 2005: 12th Internat. Conf., Nürnberg, May 2005, Proc. Vol. 2, AMA Service GmbH, Wunstorf, 2005, pp. 207–209.

[4] K. Frank et al., "Improving the analysis capability of tin oxide gas sensors by dynamic operation, appropriate additives and an advanced evaluation procedure", Sensor 2007: 13th Internat.Conf., Nürnberg, May 2007, Proc. Vol. 1, AMA Service GmbH, Wunstorf, 2007, pp.139–144.

[5] K. Frank, V. Magapu, V. Schindler, H. Kohler, H. B. Keller, and R. Seifert, "Improving the analysis capability of tin oxide gas sensors by dynamic operation", Sensors Letters 6, 2008, pp. 908-911.

[6] R. Seifert, H. Keller, and J. Matthes, "A Review on Innovative Procedures for the Analysis of Data from Gas Sensor Systems and Networks", Sensors & Transducers, Vol. 184, Issue 1, 2015, pp. 1-10.

[7] J. Matthes, L. Gröll, and H. B. Keller, "Source localization based on pointwise concentration measurements", Sensors and Actuators A 115, 2004, pp. 32–37.

[8] http://ams.com/eng/Products/Environmental-Sensors/Gas-Sensors/AS-MLV-P2

[9] R. Seifert, H. B. Keller, K. Frank, and H. Kohler, "ProSens - an Efficient Mathematical Procedure for Calibration and Evaluation of Tin Oxide Gas Sensor Data", Sensor Letters, Vol. 9/1, 2011, pp. 7-10.

Surface Acoustic Wave Sensors for Fine Particle Detection Air Quality Monitoring

Lyes Djoumi
and Virginie Blondeau-Patissier
and Meddy Vanotti
Département Temps-Fréquence
FEMTO-ST
Besançon, France
e-mail: lyes.djoumi@femto-st.fr
e-mail: virginie.blondeau@femto-st.fr
e-mail: meddy.vanotti@femto-st.fr

Etienne Quivet
and Daphne Buiron
Laboratoire de Chimie de l'Environement
Université Aix-Marseille
Marseille, France
e-mail: etienne.quivet@univ-amu.fr
e-mail: daphne.buiron@univ-amu.fr

***Abstract*—Surface acoustic wave (SAW) sensors consisting of delay lines built on Quartz are used for fine particle detection. Sensors based on either Rayleigh or Love waves using different guiding layers such as silica and resin were tested. A comparison of these different sensors capabilities has been achieved. Our SAW sensors proved to be able to detect PM10 and PM2.5 particles in the $0-100$ $\mu g/m^3$ concentration range. The influence of the guiding layer thickness on the Love wave sensors sensitivity was also investigated.**

Keywords*–*SAW sensors; Love wave; fine particles; air quality.

Figure 1. Surface Acoustic Wave sensor

I. INTRODUCTION

According to the World Health Organization (WHO), air pollution is responsible for approximately two million premature deaths per year. Therefore, it is of great importance to be able to precisely measure particle concentration in the air so that proper actions could be taken in order to reduce it. Particles smaller than 10 microns and 2.5 microns in diameter, respectively PM10 and PM2.5, are a major cause of health issues since they are likely to deeply penetrate the human lungs. Instruments currently used to measure micro particle concentration are both large and expensive. Using micro-acoustic devices for that purpose offers many possibilities in terms of cost and size. They also tend to be very sensitive as they are used for gas detection applications [1], [2]. They could also be potentially wireless [3]. The SAW sensors designed for this work are based on delay lines built on quartz (AT cut). They consist of 200 nm thick aluminum interdigited electrodes (IDTs), (cf Figure 1). The wavelength is $\lambda = 40$ μm. Since $c = f.\lambda$, the resulted frequency for Rayleigh type waves is $f = 78.5$ MHz as the wave velocity is approximately $c = 3100$ $m.s^{-1}$. On the other hand, the Love wave, which is faster $c = 5000$ $m.s^{-1}$, operates at higher frequency $f = 125$ MHz.

In this paper, the experiment setup in which the SAW sensors were tested is first described in section II. In section III, the results of these different experiements are reported and discussed before finishing with a short conclusion and a brief perspective on our ongoing works.

II. EXPERIMENTS

SAW sensors were exposed to PM2.5 particles within a VCE1000 room in which particles concentration is monitored using an Optical Particle Counter (Grimm OPC). PM10 and PM2.5 micro particles are generated from a burning candle. Particle concentration, which varies in the $0-100$ $\mu g/m^3$ range, is measured simultaneously by the OPC. The particles adsorbed on the sensitive zone induce a gravimetric effect that slows the acoustic wave down. The wave velocity decrease results in a phase shift at a constant frequency (125 MHz for Love waves and 78.5 MHz for Rayleigh waves). This phases shift is continuously monitored using dedicated electronics [4] . It is then compared with the particle concentration in the room measured with the OPC. The particles are injected the first time resulting in an increase of the concentration; the injection is stopped when the concentration reaches approximately 100 $\mu g/m^3$. As soon as the injection is stopped, particle concentration drops down. The cycle is repeated a second time during the experiment.

III. RESULTS

A. Love Wave Devices

Love waves are horizontally polarized surface waves. For the Love wave to appear, it requires a guiding layer that has a lower acoustic velocity than that of the quartz substrate. Love wave based sensors using different guiding layers were tested in this work.

1) Resin guiding layer: As shown in Figure 2, sensors using 1.8 μm thick photosensitive resin as a guiding layer responded by a phase decrease as soon as the particle concentration increased. The phase decrease is due to particle adsorption onto the sensor's surface. Conversely, the particles desorbed from the surface when particle concentration dropped down inducing the phase to increase. These sensors demonstrated a quick response and a sensitivity of 11.5 $m°.\mu g^{-1}.m^3$.

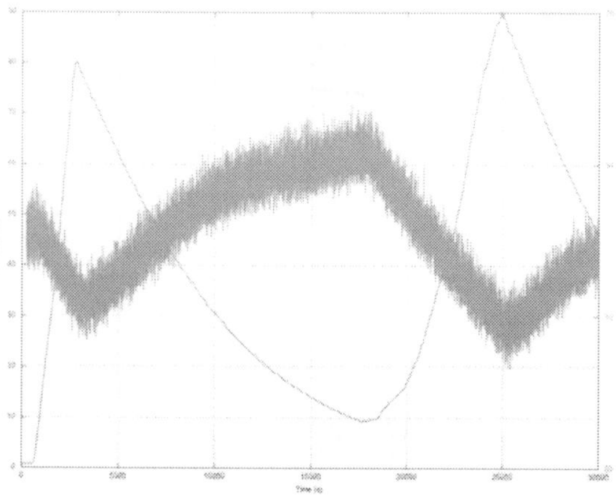

Figure 2. Phase response (green curve) with particle concentration variation (red curve) for a Love wave sensor with a photo-resistive resin guiding layer.

2) Silica guiding Layer: As it is shown in Figure 3, sensors using silica as a guiding layer also showed a quick response and exhibited a much higher sensitivity compared to the resin based sensors. It was approximately 50.9 $m°.\mu g^{-1}.m^3$. Different silica layer thicknesses from 700 nm to 1.8 μm presented a similar behaviour.

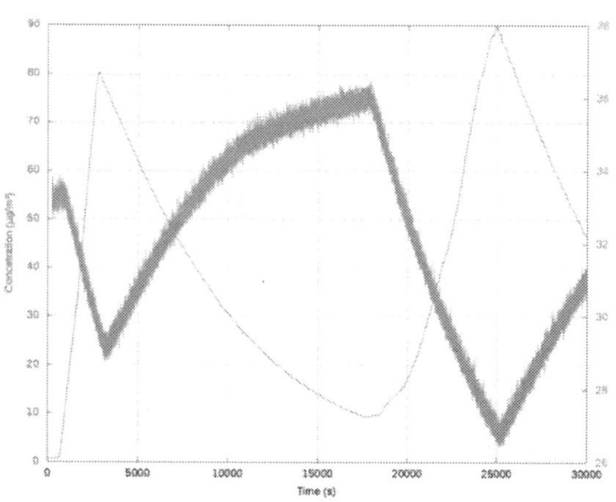

Figure 3. Phase response (green curve) with particle concentration variation (red curve) for a Love wave sensor with a 1.8 μm silica guiding layer.

B. Rayleigh Wave Devices

In constrast to Love wave based sensors, Figure 4 shows that Rayleigh wave sensors did not respond at all to the particles. Indeed, the phase was almost constant during the two particle injection cycles. This type of devices should therefore not be used for this type of applications.

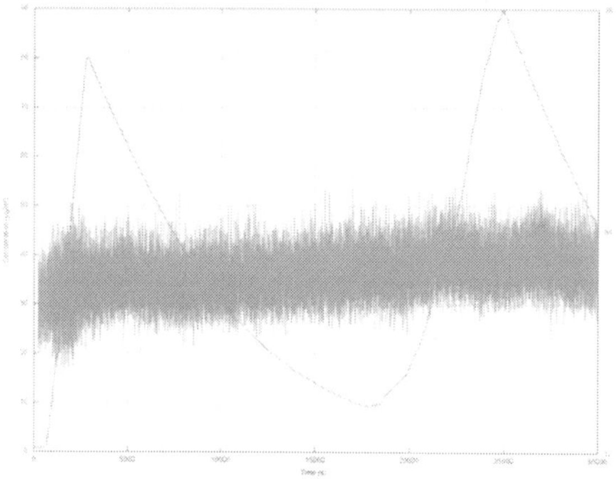

Figure 4. Phase response (green curve) with particle concentration variation (red curve) for a Rayleigh wave sensor.

IV. CONCLUSION

In this work, we demonstrated the potential of using surface acoustic wave sensors for fine particle detection in the $0 - 100$ $\mu g/m^3$ concentration range. In particular, Love wave based sensors proved to be very sensitive and quick to respond. However, this type of devices are not able to distinguish particles by size. In particular PM10 and PM2.5 particles, which represent the biggest threat to health, would induce the same response at equal mass. The SAW sensors therefore require the use of a filtering system beforehand. The design of a such filtering system and integrating it with the SAW sensors is the focus of our current research work. An operating prototype has been finalized and will soon be published.

ACKNOWLEDGMENT

This work was partly supported by the french RENATECH network and its FEMTO-ST technological facility.

REFERENCES

[1] M. Vanotti, V. Blondeau-Patissier, D. Rabus, J.-Y. Rauch, J.-M. Barbe, and S. Ballandras, "Development of acoustic devices functionalized with cobalt corroles or metalloporphyrines for the detection of carbon monoxide at low concentration," Sensors & Transducers, vol. 14, no. 1, 2012, p. 197.

[2] M. Vanotti, V. Blondeau-Patissier, D. Rabus, J.-Y. Rauch, and S. Ballandras, "Selective Detection of Hydrogen with Surface Acoustic Wave Devices Using Palladium Layer Properties," Sensors & Transducers, vol. 18, no. 1, 2013, p. 84.

[3] J.-M. Friedt, C. Droit, S. Ballandras, S. Alzuaga, G. Martin, and P. Sandoz, "Remote vibration measurement: A wireless passive surface acoustic wave resonator fast probing strategy," Review of Scientific Instruments, vol. 83, no. 5, 2012, p. 055001.

[4] D. Rabus, J. Friedt, S. Ballandras, G. Martin, E. Carry, and V. Blondeau-Patissier, "High-sensitivity open-loop electronics for gravimetric acoustic-wave-based sensors," Ultrasonics, Ferroelectrics, and Frequency Control, IEEE Transactions on, vol. 60, no. 6, 2013, pp. 1219–1226.

Gasoline Sensor Based on Piezoelectric Lateral Electric Field Resonator

Zaitsev B.D., Teplykh A.A., Borodina I.A.
Kotel'nikov Institute of Radio Engineering and Electronics of RAS, Saratov Branch
SB IRE nm.V.A.Kotelnikov RAS
Saratov, Russia
e-mail: zai-boris@yandex.ru, teplykhaa@mail.ru, borodinaia@yandex.ru

Kuznetsova I.E.
Kotel'nikov Institute of Radio Engineering and Electronics of RAS
IRE nm.V.A.Kotelnikov RAS
Moscow, Russia
e-mail: kuziren@yandex.ru

Abstract — **This paper presents a method to determine the octane number of gasoline products using a piezoelectric lateral electric field resonator. The dependence of permittivity of the gasoline on its octane number was measured. It has been shown that, for Russian gasoline grades, there is an unique dependence of aforementioned parameters. It has been found theoretically and experimentally that the frequency of the parallel resonance insignificantly changes with the change of the permittivity of gasoline contacting with free surface of the resonator. Our analysis shows that the value of the real part of the electrical impedance on the resonant frequency is unambiguously determined by the octane number of the gasoline. We provide an example of the determination of the octane number of an arbitrary mixture of different gasoline grades. We also consider the temperature of the gasoline sample under study.**

Keywords - octane number of gasoline; relative permittivity; lateral electric field excited piezoresonator; gasoline sensor.

I. Introduction

Gasoline, which is widely used as engine fuel, represents the inflammable mixture of light hydrocarbons. The most important parameter of gasoline is its octane number, which characterizes its detonation resistance. This parameter is extremely important to ensure the optimal characteristics and durability of a working engine. Detonation is a process of spontaneous inflammation of air-and-fuel mixture not from the spark plug, but from heat of the gas mixture, which is compressed by the piston. In this case, burning has an explosive nature, which leads to the temperature excursion and the premature wear of the engine. In practice, the needed octane number is achieved by using special additives, which may evaporate in time. This process will lead to changes in the octane number of gasoline. So, in a number of cases, one needs to check the octane number of gasoline. At present time, the octane number of gasoline is determined by motor and research methods on special laboratory equipment [1]. These methods are carried out under laboratory conditions, with the help of expensive instrumentation and qualified personnel. Therefore, the development of the sensor for express analysis of octane number of gasoline acquired in fuel stations represents the prospective problem. At present, there exist only several papers devoted to express methods of octane number determination. For example, it is proposed to determinate the octane number of gasoline by measuring its viscosity [2]. But this method has not been put into practice. In our laboratory we develop the sensor based on the self-excited oscillator the feedback of which contains the delay line based on the plate of Y – X lithium niobate with propagating acoustic wave with shear – horizontal polarization [3]. The liquid container with gasoline under study was placed on the path of acoustic wave. It has been shown that the frequency oscillation is unambiguously associated with the permittivity of the gasoline, which, in turn, is determined by its octane number [3]. It is well known that the lateral electric field excited piezo - resonator is sensitive to the change in the properties of contacting liquid [4]. Therefore, the aim of this paper is the development of a sensor for express analysis of gasoline octane number based on the lateral electric field excited resonator. In Section II, we measure the dielectric permittivity of gasoline. In Section III, we describe the fabrication of gasoline sensor. In Section IV, we theoretically analyze the sensor loaded by gasoline. Section V concludes the paper.

II. The Measurement of the Dependence of the Relative Permittivity of Gasoline on Its Octane Number

It is obvious that, for the development of a sensor for express analysis of the octane number of gasoline, one needs to know its parameter, which is unambiguously determined by its octane number. As it has been pointed out, this parameter is permittivity. Table 1 contains the region of admissible values of permittivity for three octane numbers: 80, 92, 95 and their averaged values [5].

TABLE I. The regions of admissible values of permittivity and their averaged values taken from [5], and also measured values of permittivity for three grades of gasoline.

Octane number	80	92	95
The regions of admissible values of permittivity [5]	2 – 2.062	2.08 – 2.115	2.145 – 2.205
Averaged values of permittivity [5]	2.031	2.0975	2.175
Measured values of permittivity	2.084	2.148	2.2

The aforementioned grades of gasoline are standard for Russian market. We have measured the values of permittivity for these grades, which are also presented in Table 1. Below, our method of measurement is described.

For measuring the permittivity, a plane air capacitor with shear dimensions of 20×20 mm^2 and with the gap of 1 mm was fabricated. The capacity of this capacitor in air was measured with the help of the LCR meter 4285A (Agilent). A LCR meter is a piece of electronic test equipment used to measure the inductance (L), capacitance (C), and, resistance (R) of a component. Then, the capacitor was immersed into a sample of the gasoline under study and the capacity was measured again. With the assumption that relative permittivity of the air is equal to 1, the sought permittivity of gasoline was determined as the ratio of capacity in gasoline and capacity in air. The obtained data for the three grades of gasoline is also presented in Table 1. One can see that they are close to the values which are taken from literature. Figure 1 shows the dependence of the measured permittivity of the gasoline on its octane number.

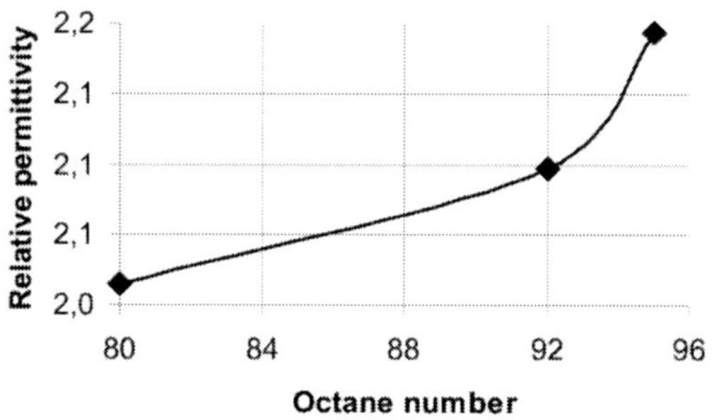

Figure 1. The dependence of measured permittivity of the gasoline on its octane number

It is evident that permittivity of gasoline insignificantly increases with increase of the octane number.

III. FABRICATION OF GASOLINE SENSOR

For fabrication of the gasoline sensor, the piezoelectric resonator with lateral electric field based on the plate of lithium niobate of X cut was used (Figure 2). The plate thickness was equal to 0.5 mm. Two rectangular aluminum electrodes with shear dimensions 5×10 mm^2 and with the gap between them of 3 mm were deposited in vacuum on the lower side of the plate.

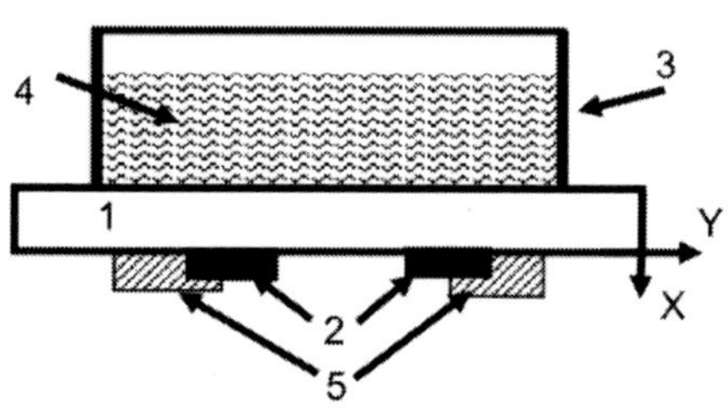

Figure 2. The gasoline sensor: 1 – piezoelectric plate, 2 – electrodes, 3 – liquid container, 4 – gasoline under study, 5 – damping layer.

The orientation of electrodes was chosen in such a way that lateral electric field was directed along crystallographic axis Y. Such orientations of the plate and lateral electric field lead to the excitation of longitudinal acoustic wave in the space between electrodes, which propagates along the normal to the surface and resounds between the sides of the plate [6]. The region around the electrodes was covered by the special damping layer. The metallic liquid container with the shear dimensions of 25 × 25 mm^2 was placed on the upper side of the plate. These dimensions exceeded the sizes of the region of damping layer. The container was fixed to the plate surface with the help of gasoline-resistant epoxy.

Figure 3 shows the frequency dependencies of the real (a) and imaginary (b) parts of the electrical impedance of the resonator with an empty liquid container. One can see that clearly expressed parallel resonance takes place at a frequency of 6.48 MHz. At that close to this frequency, the intensity of suppressed parasitic oscillations is significantly less.

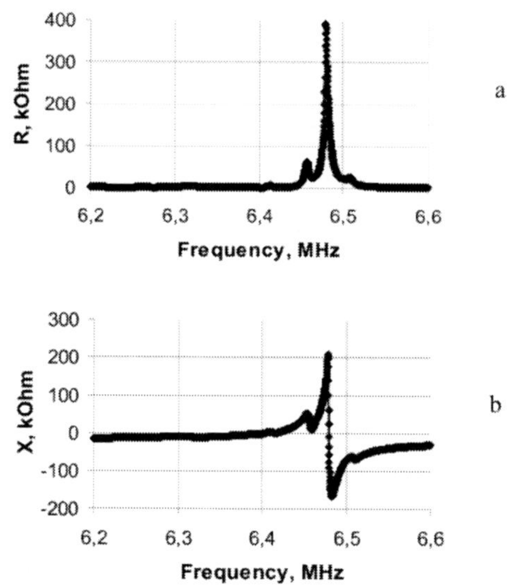

Figure 3. The frequency dependencies of the real (a) and imaginary (b) parts of the electrical impedance of the empty sensor

Then, we measured the frequency dependencies of real and imaginary parts of electrical impedance of the sensor loaded by the gasoline with a given octane number. These dependencies for values of octane numbers of 80, 92, and 95 are presented in Figures 4, 5, and 6, respectively. All measurements were carried out under a laboratory environment with the temperature of 26^{0}C and atmospheric pressure of 99.5 kPa. The detailed analysis has shown that, as an analytical parameter which is unambiguously associated with the octane number of the gasoline we can use the value of the real part of electrical impedance of the sensor on the frequency of parallel resonance. The resonant frequency does not depend on the grade of the gasoline. The dependence of the maximum of real part of the impedance on octane number is presented in Figure 7. This dependence may be used as a calibration curve of the sensor.

We have also carried out the experiment to determine the octane number of the arbitrary mixture of gasoline samples with octane values of 80 and 92. The measured value of the maximum of real part of impedance turns out to be R_{max} = 20.149 kOhm. This data corresponds to the octane number of 82.25.

It is obvious that, in practice, the estimation of the octane number of gasoline must be carried out at different values of environmental temperature and atmospheric pressure. It is well known [7] that the liquid permittivity strongly depends on the temperature and insignificantly changes with the variation in atmosphere pressure. It means that the estimation of octane number of gasoline by measuring its permittivity requires the need of temperature consideration. Our experiments have shown that the frequency of the series resonance does not depend on gasoline octane number (Figure 8) but unambiguously depends on the temperature. So, in the future work, we will measure the dependencies of R_{max} on octane number at various temperature values. In this case, we will obtain the calibration set of curves with the temperature as parameter. The dependence of the frequency of series resonance on the temperature will also be measured.

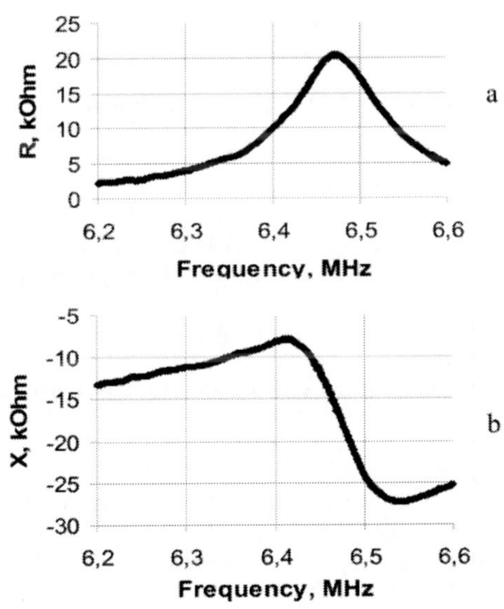

Figure 4. The frequency dependencies of the real (a) and imaginary (b) parts of the electrical impedance for the sensor loaded by gasoline with octane number of 80.

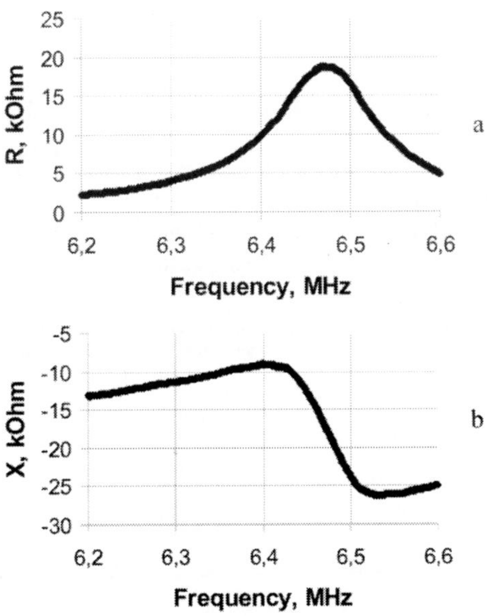

Figure 5. The frequency dependencies of the real (a) and imaginary (b) parts of the electrical impedance for the sensor loaded by gasoline with octane number of 92.

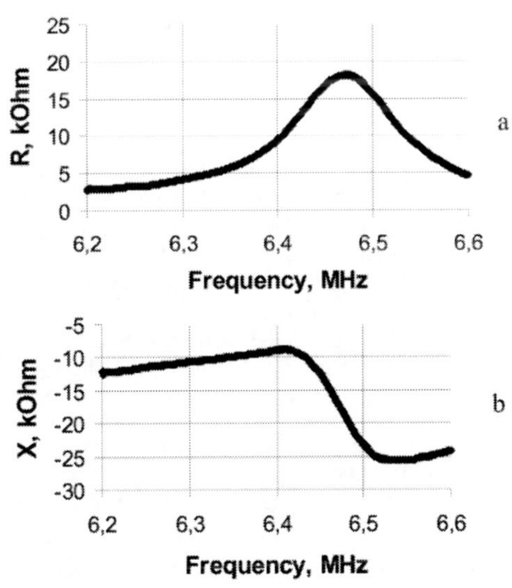

Figure 6. The frequency dependencies of the real (a) and imaginary (b) parts of the electrical impedance for the sensor loaded by gasoline with octane number of 95.

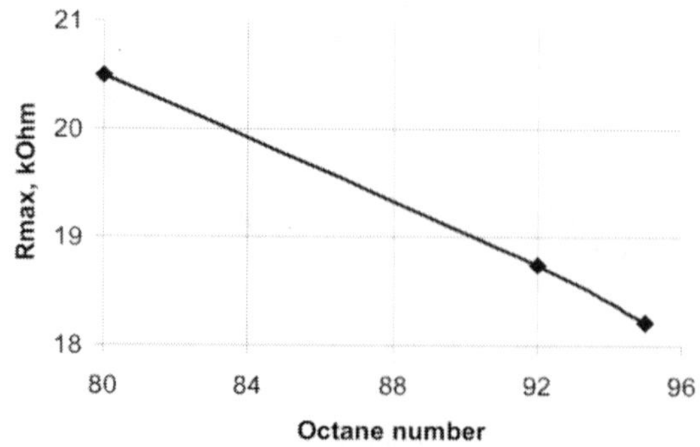

Figure 7. The dependence of the value of real part of the electrical impedance at the frequency of the parallel resonance on octane number of gasoline.

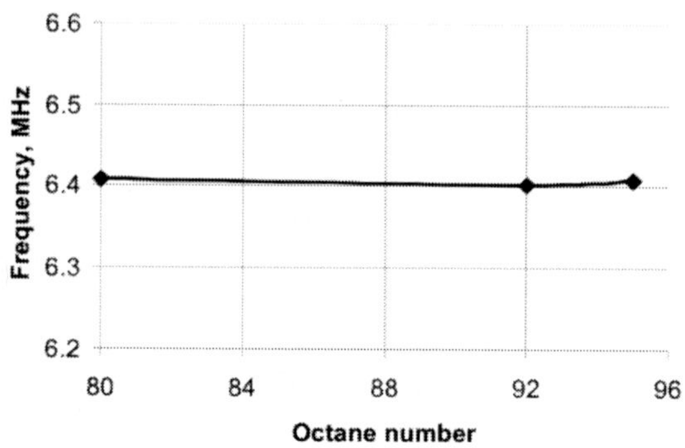

Figure 8. The dependence of the frequency of series resonance on octane number of gasoline.

Therefore, the determination of the octane number of the gasoline considering its temperature will be performed in the following way. For the sample under study, the frequency of the series resonance and the value of R_{max} will be measured. Then, by using the temperature dependence of this frequency, the temperature of the sample will be found. This will allow to choose the corresponding branch on the calibration set of curves and to determine the sought octane number by using the known value of R_{max}.

IV. THEORETICAL ANALYSIS OF REAL AND IMAGINARY PARTS OF RESONATOR LOADED BY VARIOUS GRADES OF GASOLINE

In this work, we also calculated the frequency dependences of real and imaginary parts of the resonator loaded with gasoline samples with different dielectric permittivity.

The theoretical analysis was carried out using the finite-element method [8]. The geometry of the problem is shown in Figure 9.

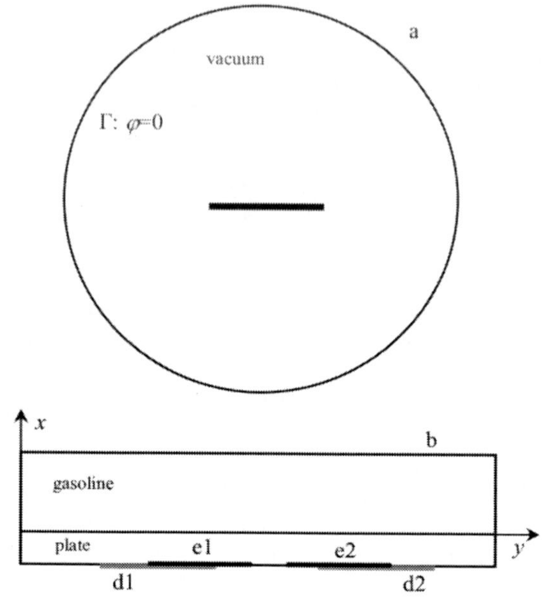

Figure 9. (a) Overview of the region of solution; (b) the central part of the region of solution: the plate of resonator and the gasoline layer, e1, e2 are electrodes, d1, d2 are damping layers.

The geometrical dimensions of all elements of the sensor and crystallographic orientations of a plate and electrodes in the XY plane are accurately equal to the experimental ones. The width of a piezoelectric plate, the electrodes and the gap between them were equal to 25 mm, 5 mm and 3 mm, respectively. The width of the area of a covering around electrodes was equal to 5 mm. The upper side of a plate was contacted with the layer of gasoline of 2 mm thick.

In the direction of the Z axis, the structure was implied to be infinite. All calculations were carried out inside a circle with a diameter of 100 mm. The elastic, piezoelectric and dielectric constants of lithium niobate and its density were taken from [9]. The speed of sound in gasoline and its density were taken from [1]. The relative permittivity of grades of gasoline were assumed to be equal to 2.0, 2.1, and 2.2 respectively. The computed dependencies of real and imaginary parts of electrical impedance for these three grades of gasoline are shown in Figure 10.

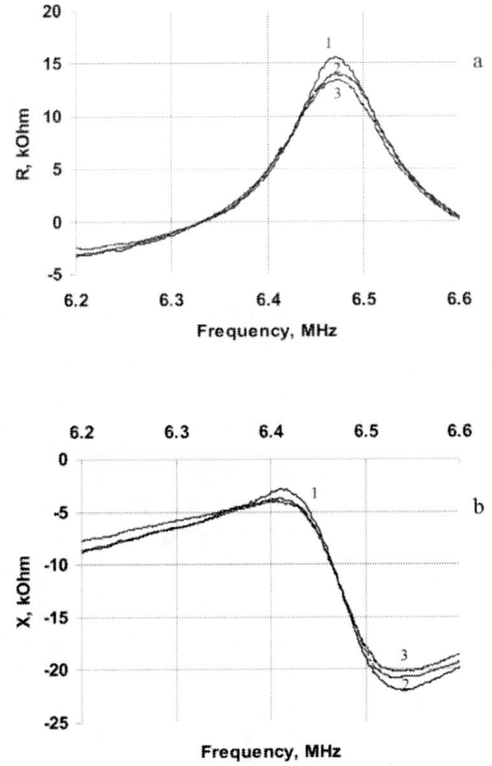

Figure 10. Theoretical frequency dependencies of real (a) and imaginary (b) parts of electrical impedance for permittivity 2.0 (1), 2.1 (2) and 2.2 (3).

So, it is shown that the theory and the experiment are in satisfactory agreement with each other.

V. CONCLUSION

In this paper, we developed a meter to measure the gasoline octane number based on the piezoelectric resonator with lateral electric field. The dependence of the relative permittivity of gasoline on its octane number was experimentally measured. It has been shown that, for Russian gasoline grades, there exists an unique relation of the aforementioned parameters. It has been theoretically and experimentally shown that the frequency of the parallel resonance insignificantly changes with the change in the gasoline permittivity. Analysis has shown that, as an analytical parameter unambiguously tied with gasoline octane number, one can use the value of real part of electrical impedance on the frequency of parallel resonance. An example of the determination of the octane number of an arbitrary mixture of different gasoline grades was given. We also considered the temperatures of the gasoline samples under study. The possibility of the consideration of the temperature of the gasoline sample under study is shown.

ACKNOWLEDGMENT

The work has been supported with the grant of Russian Science Foundation # 15-19-20046.

REFERENCES

[1] G. E. Totten, S. R. Westbrook, and R. J. Shah, Fuels and Lubricants Handbook: Technology, Properties, Performance, and Testing, Astm Manual Series, Mnl 37. West Conshokhoken: ASTM International, 2003, pp.635-648.

[2] R. M. Lec, X. J. Zhang, and J. M. Hammond, "A remote acoustic engine oil quality sensor", Proceedings of IEEE Ultrasonics Symposium, 1997, pp. 419-422.

[3] I. E. Kuznetsova, B. D. Zaitsev, E. P. Seleznev, and E. Verona "Gasoline identifier based on SH0 plate acoustic waves", Ultrasonics, vol. 70, 2015, pp. 34–37, DOI 10.1016\j.ultras.2016.04.016.

[4] B. D. Zaitsev, A. M. Shikhabudinov, A. A. Teplykh, I. E. Kuznetsova "Liquid sensor based on a piezoelectric lateral electric field-excited resonator", Ultrasonics, vol. 63, 2015, pp. 179-183.

[5] http://lib2.podelise.ru/docs/2868/index-11739-1.html?page=3 (in Russian)

[6] B. D. Zaitsev, I. E. Kuznetsova, A. M. Shikhabudinov, A. A. Teplykh and I. A. Borodina, "The Study of Piezoelectric Lateral - Electric - Field - Excited Resonator", IEEE Trans. on Ultrason. Ferroelectr. and Freq. Contr., vol. 61, №. 1, January 2014, pp. 162–172.

[7] I. E. Tamm, Fundamentals of the Theory of Electricity, Moscow, Mir Publisher, 1979.

[8] A. Teplykh, B. Zaitsev, and I. Kuznetsova. "Numerical Model of Piezoelectric Lateral Electric Field Excited Resonator", Sensors & Transducers, V. 184, Issue 1, 2015, pp. 60-65

[9] G. Kovacs, M. Anhorn, H. E. Engan, G. Visintini, and C. C. W. Ruppel, "Improved material constants for LiNbO3 and LiTaO3", Proc. IEEE Ultrasonics Symp., vol. 1, 1990, pp. 435-438

Coating Process for MEMS Based 3-axis Force Sensors

Andres Ospina and Saifeddine Aloui
Laboratory of sensor system characterization
Commissariat à l'énergie atomique
et aux énergies alternatives
Grenoble, France
Email: andres.ospina@cea.fr and
saifeddine.aloui@cea.fr

Mathieu Grossard
Interactive Robotic Laboratory
Commissariat à l'énergie atomique
et aux énergies alternatives
Saclay, France
Email: mathieu.grossard@cea.fr

Alain Micaelli
Interactive Simulation Laboratory
Commissariat à l'énergie atomique
et aux énergies alternatives
Saclay, France
Email: alain.micaelli@cea.fr

***Abstract*—The present paper discusses an experimental procedure for designing a suitable coating for Microelectromechanical systems (MEMs) based 3-axis force sensors. Several coating shapes, sizes and materials were tested. The coated sensors were calibrated and tested in order to characterize the effect of the coating on the sensor characteristics such as measurement dynamic range and resolution, the linearity of the response, as well as the impulse response of the system. Finally guidelines for optimal coating of the sensor are proposed.**

Keywords–force; sensor; MEMs; protection; coating

I. Introduction

The development of Microelectromechanical systems (MEMs) sensors was a revolution that produced small and cheap sensors. This technology allowed massive production of inexpensive and small sensors.

In tactile sensing field, force/torque MEMs based sensors such as presented in [1], [2] and [3] have allowed low cost and highly integrated touch sensing. This type of sensors has shown good characteristics such as linear behavior, low hysteresis, and good accuracy. However, because of their size and fragility, these systems suffer from two major problems:

- The sensitive area of these sensors is small
- The maximal forces and torques that this kind of system could support is low.

For example, the sensor presented in [1] has a maximum force of 1 N and the sensor presented in [3] has a maximum force of 2 N. For most tactile applications, such as object manipulation, in robotics manipulation tasks the range of forces that the sensor should support must be at least 10 N [4].

To solve the problem of measurement range, one solution consists in making bigger silicon based sensors, with bigger supports. However, due to technology considerations, the size of the sensor can not be big enough to cover a large surface which doesn't solve the small sensitive area problem. In addition, using more silicon would significantly increase the sensor cost. Another possible solution consists in protecting the sensor with an elastic coating layer, as shown in [5] or [6]. This solution distributes the forces between the sensitive part of the sensor and the area around which increases the sensor dynamic range. This solution provides protection to the sensor, increases the sensitive surface area and enables the sensor to be interfaced with an external frame for intrinsic tactile sensing such as presented in a previous work [7].

Coating the sensor can have many drawbacks such as the introduction of non linearity and hysteresis. Depending on the used elastic material, a relaxation phenomenon may appear and significantly change the sensor response to external force. The coating increases the dynamic measurement range by distributing the force between the sensor and the surface around which reduces the sensor resolution. Finally, the analysis of the forces applied on any point of the surface is complex. In [6], the authors use a spherical coating geometry to create a soft fingertip. The system could estimate the forces applied during the contact with an external object as well as detect the early slippage. In [5], the authors made a specific geometry to ensure that the contact is established on the top flat surface of the coating. Both papers use polyurethane as protection material.

In all review work about the protection of MEMs force sensors as [5], [6], [8], [9] or [10] they do not analysed more than one coating, and do not discuss why the specific coating shape, size and material has been selected. The goal of this paper is to provide guidelines for the design and construction of the coating for MEMs force sensors supported with experimental results and comparison between various predefined coatings. The objective is to identify the coating shape, size and material that provides the lowest alteration to the sensor characteristics while increasing its dynamic range and providing protection against high forces.

This paper is organized as follow: Section 2 presents the 3-axis MEMs force sensor used in our experiments as well as its initial characteristics. Section 3 presents different coatings used to protect the sensor and as well as their design and construction process. In Section 4, the characterization of each protected sensor is presented. In Section 5, the resistance to high applied forces has been tested for two of the coated sensors. Finally, optimal coating guidelines are deduced.

II. 3-axis force MEMs sensor

The force sensor operates on the principle presented in [5]. This consists of eight strain sensitive elements that are attached to a stem. All these elements are made of the same silicon crystal and have a geometry shown in Figure 1.

In this case, the sensor is made of a monocrystalline silicon element, where the sensitive elements are eight piezoresistors, i.e., the resistance value varies according to their deformation. They are made by doping the underside of the silicon membrane. The piezoresistors are divided according to the x and y

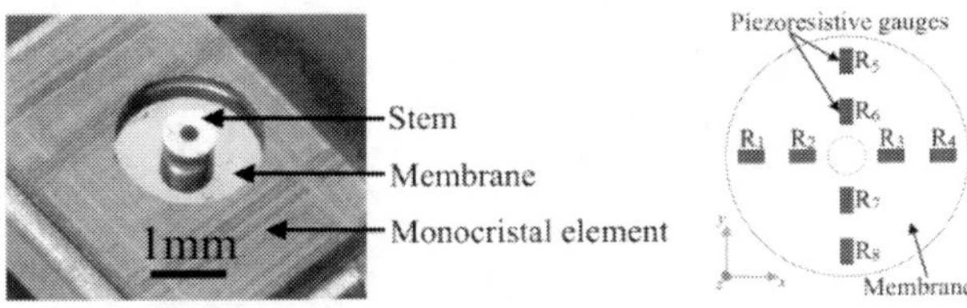

(a) Photo of the sensor (b) Piezoresistors

Figure 1. Sensor structure

axes defining the plane tangential to the membrane as shown in Figure 1b. The eight piezoresistive elements have a similar resistance value R_i at rest, and are placed so that they are constrained symmetrically upon application of a force along an axis x, y or z. Figure 2 shows schematically the deformation of the membrane during the application of a normal force F_z or tangential forces F_x, F_y in the plane of the membrane.

(a) Tangencial force (b) Normal force

Figure 2. Transversal view of the sensor

The piezoresistors are associated to each other in a Wheatstone bridge arrangement according to x and y axis, as shown in Figure 3.

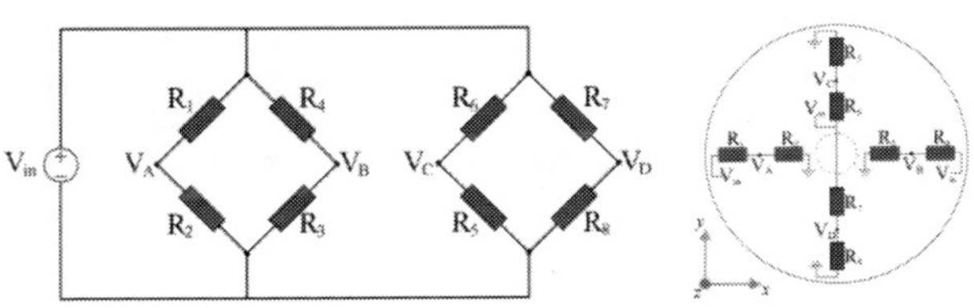

(a) Wheatstone (b) Schema connection

Figure 3. Configuration and distribution of the piezoresistors

Once a force is applied to the stem, the membrane is warped. This causes the compression or the stretching of the piezoresistors along x and y axis, leading to a change in their resistance values. The resistance variation affects the potentials $V_{A,B,C,D}$. The three voltages u_x, u_y and u_z proportional to the applied forces can be calculated as follows:

$$\vec{u} = \begin{bmatrix} u_x \\ u_y \\ u_z \end{bmatrix} = \begin{bmatrix} -a_1 & a_1 & 0 & 0 \\ 0 & 0 & a_2 & -a_2 \\ a_3 & a_3 & -a_3 & -a_3 \end{bmatrix} \begin{bmatrix} V_A \\ V_B \\ V_C \\ V_D \end{bmatrix} \quad (1)$$

where a_1, a_2 and a_3 are identified measurements gains. As presented in [5], in theory, the measurements of the forces are independent. In practice, there is a cross-talk between the axes of the sensor. The forces are estimated as follows:

$$\vec{f} = \begin{bmatrix} f_x \\ f_y \\ f_z \end{bmatrix} = \begin{bmatrix} S_{xx} & S_{xy} & S_{xz} \\ S_{yx} & S_{yy} & S_{yz} \\ S_{zx} & S_{zy} & S_{zz} \end{bmatrix} \begin{bmatrix} u_x \\ u_y \\ u_z \end{bmatrix} - \begin{bmatrix} b_x \\ b_y \\ b_z \end{bmatrix} \quad (2)$$

where S_{ij} are the components of the sensitivity matrix, $u_{x,y,z}$ is the vector of measured voltages, and $b_{x,y,z}$ are the components of the bias vector which is the voltages measured when no forces are applied.

A. *Characteristics of the sensor*

The sensor has a linear behavior with respect to normal and tangential forces because of the mono-crystalline nature of the sensor and the elasticity of silicon. The used sensor has the following characteristics:

- Membrane radius: $1000\,\mu m$
- Membrane thickness: $100\,\mu m$
- Stem radius: $575\,\mu m$
- $S^{-1}_{xx,yy}$ Sensitivity : $(42.5 \pm 1.5)\,mV/N$
- S^{-1}_{zz} Sensitivity: $(150.00 \pm 0.25)\,mV/N$
- F_z max pressure. before deteriorating: $1.5\,N$
- $F_{x,y}$ max strength. before deteriorating: $1\,N$
- $\max \Delta U_{x,y}$ maximum voltage variation before the deteriorating in tangential forces: $42.5\,mV$
- $\max \Delta U_z$ maximum voltage variation before the deteriorating in normal forces: $225\,mV$
- The sensor is $5\,mm$ long, $3.5\,mm$ wide, and $0.8\,mm$ high regardless of the stem.
- Cut-off frequency: $54\,Hz$ to $60\,Hz$

All sensitivity values are given for a supply voltage of $5\,V$.

III. Considered Sensor Coating

In order to protect the sensor and increase its sensitivity range, the sensor was protected as shown in [5]. The protection is made by deposing an elastic material over the sensor so that the forces exerted on the material will be distributed between the sensor and the support.

The chosen elastic material is polyurethane. This choice is entirely based on previous work results in determining the proper type of protection, [5] or [6]. The MEMs sensor is integrated and connected to a round PCB as shown in Figure 4 and several protections were implemented and tested.

Figure 4. MEMs force sensor connected and mounted in PCB

In this document, 5 protections are dealt with as shown in Figure 5.

These sensors were chosen to be tested in order to determine the following points:

(a) rA (b) rB (c) rC

(d) rD (e) F02

Figure 5. Coated MEMs force sensors

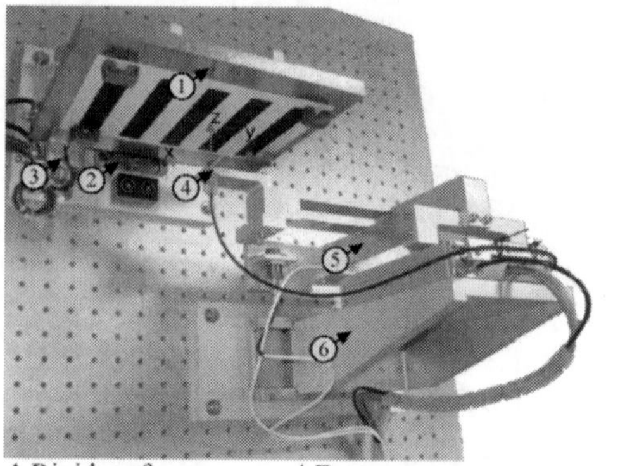

1.Rigid surface 4.Force sensor
2.Precision screw 5. Reference force sensor
3.Pneumatic actuator 6. Linear actuators

Figure 6. Testing system

The optimal construction material: The sensors are protected with two different polyurethane resins. The difference between the two tested materials is essentially in the hardness:

- the black polyurethane has a hardness of Shore 80
- the beige polyurethane has a hardness of Shore 40

The sensors rC, rD and F02 are protected with black polyurethane, rA with beige polyurethane, and the sensor rB is composed of half of each.

The influence of height: Sensors rC and rD have the same shape, the same material but different height in order to establish a relationship between the coating height and the response of the sensor.

The influence of shape: Differences in behavior between the forms of protection.

The coating procedure: Sensors rA, rB, rC and rD are made from a mold, and the protection F02 by pouring the material above the sensor.

IV. COATED SENSOR CHARACTERIZATION

In this section, a relatively low force range is used in order to determine the sensor characteristics without pushing it to its maximum supported force.

A. *Experimental test bench*

In order to calibrate and qualify the different coatings, a testing system (Figure 6) was created. This system uses a reference force sensor developed in [5] mounted on two linear actuators (Lx80F40 Linax Jenny Science) placed along the x and y axes. A precision screw and a pneumatic actuator are used to move a rigid plate parallel to the reference force system. The data acquisition system is a national instruments acquisition board (DAQ) PXI-6225 at a frequency of 1 kHz.

B. *Characterization methodology*

The following measurement methodology is performed:

- Fix the sensor to measure, in its support, in the end effector.
- Without applying any force, begin to acquire the voltages $\vec{u}$ in order to calculate the offset $\vec{b}$
- The sensor and the rigid surface are brought into contact by the precision screw, until a force of $(1.3 \pm 0.2)\,\mathrm{N}$ is exerted, and is varied manually without exceeding $1.6\,\mathrm{N}$ force.
- The two linear motors move along a predefined path, to exert tangential forces on the sensor
- When the motion terminates, the contact is automatically removed by a pneumatic actuator
- The acquisition system is stopped

The defined trajectory is designed so that the force exerted on the sensor sweeps through all of the measurable force range, i.e., explore both the positive and negative forces in the x and y axes without breaking the sensor. Unfortunately, the contact between the 3-axis force sensor and the rigid surface has a small friction coefficient, that does not allow exertion of tangential forces through all of the measurable force range. The trajectory is shown in Figure 7. The used trajectory is square in order to minimize the effects of cross-talking between the axes.

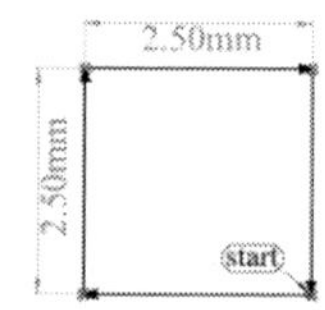

Figure 7. Trajectory for the sensor characterization

The first portion of the acquired signal is used to remove the sensor offset. At the beginning, the exerted force is null, thus the measured voltages vector $\vec{u}$ is equal to the bias vector $\vec{b}$.

$$\vec{f} = 0 \Rightarrow \vec{u} = \vec{b} \tag{3}$$

The sensitivity matrix of each sensor can be estimated using least squares method as follows :

$$\{l_i, \mathbf{S}_i\} = \underset{l_i, \mathbf{S}_i}{\operatorname{argmin}} \sum_{j=1}^{n} \left(\vec{\mathrm{ref}}_j - \vec{f}_j\right)^2 \tag{4}$$

where $\vec{\text{ref}}_j$ is the reference measurement of forces at sampling time j, and $\vec{f}_j$ is the forces calculated by equation 2 at sampling time j. n is the number of samples.

C. Characterization results

At least two measures of each of the five mentioned sensors were made. Half of the taken measures is used to calculate the sensitivity matrix and the other is used to validate the calibration.

The results of the experiments are shown in the Figure 8. The first row of the Figure 8 presents the results for the measurement set used to calibrate the sensor. The second row of Figure 8 presents the results for the measurement set used to validate the calibration. Figure 8 shows the acquired data at the point where the contact was removed. In fact, when the contact is released using the pneumatic actuator, the reference sensor begins to vibrate because the deformation due to the introduced forces creates a mass-sting system, consequently the last part of the acquired data of the measures is not used to calibrate the sensor since the reference is not accurate.

Table I presents the error statistics between the reference system and each of the 3 axis force sensors.

	Measure	Mean error	Max error	Standard deviation
rA	f_x	-3.36 mN	46.31 mN	11.82 mN
	f_y	-8.44 mN	65.00 mN	15.67 mN
	f_z	13.89 mN	52.78 mN	11.98 mN
rB	f_x	-2.09 mN	64.19 mN	12.78 mN
	f_y	9.29 mN	70.34 mN	16.56 mN
	f_z	3.90 mN	33.42 mN	7.79 mN
rC	f_x	-19.85 mN	133.14 mN	40.70 mN
	f_y	-24.37 mN	144.11 mN	35.92 mN
	f_z	5.82 mN	37.65 mN	8.19 mN
rD	f_x	-3.77 mN	54.34 mN	18.17 mN
	f_y	-2.87 mN	51.63 mN	11.92 mN
	f_z	-1.52 mN	31.25 mN	11.56 mN
F02	f_x	72.81 mN	190.33 mN	63.86 mN
	f_y	-10.53 mN	69.15 mN	16.67 mN
	f_z	28.94 mN	135.17 mN	40.19 mN

Table I. Error statistics coated sensor

The graphics of the relation between the reference forces against the calculated forces are shown in the third row of Figure 8.

To characterize the dynamic behavior of the sensor in the z axis, the reference data at the instant when the contact is released is replaced by a step function in the system input (in order to avoid the reference sensor vibration problem). Using these signals, the transfer function for each coated sensor is calculated. Taking as reference the following two characteristic transfer functions:

- Second order over-damped system

$$\frac{f_z(s)}{f_{z\text{real}}(s)} = \frac{K_p}{(1+\text{Tp}_1 s)(1+\text{Tp}_2 s)} \tag{5}$$

- System with two poles and one zero

$$\frac{f_z(s)}{f_{z\text{real}}(s)} = \frac{a_1 s + a_2}{s^2 + a_3 s + a_4} \tag{6}$$

The constant values K_p, Tp_1, Tp_2, or $a_{1,2,3,4}$ are found for each sensor. These values can be calculated in different ways. For example by the method of Harriot for over-damped second order systems or by minimizing the error between the input and output. The System Identification toolbox of MATLAB was used in order to easily determine these values. As it can be deduced from the fourth row in Figure 8, sensors rA and rB have a transfer function that fits with a second order transfer function 5. The other three sensors have a well pronounced relaxation phenomenon. As a consequence, their transfer function fits better with the one of a system with two poles and one zero presented in equation 6. The transfer functions calculated for sensors are shown in the Figure.

Bode plot and phase, calculated from systems presented in Figure 8, are shown in Figure 9.

The modelled cutoff-frequency of the sensors varies between $\approx$ 30 Hz for the F02 and $\approx$ 50 Hz for the rB. The theoretical performance of the sensors to a step signal is shown in Figure 10.

The characteristics of sensitivity and cut-off frequency of each sensor are presented in Table II.

The results were obtained using a linear model of the behavior of the sensor.

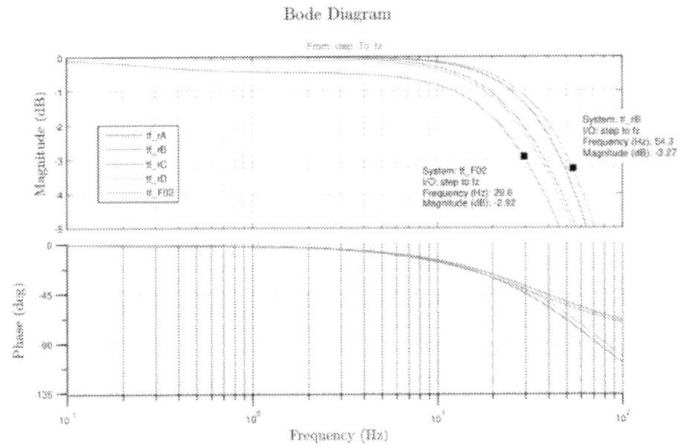

Figure 9. Frequency response and phase of the coated force sensors

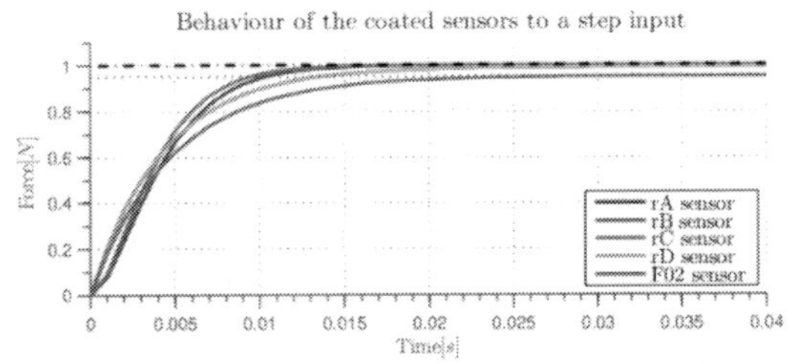

Figure 10. Behavior of the coated force sensors to a step input

	S_{xx}^{-1}	S_{yy}^{-1}	S_{zz}^{-1}	Cut-off freq
rA	0.675 mV/N	0.675 mV/N	9.5 mV/N	$\approx$ 45 Hz
rB	0.425 mV/N	0.370 mV/N	10.5 mV/N	$\approx$ 50 Hz
rC	0.8 mV/N	0.8 mV/N	15 mV/N	$\approx$ 35 Hz
rD	0.63 mV/N	0.63 mV/N	13 mV/N	$\approx$ 34 Hz
F02	0.74 mV/N	0.4 mV/N	10.5 mV/N	$\approx$ 30 Hz

Table II. Error statistics coated sensor

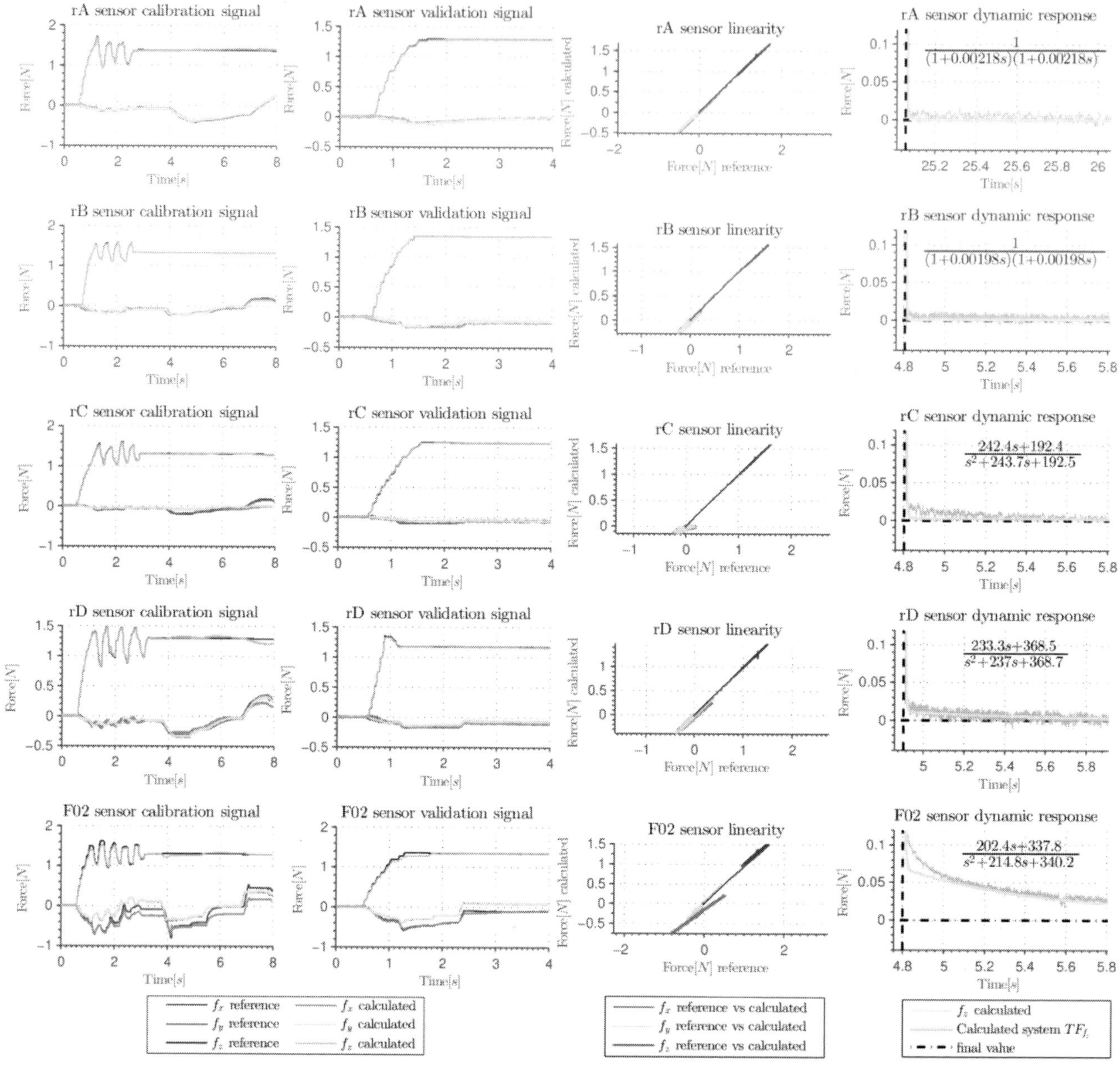

Figure 8. Results of the coated sensor characterization

D. Results Analysis

From Figure 8 and Table I, it is clear that sensors rA, rB and rD have similar behaviors and good matching of the estimated forces with respect to the reference ones. However, sensors rC and F02 have errors that are almost double compared to the others.

Figure 8 shows that sensors rA, rB and rD preserve the linear behavior between measurements. Additionally, the figure shows that the sensors rC, rD and F02 have a a more significant relaxation phenomenon.

Regarding the set-points evoked in section III. The following analyses are made:

Material to be used: For the beige polyurethane with hardness of Shore 40, the relaxation phenomenon isn't considerable as is shown in Figure 8. Sensors coated directly with this material have a better dynamic behavior (rA and rB). When two materials are combined as for the sensor rB, the problem is that the forces are not distributed evenly in all directions (as shown in the linearity analysis figures).

Influence of height: Sensors rC and rD have the same shape and the same material. However they have very different

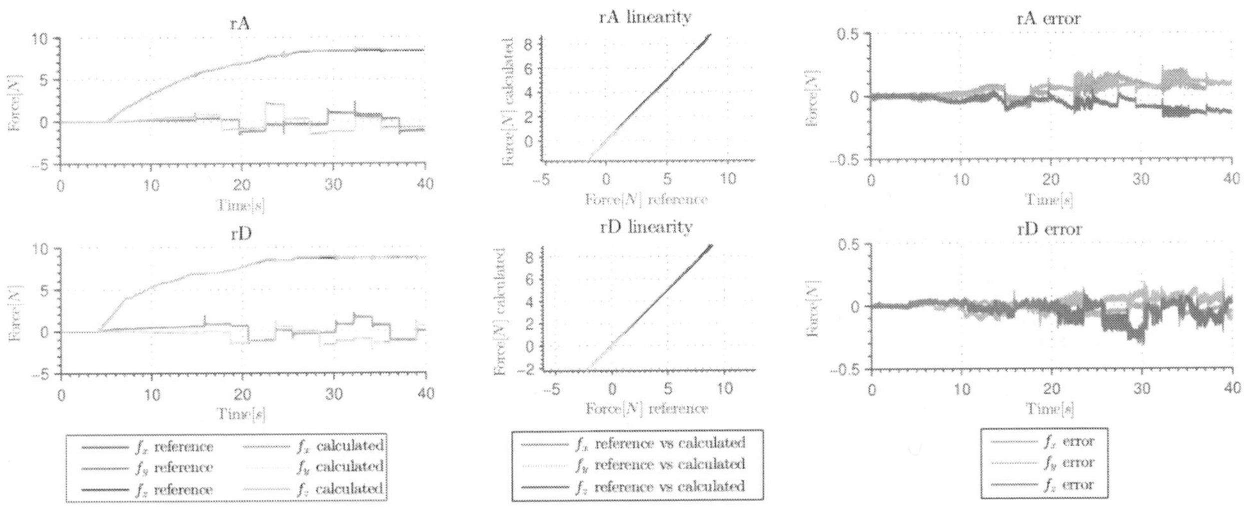

Figure 11. Results of the selected coated sensors

behaviours. The bigger coating height in sensor rC reduces its sensitivity to tangential forces.

Influence of the shape: Three different basic shapes were tested. The coating used in rA and rD has the same best linearity. Those shapes gave the best results. The shapes of sensors F02 and rC have a wide base. This significantly decreases their sensitivity in the shear axes. One of the biggest problems of the coating shape used for the F02 is that the point where the forces are applied is not centered with the sensor.

Manufacturing type of protection: The point of application of forces in the sensor must be well defined, the F02 sensor does not have this characteristic. In fact during the hardening process of the polyurethane, any disturbance in the angle affects the central point position.

V. Resistance to High Forces Test

The coated sensors that present the best characteristics (rA and rD) are selected for the high force test. The test consists of repeating the same experiment presented in the previous section by applying a higher force range. The test bench system does not allow more than 9 N. In this test, at least 8 N was applied to the sensor. The goal of this test is to verify if the coating preserves its characteristics for the range needed for object manipulation (about 10 N). The results are shown in Figure 11.

As shown in the figure, the sensors preserve their characteristics such as the linearity for the whole range of tested forces. The two systems resisted about 9 N without breaking. Clearly, they could go beyond this range without any problems. After the experiment, no hysteresis was noticed nor was there a change in their sensitivity. A more robust test bench tool could be used to determine the maximum supported force.

VI. Conclusion

This paper presents an experimental procedure for designing a suitable coating for MEMS based 3-axis force sensors. Five different coatings with different shapes, sizes and materials were calibrated, tested and characterized in order to show the effect of the coating. The analysed characteristics were the statistics of error in time, the linearity of the response as well as the impulse response of the system and the final sensitivity of the sensor.

The two sensors with the best characteristics are tested in a larger range showing that this type of coating is desirable to use in protecting MEMs force sensors.

The guidelines proposed in section III for the design and construction of the coating for MEMs force sensors supported with experimental results of section IV were analyzed and the conclusions are:

Coating material: The relaxation of the material should be the fastest possible one. Polyurethane Shore 40 meets this criterion and is advised to be used as a coating material.

Influence of height: A higher coating leads to lower sensor sensitivity to tangent forces. Thus, reducing the coating height is advised.

Influence of the shape: The point where the forces are exerted must be centered, so the tip of the protection must be pointy, and the base should not be too wide.

Manufacturing type of protection: The sensors must be made by molding.

The proposed guidelines can be used to create new coatings, with different range of forces and sensitivities. Consequently the force MEMs sensors can be applied in a larger set of applications.

Further work will focus on the creation of a new coating for a 3-axis force sensor matrix. This matrix can be used for the development of a tactile sensing system for robotics dexterous manipulation.

References

[1] F. De Boissieu, C. Godin, B. Guilhamat, D. David, C. Serviere, and D. Baudois, "Tactile texture recognition with a 3-axial force mems

integrated artificial finger," in *Robotics: Science and Systems*. Seattle, WA, 2009, pp. 49–56.

[2] D. V. Dao, T. Toriyama, J. Wells, and S. Sugiyama, "Micro force-moment sensor with six-degree of freedom," in *Proceedings of 2001 International Symposium on Micromechatronics and Human Science, 2001. MHS 2001*, 2001, pp. 93–98.

[3] K. Kim, K. R. Lee, Y. K. Kim, D. S. Lee, N. K. Cho, W. H. Kim, K. B. Park, H. D. Park, Y. K. Park, J. H. Kim, and J. J. Pak, "3-Axes Flexible Tactile Sensor Fabricated by Si Micromachining and Packaging Technology," in *19th IEEE International Conference on Micro Electro Mechanical Systems, 2006. MEMS 2006 Istanbul*, 2006, pp. 678–681.

[4] H. Yousef, M. Boukallel, and K. Althoefer, "Tactile sensing for dexterous in-hand manipulation in roboticsA review," *Sensors and Actuators A: Physical*, vol. 167, no. 2, pp. 171–187, Jun. 2011. [Online]. Available: http://linkinghub.elsevier.com/retrieve/pii/S0924424711001105

[5] F. d. Boissieu, C. Godin, L. Olmos, B. Guilhamat, D. D. C. Serviere, and D. Baudois, "Artificial touch system based on a MEMS sensor: design, characterization and application to fine texture recognition," *submitted to IEEE Trans. on Robotics*, 2011.

[6] V. A. Ho, D. V. Dao, S. Sugiyama, and S. Hirai, "Development and Analysis of a Sliding Tactile Soft Fingertip Embedded With a Microforce/Moment Sensor," *IEEE Transactions on Robotics*, vol. 27, no. 3, pp. 411–424, Jun. 2011.

[7] A. Ospina, S. Aloui, C. Godin, M. Grossard, and A. Micaelli, "Tactile sensing system for robotics dexterous manipulation based on a matrix of 3-axes force sensors," in *2015 IEEE/RSJ International Conference on Intelligent Robots and Systems (IROS)*, Sep. 2015, pp. 2105–2110.

[8] B. Gray and R. Fearing, "A surface micromachined microtactile sensor array," in , *1996 IEEE International Conference on Robotics and Automation, 1996. Proceedings*, vol. 1, Apr. 1996, pp. 1–6 vol.1.

[9] L. Beccai, S. Roccella, L. Ascari, P. Valdastri, A. Sieber, M. Carrozza, and P. Dario, "Development and Experimental Analysis of a Soft Compliant Tactile Microsensor for Anthropomorphic Artificial Hand," *Mechatronics, IEEE/ASME Transactions on*, vol. 13, no. 2, pp. 158 –168, Apr. 2008.

[10] R. Candelier, A. Prevost, and G. Debrgeas, "The Role of Exploratory Conditions in Bio-Inspired Tactile Sensing of Single Topogical Features," *Sensors (Basel, Switzerland)*, vol. 11, no. 8, pp. 7934–7953, Aug. 2011. [Online]. Available: http://www.ncbi.nlm.nih.gov/pmc/articles/PMC3231713/

Influence of Structure Configuration on Strained Devices: A Piezoelectric-oriented Survey

Irinela Chilibon
National Institute of Research and Development for Optoelectronics, INOE-2000
Bucharest-Magurele, Romania
e-mail: qilib@yahoo.com

Abstract—**This paper is a short overview of some piezoelectric materials and devices for generating renewable electricity under mechanical motion actions. Piezoelectric materials, usually crystals or ceramics, have the capability to generate a small amount of current, when they are subjected to mechanical pressure, such as pushing, bending, twisting, and turning. A vibrating piezoelectric device differs from a typical electrical power source in that it has capacitive rather than inductive source impedance, and may be driven by mechanical vibrations of varying amplitude. Several techniques have been developed to extract energy from the environment. Generally, "vibration energy" could be converted into electrical energy by three techniques: electrostatic charge, magnetic fields and piezoelectric. Mechanical resonance frequency of piezoelectric bimorph transducers depends on geometric size (length, width, and thickness of each layer), and the piezoelectric coefficients of the piezoelectric material. This paper will discuss about the manufacturing processes and intended applications of several energy harvesting devices.**

Keywords-renewable electricity; energy harvesting; vibration energy; generator; converter; piezoelectric; silicon on insulator (SOI).

I. INTRODUCTION

Renewable energy replaces conventional fuels in four distinct areas: power generation, hot water / space heating, transport fuels, and rural (off-grid) energy services.

The concept of "harvesting" is relatively recent, and presumes the capturing of the normally lost energy surrounding a system and converting it into *electrical energy* that can be used to extend the lifetime of that system's power supply or possibly provide an endless supply of energy to an electronic device, namely power harvesting.

Energy harvesting or *Scavenging energy* is an attractive concept because so many energy sources, such as: light, heat, and mechanical ambient vibrations that exist in our ambient living could be converted into usable *electricity*.

Among *alternative energy sources* can include: water energy, water waves, wind, solar, heat, random vibration, noise, nonlinear mechanical rotations, mechanical shocks, etc.

Several techniques have been proposed and developed to extract energy from the environment. In general, vibration energy could be converted into electrical energy using one of three techniques: electrostatic charge, magnetic fields and piezoelectric.

Multiple such materials, placed near each other could increase the electrical energy. The process of energy conversion in a piezoelectric material is based on the principle of the piezoelectric effect. The piezoelectric elements store electrical energy as an electric field. The *direct piezoelectric effect* describes the material's ability to transform mechanical strain into electrical charge. Many conventional systems consist of a single piezoceramic in bending mode (unimorph) or two bonded piezoelectric in bending mode (bimorph). *Cantilevered piezoelectric energy harvesters* have been investigated in the literature for energy harvesting. *Piezoelectric generators* [1] appropriate to convert the smallest mechanical deformations directly into electrical energy. This solid state effect is free of degradation in a wide operation range.

Some structures can be tuned to have two natural frequencies relatively close to each other, resulting in the possibility of a *broader band energy harvesting system*. The energy produced by these materials is in many cases far too small to directly power an electrical device.

Advances in *low-power electronics* and in *energy harvesting technologies* have enabled the conception of truly *self-powered devices* [2].

By driving one element to expand while contracting the other one, the actuator is forced to bend, creating an out-of plane motion and vibrations [3]. *Cantilevered piezoelectric energy harvesters* have been investigated in the literature for energy harvesting [4]. *MEMS (Micro-electro-mechanical System) array* with multi-cantilevers was designed with single cantilever behaving closer resonance frequency one after another [5].

The paper was structured in five sections: I. Introduction; II. Piezoelectric conversion; III. Piezoelectric generators; IV. Piezoelectric devices, and V. Conclusions and future works.

II. PIEZOELECTRIC CONVERSION

Piezoelectric materials, usually crystals or ceramics, have the capability to generate a small amount of current, when they are subjected to mechanical pressure, such as pushing, bending, twisting, and turning.

Piezoelectric materials exhibit the property that if they are mechanically strained, they generate an electric field proportional to the strain [6]. Conversely, when an electric field is applied the material undergoes strain. These anisotropic relationships are described by the piezoelectric strain constant, *d*, which gives the relationship between applied stresses while the electro-mechanical coupling coefficient, *k*, describes the efficiency (η) with which energy is converted between mechanical and electrical forms, and Q the quality factor. This latter coefficient is important in determining the efficiency of a resonant generator since the overall efficiency of a piezo element clamped to a substrate and cyclically compressed at its resonant frequency is [6]:

$$\eta = \frac{\frac{k^2}{2(1-k^2)}}{\frac{1}{Q} + \frac{k^2}{2(1-k^2)}} \tag{1}$$

A. Electrostatic convertions

Electrostatic conversion is based on the formation of a parallel plate capacitor onto which a charge is introduced from an external power source. Once the external source is disconnected then varying the capacitor configuration (plate overlap area or plate separation) causes the voltage and/or charge on the capacitor to vary. The varying voltage or charge may be extracted to provide electrical energy to a load.

For a parallel plate capacitor with plate area *A* and plate separation *d*, the capacitance is approximately

$$C = \varepsilon \frac{A}{d} = \frac{Q}{V} \tag{2}$$

where ε is the dielectric constant of the insulating material between the plates, *Q* and *V* are the charge and the voltage on the capacitor, respectively. The energy stored on the capacitor is

$$E = \frac{1}{2} QV \tag{3}$$

If the charge is held constant, then combining (9) and (10), the energy becomes

$$E = \frac{Q^2 d}{2\varepsilon A} \tag{4}$$

while if the voltage is constrained, the energy becomes

$$E = \frac{\varepsilon A V^2}{2d} \tag{5}$$

Attempts to change the stored energy by moving the capacitor plates cause a reaction force. This reaction force depends on whether the gap or the overlap area of the capacitor is varied and on whether the voltage or the charge is constrained.

III. Piezoelectric Generators

Piezoelectric generators are appropriate to convert the smallest mechanical deformations directly into *electrical energy*. This solid state effect is free of degradation in a wide operation range.

The process of energy conversion in a piezoelectric material is based on the principle of the *direct piezoelectric effect*. When a piezoelectric element is mechanically stressed it generates *electrical charges*.

Piezo energy harvesting has been investigated only since the late '90s and it remains an *emerging technology*.

The piezoelectric elements store electrical energy as an electric field. The *direct piezoelectric effect* describes the material's ability to transform mechanical strain into electrical charge. Figure 1 presents the piezoelectric generators principle.

Figure 1. Piezoelectric generators principle.

A. Piezoelectric materials

Several types of piezoelectric materials used in for energy harvesting devices are: PZT, piezoceramic / polymer composites, piezoelectric polymers, etc.

The most common types of piezoelectric materials used in power harvesting applications are:

a) *Lead zirconate titanate*, a piezoelectric ceramic, or piezoceramic, known as PZT;

b) *Poly(vinylidene fluoride) (PVDF)*. PVDF is a piezoelectric polymer that exhibits considerable flexibility when compared to PZT.

Other *piezoelectric materials* are *Fiber-based piezoelectric (piezofiber) material* consisting of PZT fibers of various diameters (15, 45, 120, and 250 μm) that were aligned, laminated, and molded in an epoxy (Macro Fiber Composite – MFC). The Macro Fiber Composite (MFC) is the leading low-profile actuator and sensor offering high performance, durability and flexibility in a cost – competitive device.

In the Table 1 we compared the electrical, piezoelectric and dielectric characteristics of piezoelectric materials from several companies (PZT - Brush Clevite Corporation, Morgan Advanced Materials; PXE – Philips; Piezolan - VEB

KKW Hermsdorf), where noted: Coupling coefficients (K_{eff}, k), piezoelectric coefficients (g_{31}, d_{31}), strain coefficients (s), mechanical quality factor (Q_m), Curie temperature (T_c).

A vibrating piezoelectric device differs from a typical electrical power source in that it has capacitive rather than inductive source impedance, and may be driven by mechanical vibrations of varying amplitude.

A more attractive configuration is to form the piezoceramic into a cantilever arrangement, as shown in Figure 2, where layers of piezoceramics are bonded to a substrate, typically made from a suitable metal. This structure allows a lower resonant frequency to be achieved while producing large strains in the piezoceramic. Where two layers of piezo material are used, the structure is referred to as a bimorph. In this case, the piezo layers may either be connected in series or parallel. If only a single piezo layer is used, the structure is referred to as a *unimorph* [6].

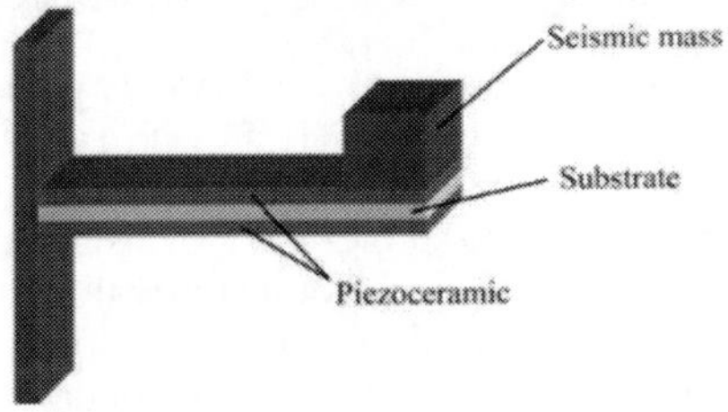

Figure 2. Piezoceramic cantilever resonator [6].

Piezoelectric unimorph cantilever consists of a piezoelectric layer which is sandwiched between two conducting electrodes and positioned on the top of shim layer. Alomari et al. [7] proposed a mathematical analysis of dynamic magnifier model for the piezoelectric unimorph beam.

Bimorph actuators consist of two independent flat piezoelectric elements, stacked on top of the other. By driving one element to expand while contracting the other one, the actuator is forced to bend, creating an out-of plane motion and vibrations. Series and parallel operation modes for bimorph actuators are function of electrical connection and the polarization (P) orientation of piezoelectric layers (Figure 3).

Series Operation refers to the case where supply voltage is applied across all piezo layers at once. The voltage on any individual layer is the supply voltage divided by the total number of layers. A 2-layer device wired for series operation uses only two wires, one attached to each outside electrode (Figure 3a). *Parallel Operation* refers to the case when a metallic blade is fixed between both piezoelectric layers and connected like in Figure 3b).

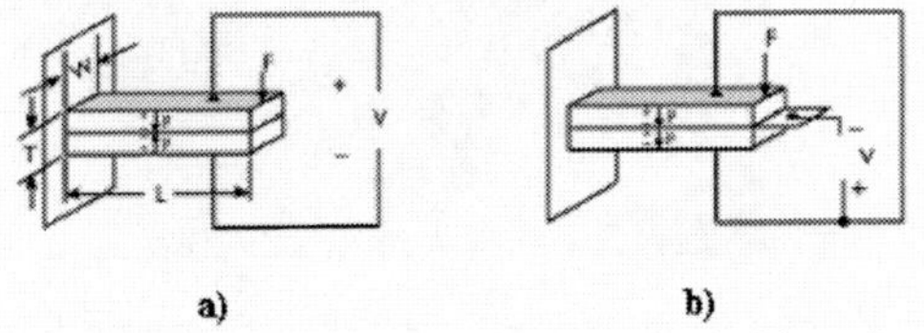

Figure 3. Series (a) and parallel (b) operation modes for bimorph actuators [2].

Figure 4 compares three piezoelectric sensor configurations: (a) A series triple layer type piezoelectric sensor. (b) A parallel triple layer type piezoelectric sensor. (c) A unimorph piezoelectric sensor [8].

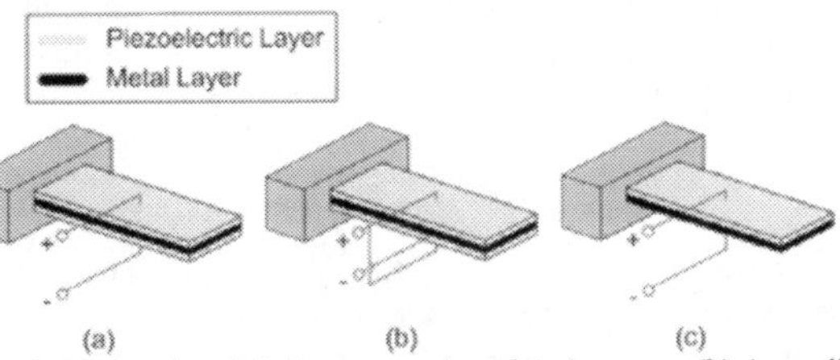

Figure 4. (a) A series triple layer type piezoelectric sensor. (b) A parallel triple layer type piezoelectric sensor. (c) A unimorph piezoelectric sensor [8].

B. Spark generation

An important application of PZT elements is the conversion of mechanical energy into electrical energy, with maximum efficiency and amount of energy [9].

A PZT cylinder hit with a mechanical shock can generate a high voltage electrical spark that processed by electronic circuits is stored in special batteries (Figure 5).

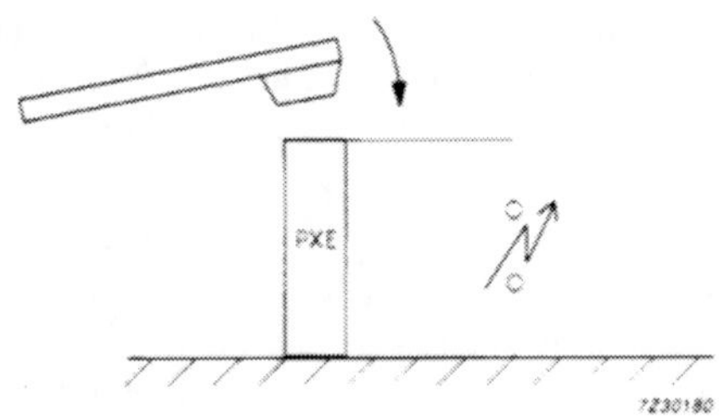

Figure 5. The principle of high voltage and spark generation [8].

In the experimental works we performed a set-up with a mechanical pendulum, which applied mechanical shocks on a fixed PZT tore of 6 mm thickness. According to the direct piezoelectric effect, PZT element converted the mechanical energy into an electrical one. The electrical signal picked up on the electrodes of PZT element has been detected and measured with a Tektronix oscilloscope with memory. The voltage peak can reach hundreds of volts (Figure 6).

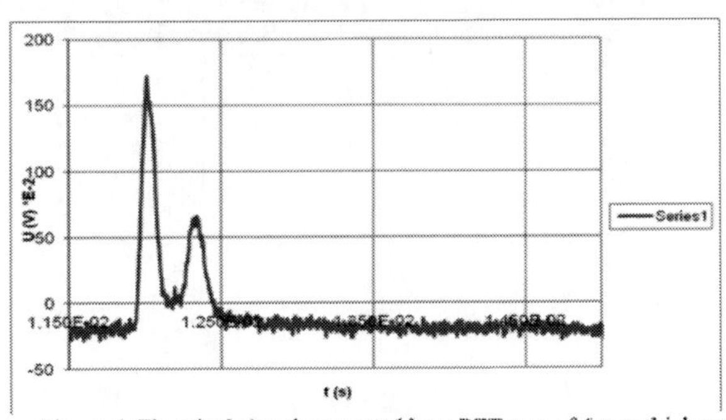

Figure 6. Electrical signal generated by a PZT tore of 6 mm thickness hit by mechanical shocks.

A piezoelectric ceramic can be depolarized by a strong electric field with polarity opposite to the original poling voltage. The typical operating limit is between 500V/mm and 1 000V/mm for continuous application.

High mechanical stress can depolarize a piezoelectric ceramic. The limit on the applied stress is dependent on the type of ceramic material, and duration of the applied stress.

A part of the energy generated by the PZT transducer can be stored in a capacitor and can be used to power a circuit.

IV. PIEZOELECTRIC DEVICES

Some examples of piezoelectric devices and their applications are presented below.

A. PVDF bimorph transducer

PVDF is a piezoelectric polymer that exhibits considerable flexibility when compared to PZT.

PVDF pre-polarized piezoelectric bimorph structure was realized on two PVDF thin films, with 25 μm thickness and 31 pC/N d31 piezoelectric coefficient. The PVDF bimorph transducer started vibration at low alternative voltage, such as 10 V, developing more than 1 mm aperture displacement at its end. The piezoelectric bimorph actuators [3] can be well suited to be implemented in devices for laser system micrometry displacement. PVDF bimorph transducers have advantages, such as: small size and weight, greater flexibility, however they do not have sufficient mechanical rigidity so they cannot bear heavy seismic masses.

B. MEMS piezoelectric energy harvesting device

Micromachined piezoelectric cantilever having low resonant frequency range between 60 Hz and 200 Hz, was developed by Shen at al. [10] appropriate for frequency range, common for environmental vibration sources.

As an application, we mention the MEMS PZT cantilever with an integrated Si proof mass, fabricated on a silicon on insulator (SOI) wafer, and a Pt/PZT/Pt/Ti/SiO_2/Si/SiO_2 multilayer device is generated for low frequency vibration energy harvesting [9]. In manufacturing MEMS, thin film deposition and etching with patterns are used, as shown in Figure 7.

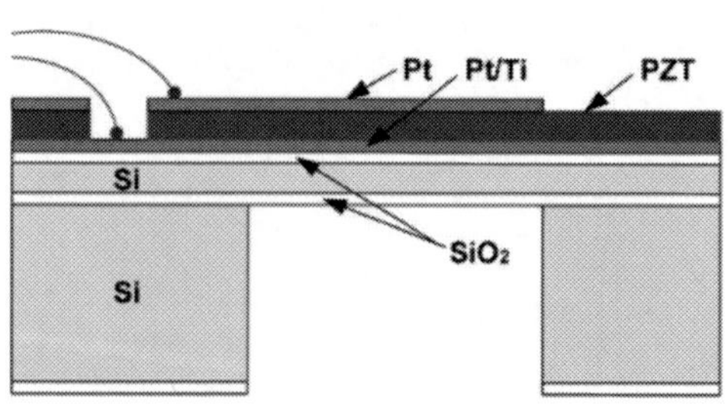

Figure 7. The schematic of the side view of a piezoelectric energy harvesting cantilever based on a silicon on insulator (SOI) wafer [9].

The measured impedance and phase angle of the PZT cantilever versus the exciting frequency are shown in Figure 8. The resonant frequency peak in the phase angle is about 184.16 Hz [10].

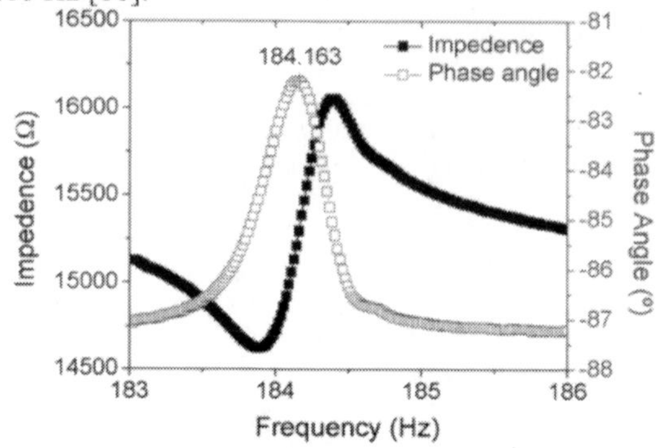

Figure 8. Measured resonant frequency of the PZT cantilever device [10].

A *MEMS (Micro-electro-mechanical System) array* with multi-cantilevers was designed with single cantilever behaving closer resonance frequency one after another [11]. Each cantilever is one spring–mass–damper system with one degree of freedom. When cantilevers with closer resonance frequency are connected together as an array, the available bandwidth covers the range of minimum to maximum resonance value of the cantilevers in the array. MEMS fabrication technology ensures the advantage of mass production of cantilevers with various structure parameters in an array.

In the application described by Shen et al. [10], a *made-up power generator array* was realized by the MEMS process using cantilevers with different sizes (Figure 9): 12 mm silicon layer thickness, 3.2 mm PZT layer thickness, the length and width in range of 2000–3500 mm and 750–1000 mm respectively, having the resonant frequency in the range of 200–400 Hz. The *micro-power generator array* device was made by many PZT film transducers, in order to capture low-level vibrations from the environment.

Serial connection among cantilevers of the array was investigated and the prototype performed well, such as: 3.98 mW effective electrical power and 3.93 V_{DC} output voltage on the load resistance. This device is promising to support networks of ultra-low-power, peer-to-peer, wireless nodes.

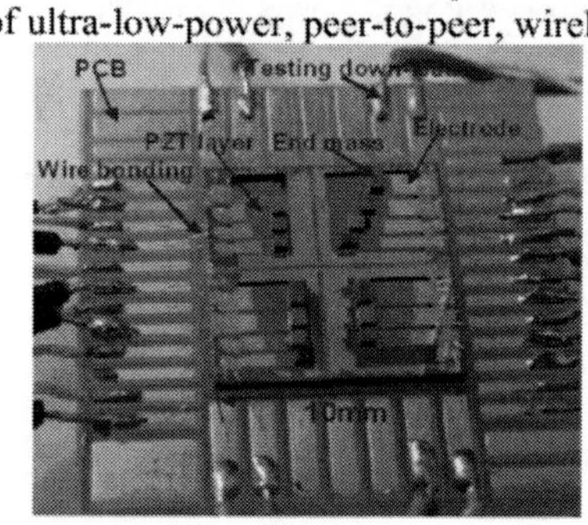

Figure 9. Picture of power generator array prototype [11].

C. Sensor network

Energy-harvesting can enable a new mode of operation, namely, the energy-neutral mode in which the system uses only as much energy as is available from the environment [12].

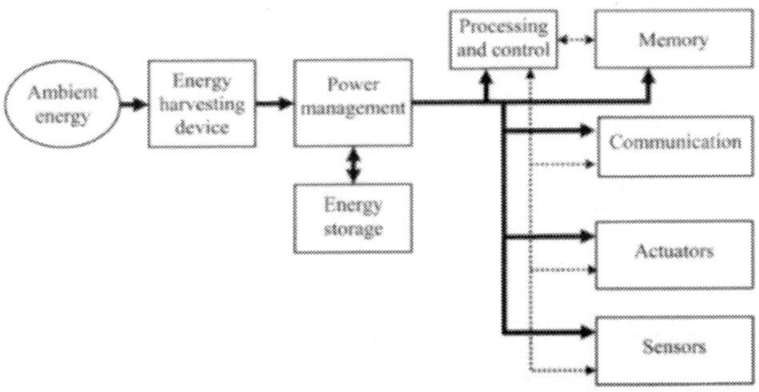

Figure 10. A generic sensor network node with energy harvesting device [13].

The power consumed by a network node can be split between the various functions. A structure of a general sensor network node is described by Benini et. al. [13], with the key elements shown in Figure 10. The power requirement of each element depends on the particular application.

D. Energy harvesting piezoelectric circuitry

Piezoelectric generators are appropriate to convert the smallest mechanical deformations directly into electrical energy. This solid state effect is free of degradation in a wide operation range. A vibrating piezoelectric device differs from a typical electrical power source in that it has capacitive rather than inductive source impedance, and may be driven by mechanical vibrations of varying amplitude. Figure 11 describes a PZT element generator with diodes and parallel capacitor.

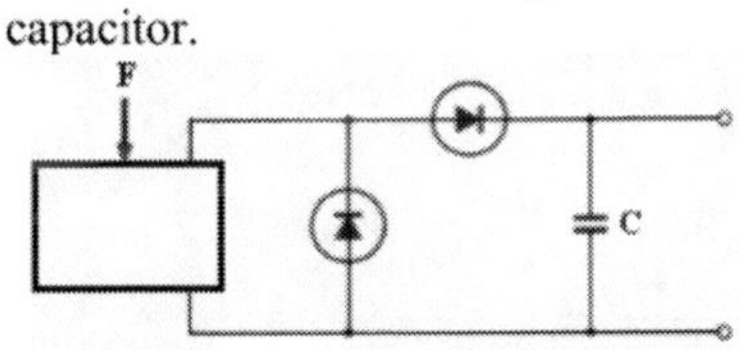

Figure 11. PZT element generator with diodes and parallel capacitor.

The principle of charge generation by a PZT disc to an electronic circuit performance are the shape of the PZT transducer, the manner in which the transducer is mounted and, of course, the nature of the electrical load (Figure 12).

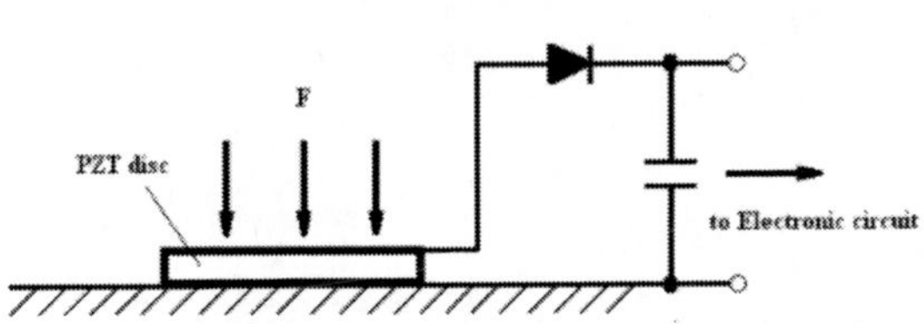

Figure 12. Mechanical force applied to a PZT disc followed by an energy converter.

A PZT disc compressed between two metal surfaces will expand in the radial direction less than a thin cylinder. So the way in which the material is mounted will directly affect the energy conversion per unit volume. The general rule therefore is to allow the PZT body some freedom to expand radially since charge generation is directly coupled to deformation.

Typical energy harvesting circuitry consists of voltage rectifier, converter and storage (Figure 13).

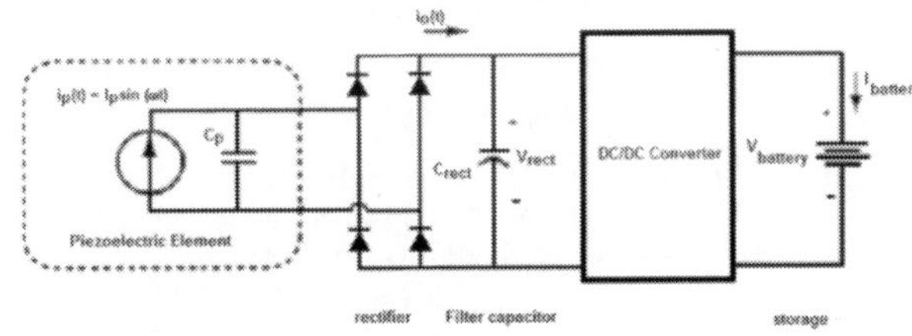

Figure 13. Typical energy harvesting circuitry.

Generally, the device will include an appropriate transducer, converter of mechanical energy to electrical one, chopper, dc-cc converter and high performance microcontroller which will control the performances, and stability of the all system.

E. Low energy harvesting power source

A self-powered autonomous wireless sensor system composed of a power source and a wireless sensing communication system (Figure 14) was realized by Marsic et. al. [14].

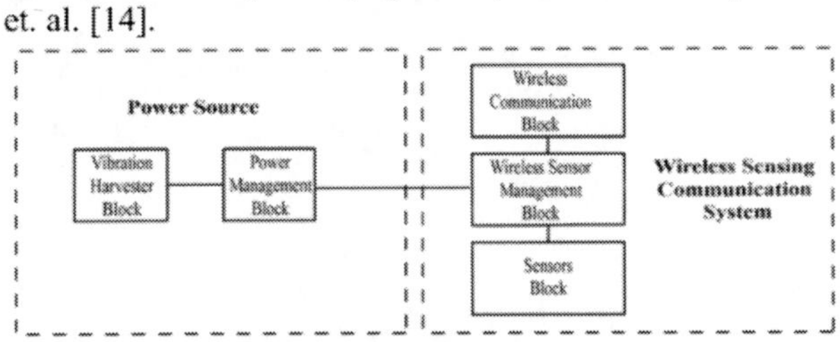

Figure 14. Block diagram of a wireless sensor node powered by a vibration energy harvester. [14]

The design optimization [14] for low power consumption minimization ensures the system's energy autonomous capability.

V. CONCLUSIONS AND FUTURE WORKS

Several techniques have been proposed and developed to extract energy from the environment. In general, "*vibration energy*" could be converted into electrical energy by three techniques: electrostatic charge, magnetic fields and piezoelectric.

Piezoelectric materials like PZT and PVDF embedded in different electronic configurations are suitable for applications, such as: unimorph, bimorph and multilayers transducers, energy harvesting circuitry, sensor network nodes with energy harvesting devices, multilayer devices generated for low frequency vibration energy harvesting, micromachining PZT cantilever, micro-power generator array, energy harvesting sensor networks, networks of ultra-low-power, peer-to-peer, wireless nodes, etc.

Mechanical resonance frequency of piezoelectric bimorph transducers depends on geometric size (length, width, and thickness of each layer), and the piezoelectric coefficients (d_{31} and s_{11}) of the piezoelectric material.

In future work we will study the influence of mechanical impacts (shocks) on the behavior of piezoelectric elements function of the piezoelectric elements characteristics (material type, size, volume, thickness, impact value, etc.); in order to increase the values of generated electrical charges and device efficiency.

ACKNOWLEDGMENT

This work was funded with support of Core Program from the National Authority for Scientific Research and Innovation, ANCSI, project nr. 5N/09.03.2016, Theme PN16-40.01.01, UEFISCDI Project ID PN-II-PT-PCCA-2013-4-2151, Contract nr. 236/2014, and Contract nr. 35/2016.

REFERENCES

[1] R. Tardiveau, et al., "Power Consideration in a Piezoelectric Generator", Smart Materials Research, vol. 2013, Article ID 410567, 7 pages, 2013.http://dx.doi.org/10.1155/2013/410567

[2] M. Lallart, D. J. Inman, and D. Guyomar, "Transient Performance of Energy Harvesting Strategies under Constant Force Magnitude Excitation", Journal of Intelligent Material Systems and Structures, vol. 21, pp. 1279-1291, 2010.

[3] I. Chilibon, C. Dias, P. Inacio, and J. Marat-Mendes, "PZT and PVDF bimorph actuators", Journal of Optoelectronics and Advanced Materials, vol. 9, Issue 6, pp. 1939-1943, June 2007.

[4] A. Erturk, J. M. Renno, and D.J. Inman, "Modeling of Piezoelectric Energy Harvesting from an L-shaped Beam-mass Structure with an Application to UAVs", Journal of Intelligent Material Systems and Structures, vol. 20, 5, pp. 529-544, March 2009.

[5] S. Z. Lulec, U. Adiyan, G. G. Yaralioglu, Y. Leblebici, and H. Urey, "MEMS cantilever sensor array oscillators: Theory and experiments", Sensors And Actuators A-Physical, vol. 237, pp. 147-154, January 2016.

[6] J. M. Gilbert and F. Balouchi, "Comparison of Energy Harvesting Systems for Wireless Sensor Networks", International Journal of Automation and Computing, vol. 05(4), pp. 334-347, October 2008, DOI: 10.1007/s11633-008-0334-2.

[7] A. Alomari, A. Batra, and C. R. Bowen, "Improving Vibration Energy Harvesting Using Dynamic Magnifier", Sensors & Transducers, vol. 196, Issue 1, pp. 57-68, January 2016.

[8] S. R Anton and H. A Sodano, "A review of power harvesting using piezoelectric materials (2003–2006)", Smart Mater. Struct., vol. 16, pp. R1–R21, 2007.

[9] Morgan, Chapter 3, http://www.morgantechnicalceramics.com/sites/default/files/documents/chapter3.pdf

[10] D. Shen, et al., "Micromachined PZT cantilever based on SOI structure for low frequency vibration energy harvesting", Sensors and Actuators A vol. 154, pp. 103–108, 2009.

[11] J-Q. Liu, et al., "A MEMS-based piezoelectric power generator array for vibration energy harvesting", Microelectronics Journal, vol. 39, pp. 802–806, 2008.

[12] A. Kansal, J. Hsu, S. Zahedi, and M. B. Srivastava, "Power management in energy harvesting sensor networks", ACM Trans. Embedd. Comput. Syst., vol. 6, 4, Article 32, 38 pages, (September 2007) DOI=10.1145/1274858.1274870 http://doi.acm.org/ 10.1145/1274858.1274870

[13] L. Benini, E. Farella, and C. Guiducci, "Wireless Sensor Networks: Enabling Technology for Ambient Intelligence", Microelectronics Journal, vol. 37, no. 12, pp. 1639–1649, 2006.

[14] V. Marsic, A. Giuliano, and M. Zhu, "Low Power Consumption Wireless Sensor Communication System Integrated with an Energy Harvesting Power Source", Sensors & Transducers, vol. 18, Special Issue, pp. 156-165, January 2013.

TABLE I. THE ELECTRIC, PIEZOELECTRIC AND DIELECTRIC CHARACTERISTICS OF SOME PIEZOCERAMIC MATERIALS

Material property	**Type of Piezoceramic Material**								
	$BaTiO_3$	*PZT - 4*	*PZT - 8*	*PXE - 4*	*PZT - 5A*	*PZT - 6*	*Piezolan*	*PXE - 7*	*PXE-11*
ρ [10^3 kg·m^{-3}]	-	7.5	7.6	7.5	7.45	7.45	7.4	7.75	4.50
K_p	0.354	0.58	0.50	0.55	0.60	0.42	0.35	0.52	0.43
K_{31}	0.208	0.33	0.295	0.32	0.34	0.25	0.21	0.31	0.25
K_{33}	0.493	0.70	0.62	0.68	0.705	0.54	0.48	0.70	0.55
K_t	-	0.51	0.44	-	0.49	0.39	0.42	-	-
ε	-	1300	1000	1500	1700	1050	950	700	400
d_{33} [10^{-12} m/V]	191	289	218	265	374	189	210	220	100
d_{31} [10^{-12} m/V]	-79	-123	-93	-141	-170	-80	-78	-86	-44.5
g_{33} [10^{-3}V·m/N]	11.4	26.1	24.5	20.0	24.8	20.4	2.0	35.4	28.2
g_{31} [10^{-3}V·m/N]	-4.7	-11.1	-10.5	-9.4	-11.4	-8.6	-7.3	-14	-11.2
s_{11E} [10^{-12} m^2/V]	8.55	12.3	11.1	13.0	16.4	10.7	12.1	12.5	8.1
s_{33E} [10^{-12} m^2/V]	8.93	15.5	1.39	12.7	18.8	13.3	17.3	15.8	9.5
s_{11S} [10^{-12} m^2/V]	8.18	10.9	10.1	11.7	14.4	10.1	11.6	-	-
s_{33S} [10^{-12} m^2/V]	6.76	7.9	8.5	6.8	9.46	9.2	13.3	-	-
Q		500	1000	500	75	450	450	80	270
$10^3 \cdot$ tg δ		4	4	6	20	20	15	20	25
T_c [^{0}C]		328	300	265	365	335	290	320	400 (195)

PLD as Possible Tool for the Fabrication of Chemosensors Based on Amorphous Membranes

Winfried Vonau, Frank Gerlach, Kristina Ahlborn
Kurt-Schwabe-Institut für Mess- und Sensortechnik
Waldheim, Germany
email: info@ksi-meinsberg.de

Abstract— **Electrochemical sensors with sensitive membranes from amorphous materials, in particular, in case of pH electrodes are traditionally fabricated by glass-blowers. For a more effective manufacturing, sometimes so-called blowing machines are used. Thereby, on the one hand a miniaturisation of these electrodes is limited due to technological reasons. On the other hand, this makes it impossible to achieve planar sensors. In addition, a relatively large amount of functional special glass is necessary for such processes. Pulsed laser deposition (PLD) could provide ideal conditions to reduce the above-mentioned drawbacks. In this contribution results of using this method for the fabrication of planar glass based electrochemical sensors are demonstrated, whereby an amorphous silicate glass is in the focus for the sensor membrane.**

Keywords- ***electrochemical sensor; pulsed laser deposition; planarity; sensor miniaturisation; thin film.***

I INTRODUCTION

Sensitive membranes are essential functional components of potentiometric chemosensors. In this respect, according to Figure 1, a distinction is made between solid-based and liquid membranes.

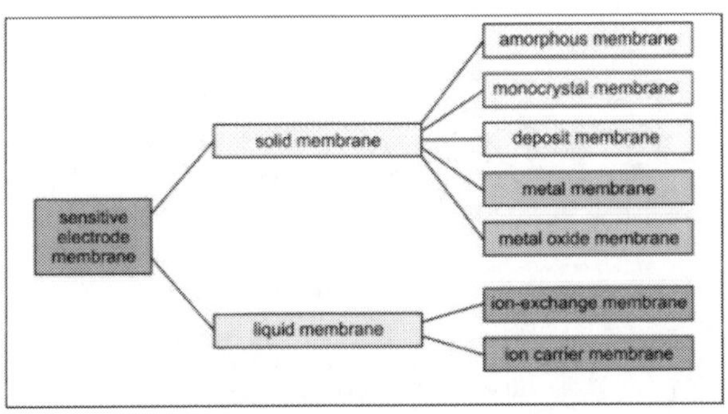

Figure 1. Classification of membrane materials for electrochemical sensors

For solid membranes, amorphous materials play a significant role. The reason is that especially the pH determination, which is one of the analyses performed most frequently worldwide, is carried out with electrochemical electrodes based on such membranes according to standards [1]. The membrane materials used here are silicated glasses with high electrolytic conductivity which mainly are achieved by using alkaline, as well as alkaline earth metal oxides, changing the silicate glass network [2] like is shown in Figure 2.

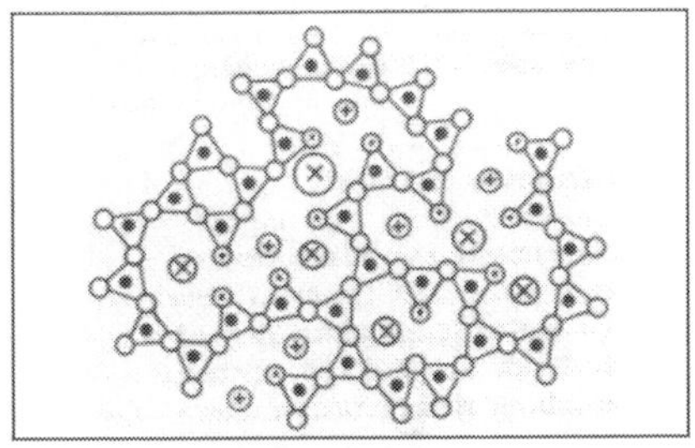

Figure 2. Two-dimensional structure of a silicate glass with network changing components
• Si, o brige oxygen bridge, ⊖ separate oxygen, ⊗ network changing component, ⊕ cation

Silica based electrode glasses, as a rule, are generated by melting their basic materials in covered platinum crucibles for several hours at temperatures > 1300 °C and subsequent quenching. For the further processing by the glassblower it is useful to outpour the liquid glass material, e.g., in a graphite flume. In this way, rods of the special glass are obtained. From these, glassblowers for the most parts produce basket or dome-shaped conventional pH electrodes in quantities of several million pieces per year in its interiors containing a buffer solution and an electrochemical reference system (as a rule an electrode of 2nd kind). Modifying the glass composition makes it possible to realise similarly constructed silicate glass based electrodes with sensitivities for a number of other cations, mainly of metals of the first group of the periodic table [3].

Beside the above mentioned sensors, whose functionality is based on electrolytic conductivity, there are also probes with electron conducting amorphous membrane materials. These include redox glass [4] and chalcogenide glass electrodes [5]. For both types of electrodes the selection of an optimal internal reference system is relatively simple. As a result of the predominant electron conductivity of the sensitive membrane materials a direct contact of the special glasses with a (noble) metal is appropriate. Liquid system components therefore are not applicable for chemosensors based on such materials. From constructional view on the one hand it is possible to fabricate compact electrodes by sticking a wire directly on the surface of the functional amorphous body, e.g., using a conductive varnish (see Figure 3); on the other hand, it is also possible to form a thin metal coating directly on the electron conducting glass by electro-plating (see Figure 4).

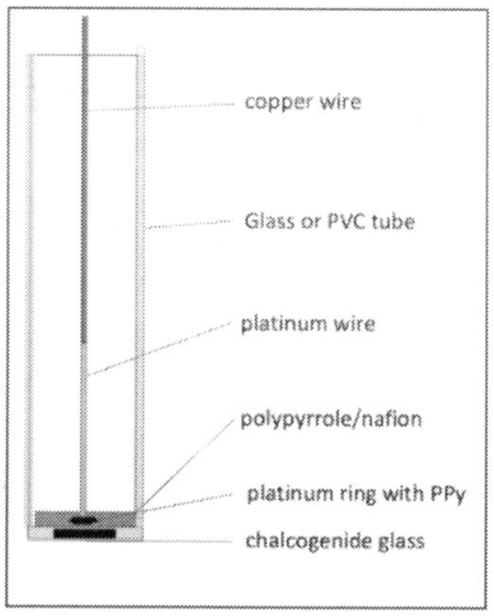

Figure 3. Schematic drawing of a chalcogenide glass electrode [6]

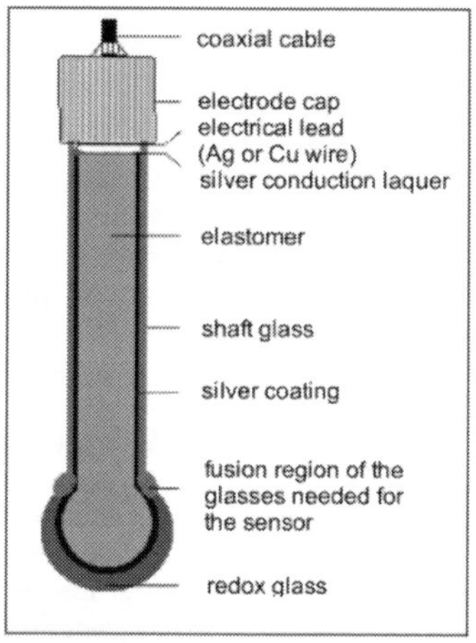

Figure 4. Schematic drawing of a redox glass electrode [7]

Also for silicate glass based cation selective electrodes, due to the purpose of their application, it is an interesting task to replace the common liquid system components by solids. The functionality causing electrolytic conductivity of siliceous pH- but also pLi-, pNa or pK-glasses [8] requires an interlayer with mixed electrical properties on the reverse side of the sensitive membrane. A transition from an ionic conducting material to an electronic conductor (for example a metal) leads to a so called blocked interface and consequently to an unfavourable measurement behaviour [9].

In the past, several suggestions were made to realise such interlayers. In the context of the investigations presented here, the possibility to form thin layers of zinc oxide or titanium oxide between sensitive glass and a noble metal should be mentioned [10]. Previous work on corresponding all solid state glass electrodes dealed with sensors fabricated with precision manufacturing techniques and screen printing (see Figure 5a+b). Here, a clear stabilisation of the half cell potentials over the time could be obtained compared to a direct metal contacting [11].

Following, it is reported on investigations using PLD as fabrication technology to realise planar all solid state pH electrodes according to above described approach, in other words to the forming of a layer design metal/ mixed conducting interlayer / cation selective amorphous membrane on dielectric substrates (SiO_2, oxide ceramic, glass).

Beside the realisation of an adherent metallic basic electrode and a semiconducting metal oxide film special attention will be paid to the transfer of the functional sensor layer from a prefabricated ion selective target material by the laser to the substrate. In this process, on the one hand, no material losses may occur. On the other hand, also the target component must be amorphous. This paper is focused on the results of research work focused on this fundamental subtask to create all solid state pH glass layers in PLD.

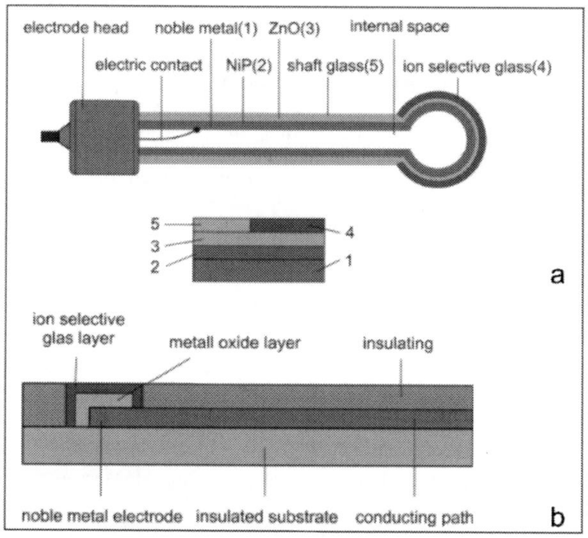

Figure 5. All solid state pH glass electrodes based on ZnO as interlayer
a fabricated in fine and glass mechanics according to [12]
b fabricated in thick film technology according to [13]

In section II, the fabrication of the glass targets, the PLD process for the glass layer deposition and the characterisation of these layers are described. Results of micro-X-ray fluorescence analysis, X-ray photoelectron spectroscopy and electrochemical impedance spectroscopy are presented in section III.

II EXPERIMENTAL

A. Fabrication of the glass targets

The targets of the sensitive pH glasses for the PLD process are obtained by pouring the molten glass in a preheated graphite mould according to Figure 6. This manufacturing method delivers homogeneous and also amorphous target materials with defined geometries. According to Figure 7 glass cylinders were fabricated that were singularised in discs with a thickness of 5 mm by means of a precision saw (Accutom-50, Fa. Struers).

Figure 6. Pouring of molten glass in a graphite mould

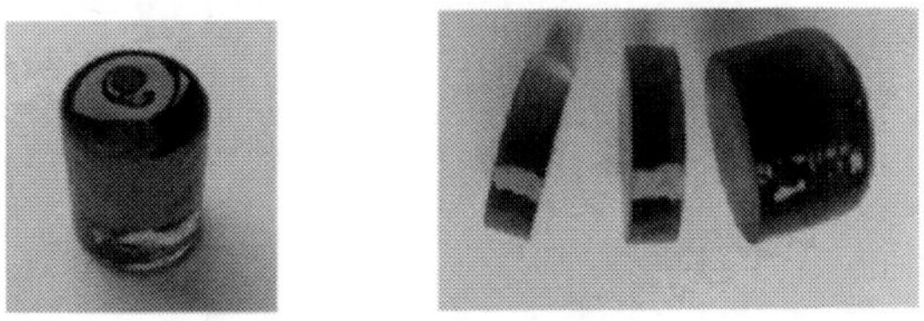

Figure 7. Targets of pH glass

B. PLD process

The preparation of the thin sensory functional layers was carried out by sputtering methods and PLD. For this purpose, a combined coating system „CREAMET 500 PLD S2" of the company Creavac (see Figure 8) was used which provides both deposition processes. Furthermore, a simultaneous substrate and mask handling is possible without an interruption of the vacuum during the coating process.

Figure 8. Combined coating system CREAMET 500 PLD S2 of the company Fa. Creavac, sputter chamber
left: mask and substrate handler and PLD chamber
right: mask und substrate handler with transfer device

With integrated substrate handler and mask change system two sputter targets, six PLD targets and altogether five changeable masks can be used and combined for the process.

As substrates pre-cleaned glass plates consisting of soda-lime glass with a size of 50 mm x 15 mm and a thickness of 1 mm were used. They were pretreated with the initial plasma process at a chamber pressure of 3.0 x 10^{-2} mbar under an argon atmosphere. As chamber pressure for the following sputtering processes of the adhesive layer (Ti) and the electrical conducting discharge electrode (Au) a value of 7.0 x 10^{-3} mbar was used. After finishing the sputtering processes the coated substrates were removed and the masks were changed in a so called „Load-Lock-Box". Prepared in this way, the substrates were transferred in the PLD coating chamber using a carrier and the PLD process was started. The deposition of the thin pH glass films was conducted by a KrF excimer laser source (ComPexPro 110 of the company Coherent) using a wave length of 248 nm, a fluence of 5.6 J/cm^2 at pulse lengths of 20 ns and a pulse frequency of 10 Hz. The determination of the laser power before and after the coating process in connection with a periodical cleaning of the entry window ensured long-term stable and reproducible basic conditions. The PLD process was carried out at a chamber pressure of 3.1 x 10^{-7} mbar in a N_2 atmosphere. The substrate was kept at room temperature. As ablation time of the sensitive layers a period from 10 to 30 minutes was selected. The substrates were positioned perpendicular to the plasma club (On-Axis-PLD).

C. Characterisation

The thin films of pH sensitive glasses prepared by PLD were comprehensively characterised with respect to material composition and electrochemical behaviour. A possibility for the nondestructive determination of homogeneity and material composition of thin pH glass films is micro-X-ray fluorescence analysis. The energy dispersive micro-X-ray fluorescence system M4 Tornado (Fa. Bruker Nano GmbH, Berlin) was used for the position-sensitive elemental analysis and allows the analysis of large and inhomogeneous samples as well as smallest particles fast and at low vacuum under environmental conditions.

With X-ray photoelectron spectroscopic measurements the chemical composition in the first few atomic layers of a material surface can be detected because of a low excitation energy of only 12.5 kV compared to values of other radiographically methods like, e.g., µ-RFA with excitation energies up to 50 kV.

The new pH thin film sensors presented here use gold as discharge material for the electrochemical potential formed at the sensor surface in contact with the analyte. This interlayer between glass substrate and pH sensitive glass layer was deposited by laser ablation. Thus, the existence of gold on the sensor surface is an indicator for the tightness of the PLD-based pH glass thin film. To demonstrate this tightness the measurement system SAGE HR 100 Compact High

Resolution (company SPECS Surface Nano Analyses GmbH) was used. The excitation of the sample was carried out with $Mg_{K\alpha}$-radiation and an X-ray power of 250 W. To evaluate the electrochemical behaviour, in particular for the estimation of the electrical conductivity of the glass thin films, impedance measurements were carried out in a neutral NBS buffer solution (pH= 6.86) by means of the potentiostat Gamry Interface 1000 (company Gamry Instruments Inc.).

In addition to the here described micro-X-ray fluorescence analysis and X-ray photoelectron spectroscopy, which allows statements about bulk properties of the target materials and adsorptive contaminations as well as surface effects, it is also possible to use energy dispersive X-ray analysis and x-ray diffraction as further radiographical research methods. Their application shows that it is possible to realise amorphous sensor membranes using PLD as thin film production method.

III RESULTS

A. Micro-X-ray fluorescence analysis (µ-RFA)

The results of µ-RFA demonstrate that PLD coated pH sensitive glass films possess a good homogeneity (see Figure 9).

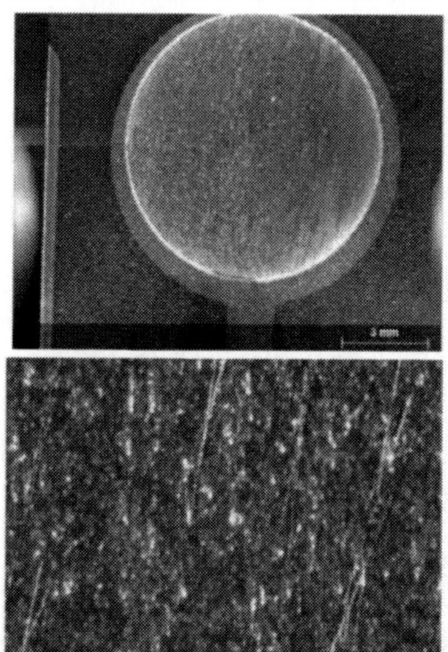

Figure 9. PLD-based pH glass thin film on glass substrate with Au/Ti-conducting path 10x magnification (a) and 100x magnification (b)

Element mappings deliver a uniform distribution of the elements over the entire analysed surface; no pronounced defects or areas with an accumulation of an element were detected (see Figure 10). This ensures compared to conventional glass electrodes identical conditions of the sensor membrane concerning the interface between measuring solution/ surface.

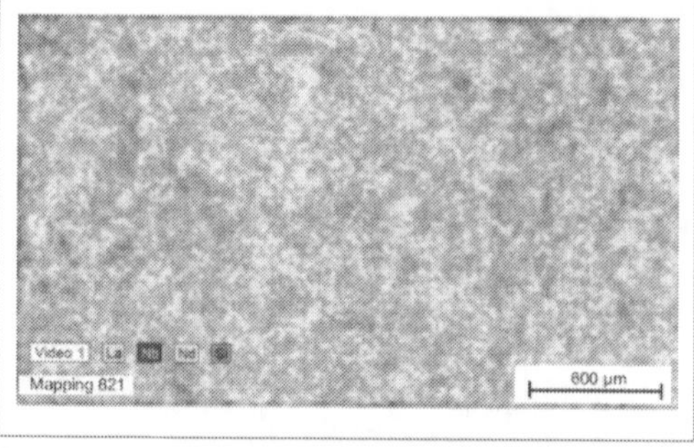

Figure 10. Element mapping of a PLD-based pH glass thin film

B. X-ray photoelectron spectroscopy (XPS)

Both the used glass targets and the fabricated PLD-based pH glass thin films were investigated by means of XPS overview spectra and spectra of the single elements in regions of their highest sensitivity. Figure 11 demonstrates in an exemplary manner a comparing presentation of the overview spectrum from a glass target and of a glass thin film deposited from this source by PLD. These spectra showed no differences in the chemical composition. In addition, a determination of the gold content on the surface of the pH thin film sensors was carried out (see Figure 12).

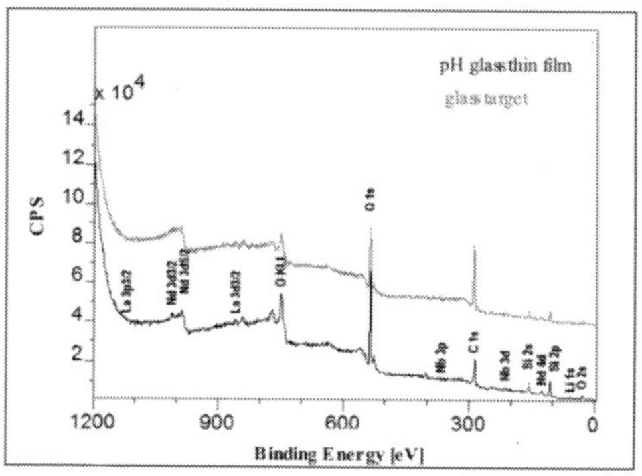

Figure 11. Comparing presentation of XPS spectra from a glass target and a pH glass thin film obtained from this target by PLD

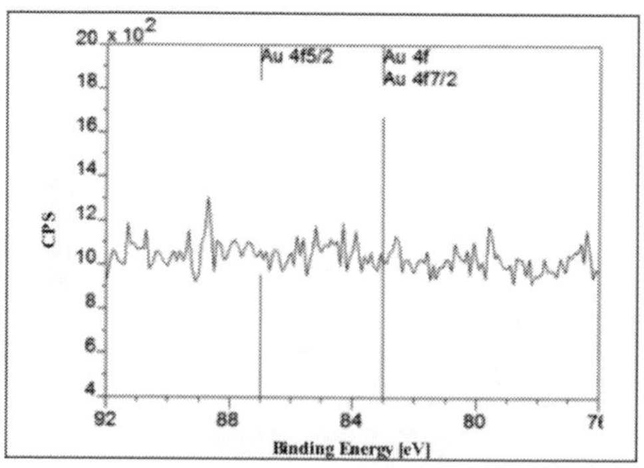

Figure 12. XPS spectrum obtained at a PLD based glass thin film, region of the highest sensitivity for gold

The spectra indicate that there are no holes in the pH sensitive layer and that this layer is tight because no peaks at the typical positions for binding energies of gold and its compounds are present.

C. Electrochemical Impedance Spectroscopy (EIS)

Figure 13 shows results of EIS determinations using a pH glass thin film and a glass bead as working electrode, in each case a KCl-saturated silver chloride electrode as reference and a platinum sheet as counter electrode. Although the phase characteristic in Figure 13a is not yet understood advantageously, a clearly lower electrode resistance can be identified for the PLD based electrode (Figure 13b). By the way, electrodes with layers produced by PLD technology deliver measurement signals with a higher repeatability. This is due to the fact that this manufacturing process provides a better reproducibility of the thicknesses of the deposits.

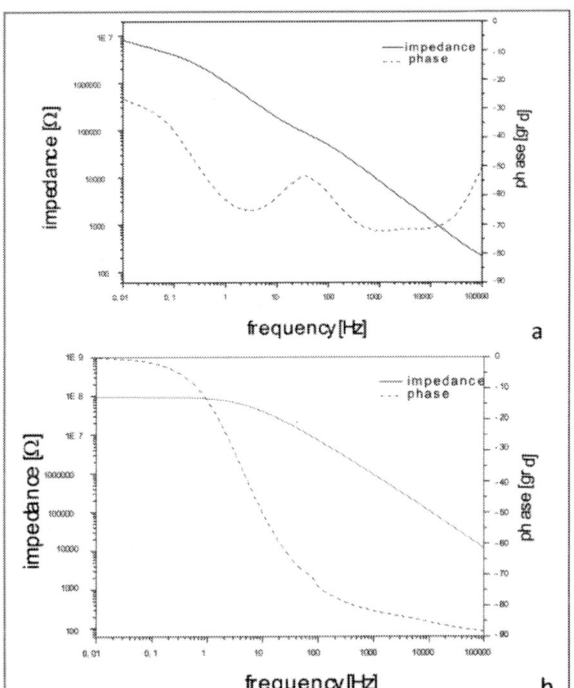

Figure 13. Impedance spectra of the 3-electrode system: thin film glass (a) and glass bead (b)/Ag/AgCl, KCl_{sat}/ Pt in a NBS-buffer solution (pH=6.86)

D. pH measurement

Previous studies, as already written above, in the main were carried out to coat planar metallised glass substrates with ion conducting selective glass films by improving and adapting PLD technology for this special purpose. For the fabrication of corresponding pH glass electrodes with constant stable electrode potentials and electrode functions following the Nernst equation the realisation of an additional semi- or mixed conducting interlayer (for example zinc oxide [12]) by the same technology is necessary [14]. This will be the subject of future projects.

However, it could already be shown, that PLD based pH glass layers in direct metal contact deliver sensor sensitivities of approximately -42 mV/pH at 25 °C. Drift behaviour and long-term stability have to be optimised for the reasons outlined above by forthcoming integration of interlayers. In case of a positive outcome of the development with respect to resolution, repeatability and accuracy, it can be expected to realise miniaturised planar all solid state glass electrodes with properties comparable to widely used sensor types.

IV CONCLUSIONS

In the present contribution, results derived from the application of PLD as a new method for the deposition of sensitive electrode glasses are described. Homogeneity and leak-tightness of thin glass films fabricated in such way could be demonstrated by µ-RFA and XPS analyses. Due to the low thickness of the glass membrane planar PLD based pH sensors possess significantly smaller electrode resistances compared to conventionally fabricated ones. This fact, as well as the possibility to deposit the sensitive membranes on different sensor substrate materials (metal, ceramics) and also on glass offer a variety of applications, e.g. in the area of cell research. Here and in a lot of biomedical and biotechnological utilisations the transparency of glass is a strong advantage.

It should also be mentioned that the previously established thin film method for the fabrication of chemosensors (CHEMFETs) is based on CMOS technology, mainly. This requires high investment and running costs and can be introduced economically only if products in large quantitites are needed. The described sensor fabrication by means of PLD allows, among others, to abstain completely from using photolithographic processes and additional encapsulation steps with simultaneous cost-efficiency also for small and medium quantities. Contrary to CHEMFETs, the sensors described in this contribution work according the potentiometric prinicple. Thus, future appliers can still use their measurement devices for conventional sensors.

REFERENCES

[1] DIN EN ISO 10523:2012-04.

[2] K. Schwabe, pH-measurement, Dresden: Theodor Steinkopff, pp. 120-186, 1976.

[3] G. Eisenman, Glass electrodes for hydrogen and other cations, New York: Marcel Dekker, 1967.

[4] B. P. Nikolsky et al., „Electron-conductive glass," Patent US 3 773 642.

[5] V. G. Vlasov, „New solid-state ion-selective electrodes-Sensors for chemical analysis of solutions," Fresenius Z. Anal. Chem., vol. 335, pp. 92-99, 1989.

[6] S. Pollrich, „Chalcogenide glasses as ion-sensitive membranes for potentiometric sensors," Diploma Thesis, Hochschule Mittweida, 2004.

[7] M. M Schults et al., „Glass electrode," Patent DE 2645623.

[8] H. Galster, pH-determination, Weinheim: VCH, pp. 115-123, 1990.

[9] F. Oehme, Ion-selective electrodes, Heidelberg: Dr. Alfred Hüthig, pp. 1-2, 1986.

[10] T. Bachmann, J. Spindler, F. Gerlach, and W. Vonau, „Glass electrode with metal contact for electrochemical applications,". Scientific Reports, J. Univ. of Appl. Sci. Mittweida, vol. 6, pp. 3-7, 2006.

[11] W. Vonau, F. Gerlach, U. Enseleit, J. Spindler, and T. Bachmann, „New solid-state glass electrodes by using zinc oxide thin films as interface layer," J. Solid State Electrochem., vol.13, pp. 91-98, 2009.

[12] T. Bachmann, J. Spindler, F. Gerlach, and W. Vonau, „Glass electrode and procedure for its fabrication," Patent DE 10 2005 059 680 A1.

[13] W. Vonau, F. Gerlach, U. Enseleit, J. Spindler, and T. Bachmann, „Chemical indicator electrode and procedure for its fabrication," Patent DE 10 2007 016 197 A1.

[14] W. Vonau, and U. Guth, "pH Monitoring: a review," J. Solid State Electrochem., vol. 10, pp. 746-752, September 2006.

Capillary Sensor with Fluorescence Reading of Effects of Diesel and Biodiesel Fuel Degradation in Storage

Michal Borecki
Institute of Microelectronics and Optoelectronics
Warsaw University of Technology
Warsaw, Poland
email: borecki@imio.pw.edu.pl

Michael L. Korwin-Pawlowski
Département d'informatique et d'ingénierie
Université du Québec en Outaouais
Gatineau, Québec, Canada
email: Michael.Korwin-Pawlowski@uqo.ca

Mateusz Gęca
Institute of Electron Technology
Warsaw, Poland
email: mati.geca@gmail.com

Przemysław Prus
Blue Oak Inventions
Wroclaw, Poland
email: pprus@boinv.com

***Abstract*-There are many standards set by national organizations and fuel producers to test and guarantee the quality of diesel fuel and its stability under storage conditions. The diesel fuel stability is related with the fuel composition that evolved to the modern fuels from the historical ones. The stability of modern diesel fuel is mainly due to the reduction of the oxidation processes, the result of the presence of unsaturated components and components with oxygen as organic components and cetane index improvers. The simple characteristic of serious degradation of diesel fuel is the appearance of resins and sediments. Traditional techniques for measuring fuel stability, like the rancimat methods, are relatively complex. On the user side, fast and low-cost sensing of the degradation of diesel and biodiesel fuel is important. The present paper concentrates on the construction of the capillary sensor which enables the examination of the presence of resin and degradation of the most widely used cetane improver (2-ethyl hexyl nitrate) in one arrangement. Results of a development of a sensor working on the principle of fluorescence excited in a disposable capillary cell with high power light emitted diodes are presented. We discuss the principle of the sensor's operation, the construction of the sensor, and the experimental results of testing diesel fuels instability.**

Keywords-biodiesel fuel stability; diesel fuel instability; cetane index improvers; capillary sensor; LED excited fluorescence.

I. INTRODUCTION

A. *Modern diesel fuels*

Classical petro-diesel fuels are made from stable components of straight run distillate products of crude oil (alkanes) with an addition of improvers [1]. Biodiesel fuel is a mixture of classical petro-diesel fuel and bio-components.

It was historically postulated that petro-diesel fuel may be kept in storage for prolonged periods. But modern petro-diesel fuels include stable components (alkanes) and cracked material which contains olefins (alkenes) characterized by a double bond chemical. Alkenes are more reactive than alkanes. Bio-diesel components include significant amounts of fatty acids esters that are also characterized by the presence of double bonds. Oxidation of hydrocarbons with double bonds may lead to waxy solids or gums emerge [2].

One of the most important diesel fuel quality parameters is the ignition quality. The ignition quality depends on the molecular composition of the fuel and is characterized by the ignition delay time, which is the time between the start of injection and the start of combustion. The minimum cetane number of diesel fuel differs by region, for example in Europe the minimum value is 51, but in some regions of United States it is 40. In Europe, the major problem of the refineries is obtaining fuel with high cetane number.

There are two methods to increase the cetane number. The first method is to reduce the content of aromatic and/or double bonds of fuel by hydrogenation - this is usually not done because of a high cost. The second method is using cetane improving additives – this method is preferred due to its low cost [3]. The alkyl nitrates and peroxides cetane improvers have been in use since 1921. Cetane improvers decompose rapidly and form free radicals when exposed to temperatures above 100°C. As these radicals increase the rate of main fuel components decomposition, the ignition delay is negatively affected. The use of cetane improvers in diesel fuel of high quality increases the engine durability [4].

The 2-ethyl hexyl nitrate (2-EHN) is the most popular cetane index additive. Its production volume in 2014 was about 100,000 tons. The ASTM D 4046 standard test method is used for determining the amount of alkyl nitrate added to diesel fuel to judge compliance with specifications covering alkyl nitrates. Unimolecular decomposition of 2-EHN creates nitrogen dioxide (NO_2), which further reacts with available hydrogen atoms to produce hydroxyl radicals. This effect is greatest at temperature and density conditions, matching the start-up conditions in a diesel engine, and becomes negligible at the highest temperature–density conditions found in standard engine working conditions [7]. On the other hand, the addition of 2-EHN to fuel improves the spray formation in diesel engines [8]. Therefore, 2-EHN performs well physically and chemically during the combustion of fuel, but can also decompose slowly even at temperatures below 100°C [9]. Thus, 2-EHN can be an additional reason of the fuel instability, introducing temperature instability and being the initiator and promotor of oxidation of fuel.

The results of diesel fuel instability are sediments and gum formation. The bio-diesel fuel has been found to be more prone to oxidation than the vegetable oils or petro-diesel fuel. The effects of bio-diesel fuel instability may be the presence in the fuel tank of a wide variety of alcohols, aldehydes, peroxides, polymers, as well as the previously mentioned insoluble gum and sediments. The results of polymer and soluble waxes formation is the increase in the diesel fuel viscosity [5]. The changes in molecular composition of fuel affect its ignition characteristics. Therefore, fuel instability is of concern when the modern diesel fuel is stored over an extended period of time. Diesel fuel stability may be affected by a large number of parameters which can be categorized by oxidation, thermal and storage conditions [2]. The storage conditions can be described as exposure to air and/or light at the environment temperature. Oxidative properties of biodiesel are commonly tested according to the EN 14112 standard as rancimat and Iodine values, but several other methods have also been used in the analysis of oxidation state of oil and biodiesel [6].

The visible effects of serious diesel fuel instability may be described as fuel darkening and sediments presence, as presented in Figure 1, on which the degradation is the effect of two years fuels samples storage in transparent glass vessels exposed to ambient light at room temperature. The sediments and darkening are present in cases of premium (Cetane Number = 59.6) and standard fuel (Cetane Number = 54.1) bought at a fuel station, while the own-mixed fuel does not seem affected by instability. All fuels above the formed sediment layer are transparent. The own-mixed fuel at the beginning of the examination was characterized by a worse fit for use parameters than the fuels bought at the fuel station. However, the mixed fuel was prepared with clear and fresh components with the maximum permissible concentration of antioxidants and the smallest concentration of 2-EHN (Cetane Number = 51.2). Some fuels prepared in such way show visual effects of instability as a conversion into pale and cloudy liquid. The visible effects of four weeks exposition to ambient light of premium fuel are presented in Figure 2. At first, the fuel instability process leads to fuel fading and cloudiness, next the dark phase forms at vessel's bottom and separates from the clear fuel. Hence simple a fuel color evaluation is not sufficient for fuel instability discrimination.

Figure 1. Visible effects of fuel instability.

Figure 2. Visible effects of premium fuel cloudiness after exposition to ambient light for four weeks. Fuel sample in the left side container has been exposed to light. The sample in right side container has been keept in dark conditions.

B. *Optical methods and sensors for diesel fuel testing*

These are a set of spectrophotometric method used for diesel fuel testing. The examinations of light absorption, scattering, fluorescence, and chemiluminescence are performed. Some of them are executed in a combustion chamber as evidence of the combustion process [10][11]. Many of them are performed on processed diesel fuel sample and include a tedious liquid to liquid extraction with organic solvents. Biodiesel and diesel fuels show native fluorescence [12], but with very limited excitation efficiency. However, the diesel fuel may contain many fluorophores. The task of the determination of the fuel`s condition is further complicated by the fact that the fluorophores have different characteristic excitation and emission ranges in different samples. Despite this, ultraviolet fluorescence spectroscopy methods were developed to identify oils by the differences of their aromatic compositions. For this purpose, advanced measurement technology as synchronous fluorescence spectroscopy and time-resolved fluorescence have been developed. They demonstrate an improved potential for classification of fuels than the classic fluorescence spectroscopy [13][14]. But presently available spectroscopic methods are still characterized with some disadvantages. Mathematical models proposed to convert spectroscopic examination results into diesel fuel set of parameters work only with known and examined previously components [15]. Also, plastic disposable cuvettes are not fit for examination as they are slowly dissolved by diesel fuel. Quartz cuvettes used in spectroscopic examination require precise maintenance between measurements. The light sources are costly when as laser or lamp excitation is used. Despite these drawbacks, dedicated components for spectroscopic sensors are under development [16][17].

Alternative methods to spectroscopy, which include an examination of diesel fuel with local heating in a closed capillary vessel and the examination of the dynamical rise of fuel in a inclined capillary, show a potential of a fast fuel fit for use determination [18-22]. Also, for these methods dedicated components have been developed [23][24].

But in the routine daily work, the transport business still demands the development of new rapid and low-cost sensors for reliable determination of fuel fit for use or fuel degradation below usefulness.

The rest of this paper is organized as follows. Section II describes the idea of a multiparametric sensor for diesel fuel instability effects testing. Section III describes the sensor construction including sensor head with optrode as well as optoelectronics system set-up. Section IV addresses the experimental results of the fluorescent signal analysis. Section V goes into short conclusions.

II. Idea of a Multiparametric Sensor for Diesel Fuel Instability Effects Testing

The idea of the sensor was inspired by the need to come up with a low-cost measurement method of a set of diesel fuel instability effects in one system that would require the minimum of automated mechanical elements.

The aimed-at set of diesel fuel parameters includes the initial state of oxidation and the serious instability effects. Both effects are characterized by a transparent liquid state. As the fuel is transparent the both fraction may be mixed resulting in a visibly uniform color of the fuel. The cloudiness of fuel is considered as an intermediate state and can be easily determined by human observation or with white light scattering measurements.

The initial state of oxidation may be connected with 2-EHN degradation that should lead to a reduction of its concentration. The concentration of 2-EHN may be evaluated with the direct analysis of fluorescence signal excited with 366nm wavelength light, selected from the output of the xenon discharge light source of 150W power with a 3nm slit [15]. Due to the relatively low power of the signal, the detection is made with a photon multiplying tube. The exit signal with a characteristic shape of double-hump is in the range from 380nm to 450nm.

The serious effect of fuel instability is the presence in it of soluble and insoluble gums. Insoluble gums create sediments in tanks, while soluble gums can degrade the injection system. The laser inducted fluorescence, with argon-ion laser operating at 488 nm with the constant power of 100mW used as the excitation source, is presently the proven measurement method [25]. Due to high laser power, the detection is performed with a photodiode array. The emitted signals range from 510nm to 750nm with a maximum at 570nm. For the real fuels, there was always observed some background fluorescence, but its intensity was usually low compared to that of the degraded fuel.

Both the fluorescent measurements were performed in our work in standard fluorescence cuvettes, 10mm x 10mm x 45mm. A cuvette was mounted in place with a shielded holder, which also minimized scattered light from the cuvette input and output faces. The aperture for the fluorescence measurement was 7mm in the central portion of the cuvette.

III. Sensor Construction

A. *Sensor head*

The set of parameters of interest may be observed using the fluorescence excited with 488nm and 366nm radiation in the sample of liquid positioned in a capillary vessel using optical fibers as probes (Figure 3).

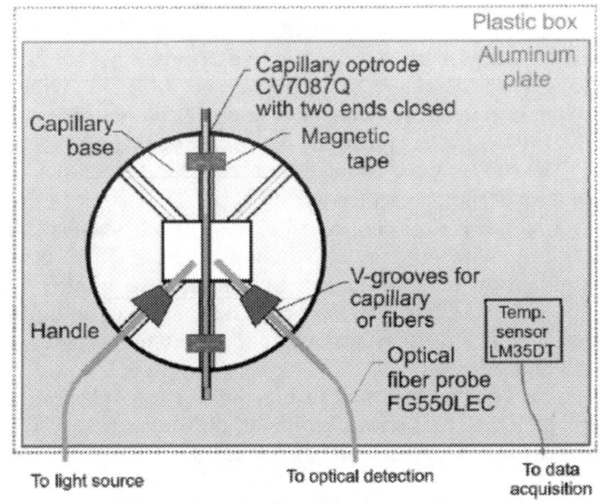

Figure 3. Scheme of the capillary sensor head.

The use of capillary reduces significantly costs of measurement and in two ways.

First, the measurement of degraded diesel fuel that is characterized by the presence of adhesive gums required the use of disposable cuvettes or a specific cleaning and washing process. Moreover, disposable plastic cuvettes are affected by diesel and biodiesel fuels. Therefore, the capillary optrode CV7087Q is used here as a replaceable and disposable vessel that is of considerably lower cost than a classical fluorescence cuvette.

When a capillary optrode CV7087Q is considered, the approximated fluorescent aperture is 0.7mm. This fluorescent aperture is 10 times lower than when a classical cuvette is used. Therefore, the optical power used for excitation of fluorescence in the proposed head may be significantly lower (100 times) than when a commercial spectrophotometer is used. In the case of the laser inducted fluorescence and a spectroscopic cuvette, the excitation power is about 100mW. Therefore, in the presented case the high power light emitted diodes can be used as their minimal specified powers are 3mW from M365FP1 working at 365nm range, and 1.5mW from M490F2 working at 490nm.

The FG550LEC step-index multimode fiber was used as the light probe, as it enables positioning of the optical axis of the probes and the optrode in one plane. Moreover, the fiber is characterized by a 550μm diameter of the core, which allows the effective coupling with high power light emitting diodes, and a low numerical aperture, that reduces the fluorescent aperture of the head. This fiber is characterized by high attenuation below 400nm, but in the sections used of 0.5m long, the attenuation is acceptable.

The head was also equipped with a temperature sensor made with LM35DT circuits.

B. Optoelectronic system set-up.

The sensor's head consists of two functional blocks: the head proper and the optoelectronic set-up, shown in Figure 4.

The optoelectronic set-up is divided into two parts, the light source and light detector, both connected to a personal computer equipped with spectra acquisition software and system script designed for measurement automation.

As the light source, two fiber-coupled LEDs were used. The high power LEDs selected were Thorlabs M490F2, with the 490nm dominant wavelength and M365F1 with the 365nm dominant wavelength. The diodes were connected to DC2100 controllers operating in the constant current mode.

The diodes were coupled into the optical fiber switch of our own design, presented in [26].

The head was connected to two spectrometers Maya 2000pro with an optical signal divider. This enables simultaneous monitoring of the signal of light emitted diode and of the excited fluorescence. The fluorescence signal is measured in a 6-fibers arm, while the excitation signal uses a 1-fiber arm.

The system element causing the highest light damping was the DMC1-02 monochromator, the attenuation of which is about 1:1000 at analyzed wavelengths.

IV. EXPERIMENTAL RESULTS

In this section are presented the experimental procedures and the results of examination of different diesel and biodiesel fuels.

The measurement procedure consists of a few steps. First, the background signal of for the empty optrode is measured, then the optrode is directly filled from the desired layer of the fuel in the tank and the outer optrode wall is wiped. Next, the signal of fluorescence is measured. Last, the spectra are calculated as the difference between the fluorescence and the background signals.

A. Diesel and biodiesel fuels used for examination

The operation of the sensor was examined with fuels that are bought at a petrol station and with mixtures prepared from components. These fuels were not aged. Reference fuels were stored at room temperature in glass tanks in closed dark containers exposed to natural light. The fuel samples that are subject to degradation were stored in transparent glass tanks also exposed the same light. The exposition was made on a windowsill with direct sun view on from south direction in Warsaw. The short term aging of 4 weeks duration was performed in winter conditions of sunlight, for visible effects see Figure 2. Fuels aged for two years were exposed to full year cycles, visible effects can be observed in Figure 1.

The four different premium diesel fuels were selected for tests. One was a clear mixture of alkanes with no additives (CN=49.8), and the three others were mixtures of petrodiesel with additives including 2EHN – one commercial with no bio-component (CN=59.6) and two with a bio-component, one with 1% of fatty acids methyl esters (FAME) (CN=59.1) and second with 7% of hydrogenated vegetable oil (HVO) (CN=59.2). The standard commercial diesel fuel includes 7% of FAME (CN=54.1).

B. Boundary examinations

Boundary examinations included measurements of fluorescence of fresh fuels and two years aged fuels. In all mentioned in this section cases, the outer walls of the capillaries were cleaned after the test. Spectra of fresh fuels, scanned with a 1-second time frame of scanning, and excited with 366nm wavelength, were presented in Figure 5.

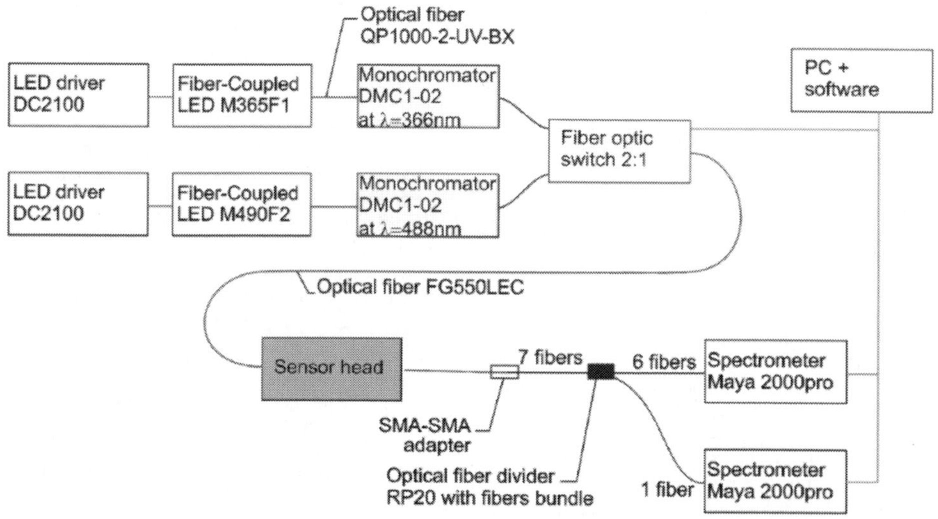

Figure 4. Sensor system scheme.

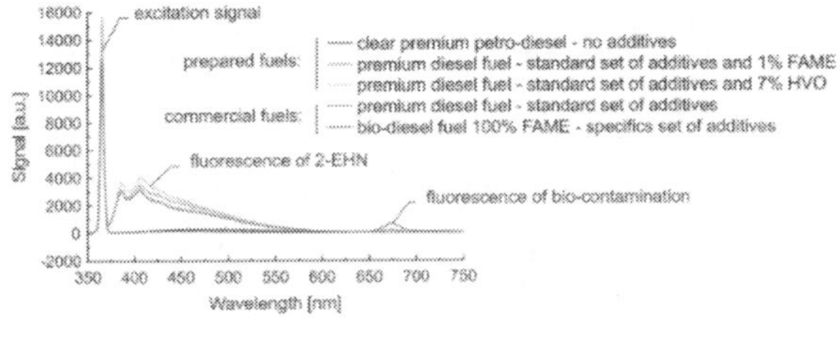

Figure 5. Spectra of fresh fuels excited with 366nm wavelength.

As stated previously, the excitation and fluorescence signals differ significantly, but the signal received from 2-EHN is relatively high. The 2-EHN signal is not present in the 100% FAME bio-diesel fuel and in the clear premium petro-diesel, which can be expected as EHN is not an additive for such fuels. Except for the 2-EHN, the fluorescence signal of bio-contaminants is observed for commercial fuels, while the bio-diesel fuel is characterized with a higher signal than the premium petrodiesel. The biodiesel shows a small fluorescence in the range of 450-700nm, due to aromatic components. Such fluorescence is not observed in the clear premium petro-diesel, which as previously stated is prepared from alkanes.

In the case of gum presence examination with excitation at 488nm, the power of excitation and fluorescence signals differ so much that their observation requires using both arms of photo-detection with different times of scanning. In the presented case, the fluorescence was measured with 10-second scanning and the excitation was measured with 5-second scanning.

Spectra of fuels stored for two years on windowsill measured with 488nm wavelength excitation are presented in Figure 6. The excitation signals are the same in both cases and do not affect the fluorescence characteristics. The presence of gums is evident, as a fluorescence signal in the range from 530nm to 700nm is present.

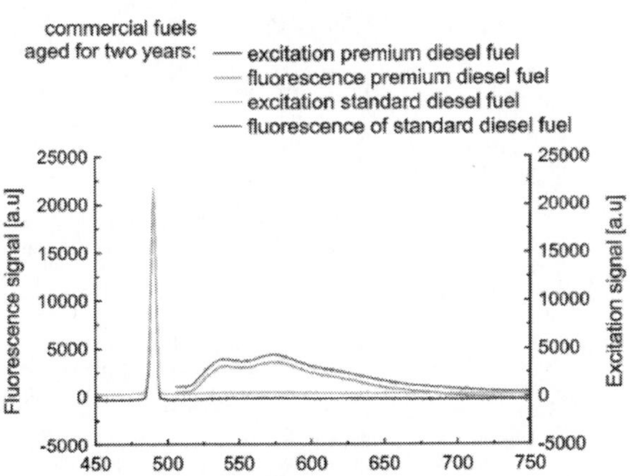

Figure 6. Spectra of commercial fuels stored two years on windowsill excited with 488nm vawelenght.

In both samples, the signal is almost the same, which means that the concentration of gums in both cases is the same. That at first view may seem strange. The vertical shift of signals can be the result of a difference between radii of used capillaries, as a small variation of this parameter is normal. In such case, the examination of the excitation signal at the receiver arm enables a simple mathematical correction.

Examinations of fresh fuels do not show any fluorescence signals comparable to results presented in Figure 6.

C. *Examination of premium commercial fuel exposed for light for few weeks*

We examined premium commercial diesel fuel stored at windowsill for up to five weeks and compared the results to storage of the same fuel in dark conditions. The fuel stored in dark condition does not show any visible changes or any changes when measured using the method described above. The change of appearance of fuel exposed to light can be described as follow: after one week the sample color started fading, after two weeks the sample becomes cloudy, and after five weeks there is an emergence of sludge. The sludge color is dark brown, similar to that of buckwheat honey, and it is sticky to the touch. The cleaning of outer capillary walls after probing of fuel exposed for five weeks need some attention, as sticky areas are palpable. Thus one can conclude that some reactions occurred in the sample under storage. It is interesting, that the examination of fluorescence excited at 488nm did not show any fluorescence signals.

The examination results of fluorescence excited at 366nm when the fuel was stored at a windowsill are presented in Figure 7. The observed fluorescence signals show significant changes of shape and power. The signal of bio-contamination disappeared. The signal power has not monotonically reduced. The initial spectrum maxima (point 4 in Figure 7.) after consecutive weeks of exposition shifted toward lower wavelength which was stable for some time (wavelength point 3 in Figure 7.). Local signal minima wavelength (point 2 in Figure 7.) were stable for some time, and then minima disappeared. The same effect applied to the first local maxima (wavelength point 1 in Figure 7).

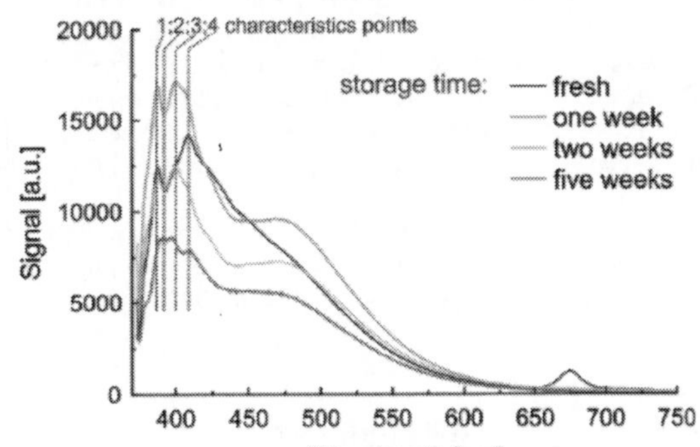

Figure 7. Measurement data of fluorescence excited at 366nm for premium commercial fuel stored at windowsill.

Therefore, in the described sensor device, the difference of signals S(4)-S(2) values measured in point 4 and in point 2 may be a good measure of fuel degradation. The wavelength at the point 4 was 408nm, and at the point 2 was 392nm. The results of examinations are presented in Table 1, including results for fresh fuels, fuels degraded to five weeks as well as seriously degraded fuels with gum presence the fluorescence of which was presented in Figure 6.

TABLE I. FUELS CLASSYFICATION

Fuel type	Exposition for light [weeks]	Visual report	Difference of signals; S(4)-S(2) [a.u.]
Premium - no additives	0	transparent, light yellow	0
Premium commercial	0	transparent, yellow	2585
Premium commercial	1	transparent, light yellow	847
Premium commercial	2	turbid, light yellow	-18
Premium commercial	5	turbid, light yellow, sludge stains	-523
Premium commercial	104	transparent, buckwheat honey, sediment	-563
Standard commercial	104	transparent, buckwheat honey, sediment	-346

The proposed measure is lower than zero for degraded fuels with are characterized by the presence of turbidity and first appearance of gum sludge. The difference is greater than zero for transparent fluids. It should be noted that premium fuels, that do not shows fluorescence, show zero difference the mentioned signals. The measured signal at the excitation wavelength (366nm) changes significantly, as can be expected for fuel transparency changes.

V. CONCLUSIONS

We proposed a sensor of diesel fuel degradation with fluorescence examination in a capillary optrode. The analysis of the measured signals of fresh and degraded diesel and biodiesel fuels showed the relationship of the degradation with measured and processed signals.

On the base of data collected in the experiments we can set the parameters determining the initial diesel fuel degradation level as the difference of signals registered at 408nm and 392nm for fuel sample excitation and 366nm. The seriously degraded diesel fuel is characterized by fluorescence signals in the range of 530nm to 700nm when the excitation signal is at 488nm.

We conclude that the proposed instrumentation may be in future a valuable added module to the capillary sensor system for diesel fuel fit-for- use examinations.

ACKNOWLEDGMENT

This work was partially supported by the NCBiR/PGNiG grant Polish Technology for Shale Gas, task T3.1.

REFERENCES

[1] Technical Committee of Petroleum Additive Manufactures in Europe, "Fuel Additives: Use and Benefits," ATC Document, vol. 113, 2013, pp. 1-68.

[2] S. Jain and M. P. Sharma, "Stability of biodiesel and its blends: A review," Renewable and Sustainable Energy Reviews, vol. 14, 2010, pp. 667–678.

[3] T. Herold, "Next Generation Derivered Cetane Analysis: High Precision Enables Refineries to Operate Close to Specifications and Increase Profitability," Petro Industry News, vol. 15, 2014, pp. 6-7.

[4] A. Kulinowski, T. Henly, and T. Stocky, "The Effect of 2-Ethylhexyl Nitrate Cetane Improver on Engine Durability," SAE Technical Paper 981364, 1998, pp. 1-9.

[5] R. A. Korus, T. L. Mousetis, and L. Lloyd, "Polymerization of vegetable oils," American Society of Agricultural Engineering vol. 4, 1982, pp. 127-137.

[6] M. G. Fonseca, et al., "Advanced Techniques in Soybean Biodiesel," in H. El-Shemy (Ed.), Soybean - Bio-Active Compounds, , InTech, Rijeka, Croatia, 2013, pp. 23-45, ISBN: 978-953-51-0977-8

[7] D. J. Bogan and R. Guirguis, "Mechanism of ignition enchancement by nitro and nitrade compounds,"Preprints – ACS, Division of Petroleum Chemistry, vol. 30, 1985, pp. 327

[8] B. S. Higgins, D. L. Siebers, and A. A. Aradi, "Comparison of 2-ethylhexyl nitrate and fuel composition induced changes in the diesel spray ignition process," International Journal of Engine Research, vol. 2, 2001, pp. 47-67.

[9] H. Bornemann, F. Scheidt and W. Sander, "Thermal decomposition of 2-ethylhexyl nitrate (2-EHN). Int. J. Chem. Kinet., vol. 34, 2002, pp. 34–38.

[10] A. G Gaydon, The Spectroscopy of Flames, John Wiley and Sons, Inc., New York, USA, 1957

[11] S. S. Merola, L.uca Marchitto, C. Tornatoe, and G. Valentino, "Chemiluminescence analysis of the effect of butanol-diesel fuel blends on the spray combustion process in an experimental common rail diesel engine," Thermal Science, vol. 19, 2015, pp. 1943-1957.

[12] A. R. L. Caires, V. S. Lima, and S. L. Oliveira, "Quantification of biodiesel content in diesel/biodiesel blends by fluorescence spectroscopy: Evaluation of the dependence on biodiesel feedstock," Renewable Energy, vol. 46, 2012, pp. 137–140.

[13] S. G. Wakeham, "Synchronous fluorescence spectroscopy and its application to indigenous and petroleum-derived hydrocarbons in lacustrine sediments," Environ. Sci. Technol., vol. 11, 1977, pp. 272–276.

[14] M. Wlodarski, A. Bombalska, M. Mularczyk-Oliwa; M. Kaliszewski, and K. Kopczyński, , "Fluorimetric techniques in analysis and classification of fuels," Proc. SPIE vol. 8703, 2012, pp. 87030B.

[15] M. Insausti and B. S. Fernández Band, "Determination of 2-ethylhexyl Nitrate in Diesel Oil Using a Single Excitation Emission Fluorescence Spectra (EEF) and Chemometrics Analysis," J Fundam. Renewable Energy Appl., vol. 4, 2014, pp. 1000137

[16] A. Kociubiński, M. Borecki, M. Duk, M. Sochacki, and M. L. Korwin-Pawlowski, "3D photodetecting structure with adjustable sensitivity ratio in UV – VIS range," Microelectronic Engineering, vol. 154, 2016, pp. 48–52.

[17] M Borecki, et al., "Large-area transparent in visible range silicon carbide photodiode," Proc. SPIE, vol. 8903, 2013, pp. 89030H.

[18] M. Borecki and M. L. Korwin-Pawlowski, "Optical capillary sensors for intelligent microfluidic sample classification," in

Nanosensors: Theory and Applications in Industry, Healthcare and Defence, T.C. Lim, Ed., CRC Press, Boca Raton, FL, USA, 2011, pp. 215–245.

[19] M. Borecki, et al., "Fiber Optic Capillary Sensor with Smart Optode for Rapid Testing of the Quality of Diesel and Biodiesel Fuel," IJASM, vol. 7, 2014, pp. 57–67.

[20] P. Prus, M. Borecki, M. L. Korwin-Pawlowski, A. Kociubiński, and M. Duk, "Automatic detection of characteristic points and form of optical signals in multiparametric capillary sensors," Proc. SPIE, vol. 9290, 2014, pp. 929009.

[21] M. Borecki, et al., "Sensing Method and Fiber Optic Capillary Sensor for Testing the Quality of Biodiesel Fuel," IARIA, Proc. Sensordevices 2013, pp. 19–24.

[22] M. Borecki, et al., "Dynamical Capillary Rise Photonic Sensor for Testing of Diesel and Biodiesel Fuel," Sensors & Transducers Journal, vol. 193, 2015, pp. 11-22.

[23] A. Baranowska, P. Miluski, M. Kochanowicz, J. Zmojda, and D. Dorosz, "Capillary optical fibre with Sm3+ doped ribbon core," Proc. SPIE, vol. 9662, 2015, pp. 96620Z.

[24] M. Geca, M. Borecki, M. L. Korwin-Pawlowski, and A. Kociubiński, "Local liquid sample heating: integration and isolation of a micro-heater," Proc. SPIE, vol. 9662, 2015, pp. 96620E.

[25] D. W. Naegell and R. H. Hill, "Laser inducted fluorescence detection of gums in jet fuels," Aero Propulsion and Power Directorate, Wright Laboratory, Air Force Systems Command, Wright-Patterson Air Force Base, WL-TR-92-2015, 1992, pp. 1-50.

[26] M. Borecki, J. Szmidt, P. Wrzosek, and M. Beblowska, "Optical fiber switch for sensor networks: design principles," Proc. SPIE, vol. 6347, 2006, pp. 63471Q.

Development of Methanol Sensors: Carbon Nanotubes Blended Hydroxyapatite Nano-Ceramics

S. R. Anjum and R. S. Khairnar
School of Physical Sciences,
Swami Ramanand Teerth Marathwada University
Nanded-431606, INDIA
{sraanjum, rskhairnarsps}@gmail.com

Abstract—**The experimental study reports the performance of Carbon nanotubes (CNT) blended Hydroxyapatite (HAp) composites as a sensing material for the detection of methanol vapours. The main objective of the work is to improve the temperature dependent sensitivity of the sensor for lower methanol concentration. Moreover, the sensing ability of native HAp and CNT blended HAp thick films is studied in terms of operating temperature, response / recovery time, maximum detection limit. Thick films of the native and blended materials are fabricated via screen printing technique. The sensing parameters are studied using two probe electrical methods. The sensor substrate is made by means of doping of various concentrations of CNT in HAp. The sensing of methanol vapours is studied at a fixed concentration of 100 ppm. Native HAp substrate shows good sensitivity for methanol at room temperature; however its sensing performance is inferior to the CNT blended materials. The blended composites exhibit impressive sensing ability compared with native HAp in terms of sensitivity, response/ recovery time and maximum uptake the limit. The sensing mechanism for methanol detection, the role of HAp as a parent material and CNT as an additive, is explained using a suitable sensing mechanism.**

Keywords- Carbon nanotubes; Gas sensor; Hydroxyapatite; Methanol sensor

I. INTRODUCTION

Methanol is a liquid petrochemical volatile organic compound. It is one of the most versatile compounds having a variety of applications in various fields. Methanol is a building block for many industrial applications. It is used as an antifreeze, solvent, fuel, and also denaturant for ethanol. The chemical is also a key component of biodiesel production. Like most of the organic volatile chemicals, methanol must be handled, transported and used with great care. It has significant toxic, flammable and reactive properties, produces harmful effects on human health and the environment. Thus, to reduce methanol exposure, one should need a sensor that detects these vapours at low detection limit with accuracy and efficiency. The present work elucidates the development of nano material based sensing substrate which works at the low operating temperatures and shows better sensitivity for organic vapours at the lower detection limit. Carbon nanotubes are the most desirable sensor substrate with enhanced surface to volume ratio, small grain size and remarkable electrical characteristics [1]-[4]. However, the surface of native CNT is not ideal for gas sensing application as it has less number of active reaction sites available for the adsorption of gas molecules [5]-[6]. This is because it has a perfect carbon-carbon network. The introduction of defects via; vacancies, functionalization or dopant, in carbon network, make it a desirable surface for sensing application by providing many active adsorption/ reaction sites [7]-[8]. The presence of defects drastically modifies the structure and electrical properties of this material, thus creating a potential sensor substrate. The sensors, which are developed using carbon nanotubes as a dopant or functionalized CNT as supportive material, show excellent sensing characteristics. These sensors work at lower operating temperature compared to metal oxide doped material. Also, the response / recovery time for such sensors are found to be less long. Calcium Hydroxyapatite [$Ca_{10}(PO_4)_6(OH)_2$], having properties such as porous hexagonal network, nano grain size, and higher specific surface area, is utilized as sensing substrate [9]-[14]. The surface of HAp is considered as an ionic conductor. The presence of H^+ and OH^- ions (hydroxyl group) is found to be responsible for its conductivity at elevated temperature [15]-[17]. At low temperature, the conductivity is either because of proton transfer among OH^- ions or migration of protons from OH^- to PO_4^{3-} ion [11], [18].

$$OH^- + OH^- \leftrightarrow O^{2-} + H_2O$$

or

$$OH^- + PO_4^{3-} \leftrightarrow O^{2-} + HPO_4^{2-} + OH \leftrightarrow O^{2-} + PO_4^{3-} + H_2O + \text{vacancy OH}$$

The protons (H^+), hydroxyl ions (OH^-), and oxides ions (O^-) control the reactivity when the adsorbed molecules come in contact with the surface. The interaction of volatile organic vapours ($C_xH_yO_z$) like methanol, ethanol and propanol etc with HAp surface increases its conductivity since these vapours donate a proton to the surface resulting in decreasing the electrical resistance of the material. The present study deals with the utilization of sensing ability of HAp and CNT in order to get desirable sensing substrates for the detection of methanol vapor at 30^0C.

II. EXPERIMENTAL

Calcium Hydroxyapatite is synthesised by following the path reported in our earlier publications [9]-[10]. In order to achieve the best sensing substrate, CNT in various weight concentrations is blended in HAp via liquid phase reinforce method under similar experimental condition. A known quantity of CNT with nano HAp is dissolved in alcohol is and kept under magnetic stirring followed by sonication and allowed to dry at room temperature. The dried nano powder is sintered at 100^0C for 1h in a programmable furnace to remove volatile compounds and water vapours. The powder is then mixed mechanically in an agate mortar continually for 4-5 hours. Scanning Electron Microscopy (SEM), X-Ray Diffraction (XRD) and Brunauer-Emmett-Teller (BET) surface analysis are carried out to analyze the morphological and structural characterization of the material. The prepared composite materials along with native HAp is deposited in the form of thick films by screen printing technique. The area for each prepared film is kept constant. A schematic sensing setup is employed to examine the sensing ability of the material [19]. The variation in resistance in the presence of atmospheric air and tested vapours is measured for a preset concentration of methanol under similar experimental conditions. The sensitivity factor (gas response) is calculated by using the equation

$$Gas\ response\ S(\%) = \frac{Rg - Ra}{Ra} \times 100$$

where Ra and R_g represent the sensor resistance in the presence of atmospheric air and test gas respectively.

III. RESULTS AND DISCUSSION

A. Morphological Analysis

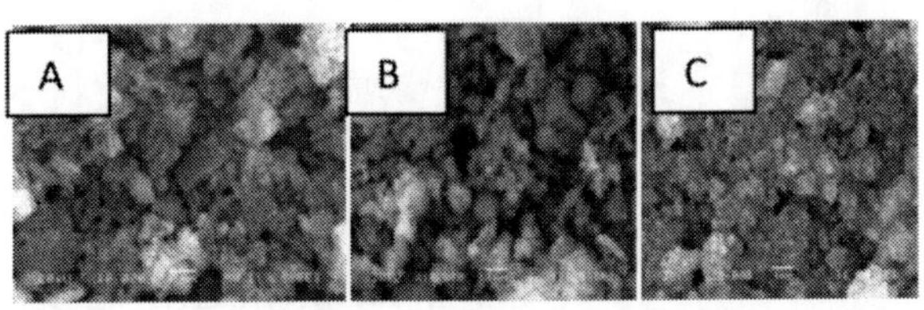

Figure 1. SEM micrographs for (A) Native HAp, (B) 0.5wt% CNT blended HAp, (C) 0.7wt% CNT bended HAp showing variations in surface topography due to the presence of CNT.

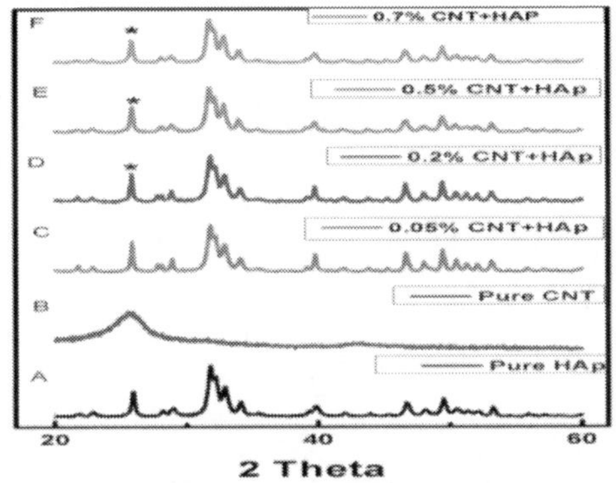

Figure 2. X-ray diffraction pattern of native HAp, CNT and CNT blended HAp material (* represents the peak for CNT): Y-axis has arbitrary units.

The surface morphology for native HAp and CNT blended HAp is shown in Fig. 1. The surface of HAp is covered with a large number of small grain sized particles. These small grains are closely arranged in a circular pattern over a large area. The presence of CNT in various concentrations significantly affects the surface property. 0.5wt% CNT blended HAp surface shows a porous structure with the small sized particle. Such surface increases the possibility of interaction between organic vapours and the sensing substrate. It seems that there is more compactness on the surface for 0.7wt% CNT, reducing the porosity.

B. Structural Analysis

X-ray diffraction pattern of native HAp, CNT and CNT blended HAp material is recorded for 2θ value 20 to 60 degree with a scan rate 2^0/min on Rigaku diffractometer with Cu $K\alpha_1$ radiation (λ=1.54Å). Fig. 2(A) shows X-rd diffractogram of native HAp synthesized by weight chemical precipitation method. The (2 1 1), (3 0 0), ((0 0 2), (2 1 3), (2 2 2) planes of HAp are clearly observed in the diffraction pattern. All peaks exhibit hexagonal phase structure of HAp (JCPDS card No. 00-009-0432) [9]-[11], [14], [15], [17]. The CNT blended HAp material also exhibits similar patterns. The peak for CNT with the plane (0 0 2) at 26^0 is not clearly discerned by diffraction pattern may be due to the small weight concentration of CNT in the composite material or presence HAp peak at the same plane.

C. Surface area Analysis

The adsorption-desorption isotherm along with the pore size distribution is displayed in Fig.3. The isotherm for both native HAp and 0.5wt% CNT blended HAp is identified as type III as it exhibits type III hysteresis loop having weak interaction between adsorbent and adsorbate.

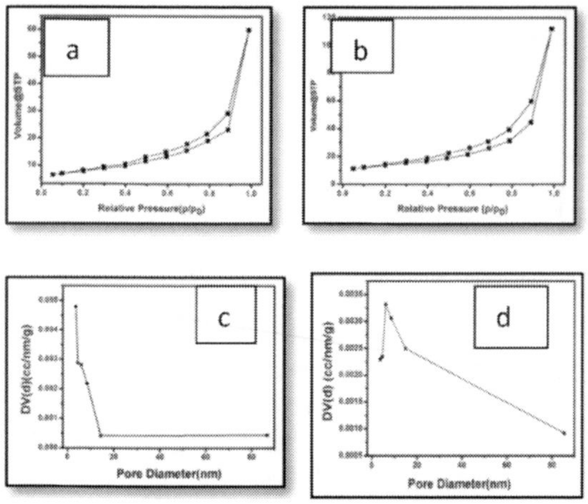

Figure 3. N_2 adsorption/desorption isotherm (a) native HAp, (b) 0.5wt% CNT blended HAp and BJH pore size distribution curve (c) native HAp, (d) 0.5wt% CNT blended HAp.

The BJH pore distribution suggests the mesoporous nature of the material. The measured specific surface area of native HAp is 22.069 m^2/g, while that of 0.5%CNT blended HAp is found to be 49.99 m^2/g which is twice the surface area of HAp.

D. Methanol Sensing Properties

The response of the sensing substrate is tested at elevated temperature in order to select the operating temperature. The operating temperature is defined as the temperature at which the sensor has a maximum gas response. A profile of gas response as a function of temperature for a fixed concentration of methanol is plotted in Fig. 4(A).

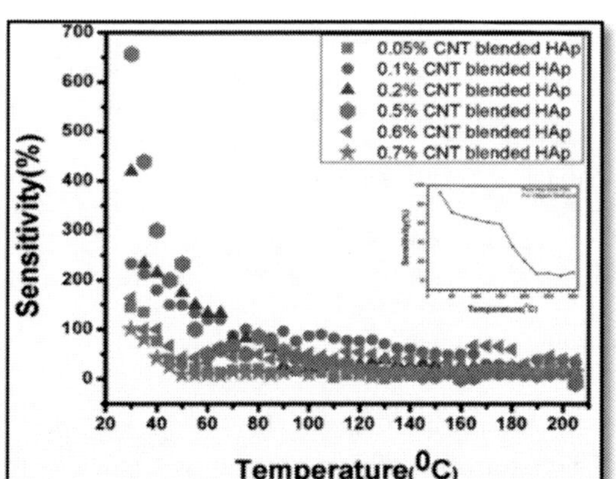

Figure 4(A). Sensor sensitivity (response) of native HAp and CNT blended HAp at variable temperature for 100 ppm concentration of methanol

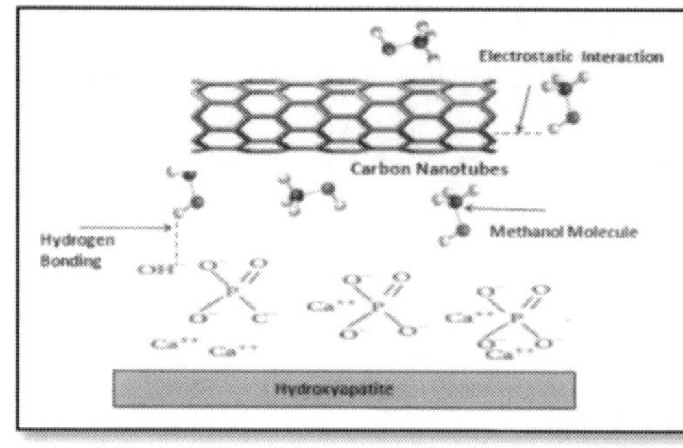

Figure 4(B). Formation of hydrogen bonding, due to dipole- dipole interaction between polar methanol molecule and hydroxyl ions on HAp surface. Electrostatic interaction between methanol and CNT molecules leads to enhance the sensing property of the substrate material

Both the native HAp and CNT blended HAp materials show the same substrate temperature of 30 °C for getting maximum sensitivity in presence of 100 ppm methanol. The interaction of methanol molecules with HAp surface increases the sensitivity of the device by forming hydrogen bonding with HAp molecules. The methanol molecules interact with CNT via electrostatic interaction. It is believed that this interaction assists the unidirectional flow of electric current flowing through the tube (See Fig. 4(B)) increasing the sensitivity of the device. The alteration in sensitivity as a function of CNT concentration in composite at room temperature (30 °C) for 100ppm methanol is shown in Fig 5. The response varies linearly with CNT concentration, attains peak value for 0.5wt% of CNT concentration, and afterwards, it decreases with increase in concentration. It shows that each composite material has its own impact on the sensitivity of the material. However, the response of 0.5 wt% of CNT concentration is superior with a magnitude~ 600%, when exposed to methanol at room temperature (30 °C). This particular concentration leads to provide a balanced sensing layer for the gas sensing application. For higher concentrations, the surface modification doesn't support the effective sensing phenomenon.

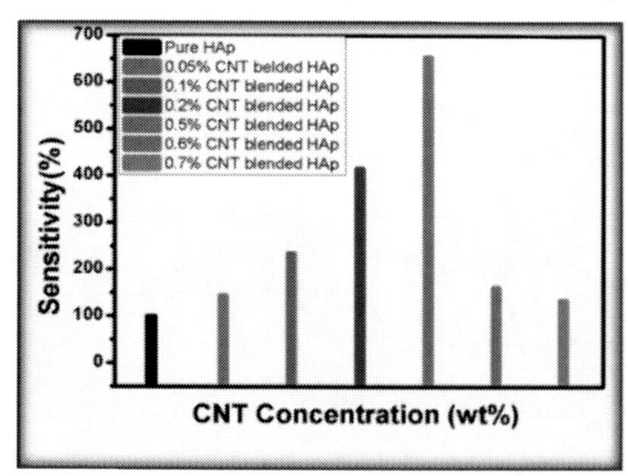

Figure 5. Variation in sensitivity for different CNT concentrations in HAp, at room temperature (30 °C) for 100 ppm methanol

A comparative study of the response/ recovery time characteristics of native HAp and 0.5 %CNT blended HAp material at room temperature (30 °C) is carried out. The response of the material as a function of time is recorded by exposing the sample to detecting vapours and atmospheric air, respectively as shown in Fig. 6. The response time is 160 sec for native HAp substrate and 60 sec for 0.5wt% of CNT concentration respectively. The material recovers more than 90% of its initial value after exposing to atmospheric air. Native HAp shows sluggish desorption rate due to the polar affinity (hydrogen bonding between methanol molecules and HAp surface). In case of CNT blended HAp composite material two possible types of physisorption may occur upon exposure to target molecule. One is a weak physisorption (van der Waals dispersion forces) between CNT molecules and target molecules. Being weak, forces such adsorption to be easily desorbed after exposing to atmospheric air at room temperature without any need for extra heat or energy resulting faster recovery time. The other is the formation of hydrogen bonding (stronger than van der Waals dispersion forces) due to the dipole-dipole attraction between polar methanol molecule and hydroxyl ions on HAp surface. It requires few minutes to recover its original state when the sensor is exposed to atmospheric air.

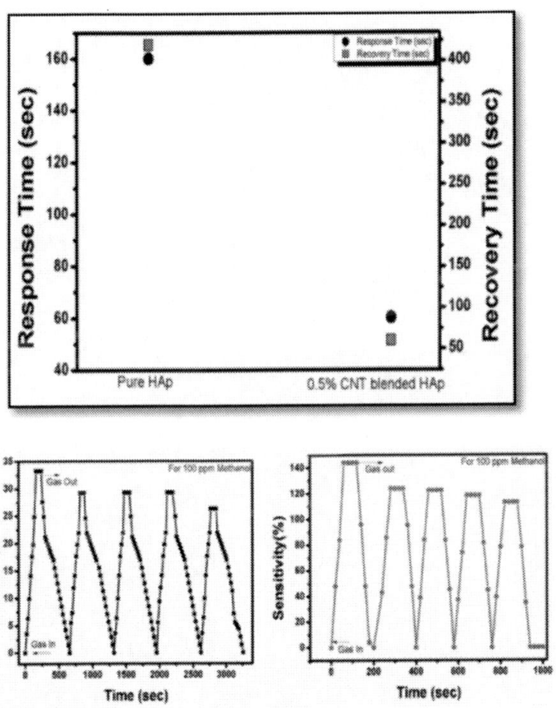

(a) (b)

Figure 6. Response/ recovery time plot for native HAp and 0.5wt% CNT blended HAp thick film in the presence of 100 ppm methanol. Continuous repeated cycles for response / recovery time at room temperature (30 °C), (a) native HAp, (b) 0.5% CNT blended HAp.

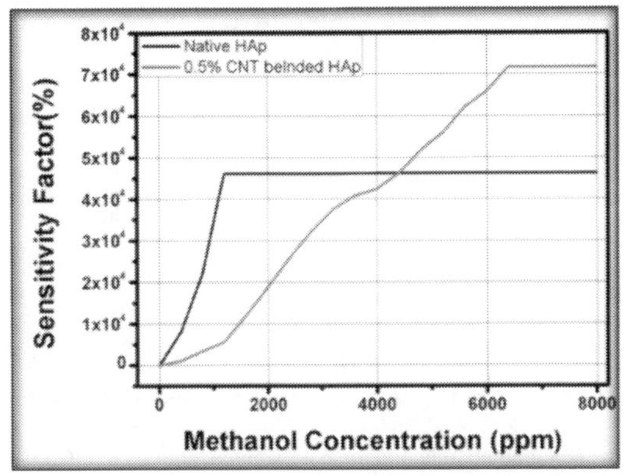

Figure 7. Sensitivity of native HAp and 0.5% CNT blended HAp thick films for various concentrations of methanol vapours at room temperature (30°C).

The sensitivity of native HAp and 0.5% CNT blended HAp material to different methanol concentrations is also recorded to compare the maximum methanol detecting limit of the materials. The sensor is held at room temperature (30 °C) and exposed to various concentrations of methanol ranging from 100 ppm to 6500 ppm. The nature of the graph in Fig. 7 depicts significant changes with increasing methanol concentration. The surface area and available active reacting sites of the HAp and CNT play an important role in the deposition of methanol. Sensitivity depends on adsorption of the gas molecule at the available adsorption sites. Therefore, 0.5% CNT blended HAp shows much higher uptake capacity than HAp. Saturation occurs due to lack of adsorption sites with increasing concentration since the surface is covered with methanol vapours.

IV. CONCLUSIONS AND FUTURE WORK

The influence of CNT blending on HAp surface, for enhancement in sensing properties of methanol, has been studied. The sensing performance of the native HAp thick film and 0.5wt% CNT blended HAp thick film are compared in terms of sensitivity (maximum response), response time and reproducibility for a fixed concentration of methanol. The response of the material in the presence of various concentrations of methanol is recorded to find out its maximum detection limit. The results corroborate that addition of CNT in small weight concentration dramatically ameliorates the sensing property of native HAp. The enhancement is attributed to increment in surface area and possible immobilisation of methanol molecules on the peripheral end corners of CNTs. The study indicates the potential use of such blended matrix in practical sensing devices operating at around room temperature (30 °C). This work represents the first report in a series of experimentations. This work will be followed by the sensing studies for higher alcohols such as ethanol, propanol, and butanol. In addition to this, oriented deposition of the CNT on HAp surface may be carried out in the future for the enhancement of sensitivity and detecting the lowest concentration of organic vapours.

REFERENCES

[1] B. S. Dasari, W. Taube, P. Agarwal, M. Rajput, and A. Kumar, J. Akhtar, "Room Temperature Single Walled Nano tubes (SWCNT) Chemo resistive Ammonia Gas Sensor," Sensors and transducer, vol. 190, Issue 7, pp. 24-30, 2015.

[2] Joseph C. Obirai, Gray Hunter, and Prebir Dutta, "Multi-walled carbon nanotubes as high temperature carbon monoxide sensors," Sensors and actuators B, vol. 134, pp. 640-646, 2008.

[3] A. Ghasemi, and M. Molla, "Highly sensitive single walled carbon nanotubes (5, 0) for adsorption gases CO_2, CO and N2: a DFT study," J. Chem. Tech. Research, vol. 4(4), pp. 1302-1308, 2012.

[4] Y. Du, Q. Xue, Z. Zhang, F. Xia, Z. Liu, and W. Xing, "Enhanced hydrogen gas response of pd nano particles decorated single walled carbon nanotubes films/SiO2/Si hetero structure," AIP Advan., vol. 5, pp. 027136, 2015.

[5] P. Kar, and A. Chaudhury, "Carboxylic acid functionalized multi-walled carbon nanotubes doped polyaniline for chloroform sensor," Sensors and actuators B, vol. 183, pp. 25-33, 2013.

[6] M. Humayun, R. Divan, Y. Lui, L. Gundel, P. Solomon, and I. Paproty, "Novel chemo resistive CH4 sensor with 10ppm sensitivity based on multi-walled carbon nanotubes functionalized with Sno2 nano crystals," J. vacuum Sci. and Tech., vol. 34, pp.01A131, 2016.

[7] L. Shobin, B. Renganathan, D. Sastikumar, K. park, and S. Manivannan, "Pure and isobutyl methyl ketone treated multi-walled carbon nanotubes for ethanol and methanol vapor sensing," IIEEE sensor journal, vol. 14 (4), pp.1248-1243, 2014.

[8] Akbari, Z. Buntal, M. Ahmed, A. Enzevaee, R. Yousof, S. Iqbal, M. Ahmei, M. Sidik, and H. Karimi, "Analytical calculation of sensing parameters on carbon nanotubes based gas sensor," Sensors, vol. 14, pp. 5502-5515, 2014.

[9] R. U. Mene, M. P. Mahabole, K. C. Mohite, and R. S. Khairnar, "Fe doped Hydroxyapatite thick films modified via swift heavy ion irradiation for CO and CO_2 gas sensing application," J. Alloys Comp., vol. 584, pp. 487-493, 2014.

[10] R. U. Mene, M. P. Mahabole, R. C. Aiyer, and R. S. Khairnar, "Hydroxyapatite nano ceramics thick film: An efficient CO_2 gas sensor," Open Appl. Phys. J., vol. 3, pp.10-16, 2010.

[11] Li Huixia, Liu Yong, Tan Yanni, Luo Lantan, Zhang Qing, Li Kun, and Tang Hanchunl "Room temperature gas sensing properties of tubular Hydroxyapatite," New. J. Chem., vol. 39, pp. 3865-3874, 2015.

[12] R. U. Mene, M. P. Mahabole, and R. S. Khairnar, "Surface modified Hydroxyapatite thick film for CO_2 gas sensing application: Effect of swift heavy ion irradiation," Radi. Phys. Chem., vol. 80 (6), pp.682-687, 2011.

[13] R. U. Mene, M. P. Mahabole, Ramphal Sharma, and R. S. Khairnar, "Enhancement in CO gas sensing properties of Hydroxyapatite thick films: Effect of swift heavy ion irradiation," Vacuum, vol. 86 (1), pp.66-71, 2011.

[14] Rajendra S. Khairnar, Vanja Kokol, and S. R. Anjum, "Development of Hydroxyapatite nano ceramics for methanol and ethanol sensor," Int. J. Pure Appl. Res. Eng. Tech., vol. 3 (8), pp.379-86, 2015.

[15] Lanlan Luo, Yong Liu, Tan Yanni, Li Huixia, Zhang Qing, and Li Kun, "Room temperature gas sensor based on tube-like Hydroxyapatite modified with gold particles," J. Cent. South Univ., vol. 23, pp.18-26, 2016.

[16] S. Suresh, "Theoretical studies of solid state dielectric parameter of Hydroxyapatite," Mater. Phys Mech., vol. 14, pp.145-151, 2012.

[17] Qing Zhang, Yong Liu, Ying Zhang, Huixia Li, Yanni Taqn, Lanlan Luo, Junhao Duan, Kaiyang Li, and Craig Banks, "Facile and controllable synthesis of Hydroxyapatite / graphene hybrid materials with enhanced sensing performance towards ammonia," Analyst, vol. 140, pp.5235-5242, 2015.

[18] R. Ramli, R. Adnan, M. Abubakar, and S. Masudi, "Synthesis and characterization of nano porous Hydroxyapatite," J. Phy. Sci., vol. 22 (1), pp.20-37, 2011.

[19] Rajendra S. Khairnar, S. R. Anjum, and M. P. Mahabole, "Development of CNT doped nano-HAp thick film gas sensor," Inter. J. Eng. Sci. Inno. Tech., vol. 3 (3), pp.3253-261, 2014.

Development of a Mechanical Sleeve Diagnosis Test

André Borges
School of Technology
Polytechnic Institute of Cávado and Ave (IPCA)
Barcelos, Portugal
e-mail: a8685@alunos.ipca.pt

Vítor Carvalho
School of Technology & Algoritmi R&D
IPCA & Minho University
Barcelos & Guimarães, Portugal
e-mail: vcarvalho@ipca.pt

***Abstract*— This paper presents the development of a system to assist the inspection, repair and calibration of mechanical sleeves. This system contemplates a mechanical device and the underlying software in which the main data acquisition is carried out through a force sensor. The developed system implied the development of specific hardware, based on the platform Arduino, and dedicated software based on C programming language. A user interface to register and store the fulfilled tests was developed. The system allowed to optimize the performance and the efficiency of a manufacturing unit, which, until now, was done using a manual procedure.**

Keywords-sleeve; nozzle; force sensor; Arduino.

I. INTRODUCTION

This section presents the state or art, the motivation and the background of the project, as well as its purposes and the paper structure.

A. State of Art

Verhagen et al. (2015) [1] argue that automation of engineering processes is increasingly prevalent in multiple lifecycle phases such as design, manufacturing and service. The automation of physical tasks is a long-standing characteristic of enterprises striving to remain competitive. For mass production systems in particular, the majority of manual labour has been replaced by automated production equipment, a trend that is increasingly replicated in series production systems.

Limoncelli (2016) [2] tells that care should be taken when a process is automated because the human component of the process could be very important for the entire system. "When a process is automated the automation encapsulates learning thus far, permitting new people to perform the task without having to experience that learning."

Luz and Kuiawinski (2006) [3] expose that, with the industry evolution, relevant events were observed in the development of Production Engineering settings and the presence of the machines, manufacturing processes and production systems increased. Using these concepts, expanded methods have been created to the other branches of the organization, such as the commercial and services branches.

Zuboff (1994) [4] quoting H. L. Arnold, an industrial journalist, wrote with excitement about Ford's innovations that maximize the continuity of the assembly. He summarized the main elements of that productivity strategy, initially, all unnecessary movements were eliminated from the actions of the workers. The task was organized in order to require the least amount of will power consumption and mental effort.

From the above, it can be assumed that automating a manual process can be very advantageous although it should be pondered if this action is beneficial to the company as it is to the human element. In the case of this paper, it will be clearly demonstrated that the developed system brings numberless advantages to both sides because it will reduce the error margin and increase the efficiency, resulting in an increase of effective working time of the operator.

B. Motivation and Background

The motivation associated with this study fits in upgrading/automating a mechanical sleeves test procedure of a multinational technological company, located in the city of Braga, northern Portugal. The sleeves are used by an electronic components assembly industrial machine; this machine controls the segments in order to pick the components and drop them in the right place of a PCB (printed circuit board). They have a spring inside with a defined pressure, which is responsible for absorbing the impact of SMD components (Surface Mounting Devices) both in the collection as well as in the placement. The state of this spring is critical to ensure the components application accuracy as well as to prevent the rejection of the electronic components. The spring pressure can only be applied after placing a nozzle (Fig. 1).

The previous method that was used for the detection of the spring state was a manual process using a testing instrument in which the result of the applied force in the spring was shown using a manometer. To observe that, some individual weights of 200 g each were used, who exercise force exclusively on the spring. The pointer of the manometer must be between 15 and 25, resulting in a maximum force applied of 2.2 N. That range is recommended by the buyer which is also the manufacturer of the industrial machine referenced above. This measurement system has no units which gives a non-scientific approval.

Figure 1. Example of a sleeve with the nozzle applied.

C. *Project purposes*

As the manual diagnostic test is a time consuming process and it may not offer the same test conditions to all sleeves - this is a consequence of the weights that might be dropped at different heights resulting in a change in the force exerted in the spring. So, to address these issues, the purpose of this project is to develop a device associated with a graphical application, allowing direct contact between the data acquired with the operator, which results into less manual labour on the side of the user.

This project contemplates two main parts, hardware and software. The hardware to be developed will comprise:

- A support structure to backing the tool in the repair bench;
- A motor for controlling the force to apply to the sleeve to be evaluated;
- A sensor for measuring strength and all electronic components required.

The software to be developed should provide:

- An interface for interaction with the operator to control and analysis of the measures;
- Graphical presentation of the force measured;
- Organization and storage of the data acquired.

D. *Paper structure*

This paper is structured in 4 sections. In the second section, Technical Description, the problem analysis is presented as well as the way it was approached, demonstrating how problems were solved and which are the reasons that led to the chosen solutions. This section exposes the most important points of the development of this project. In the third section, Final Tests and Installation, we describe the final tests carried out and the method how the installation of the device was executed in production. In the fourth section, Conclusion and Future Work, we present the conclusions of the work carried out, as well as indicate some improvement proposals.

II. TECHNICAL DESCRIPTION

The problem to be solved arises from the need to replace the manual performed sleeve spring diagnostic test that, can be susceptible to human error, for a new device capable to streamline resulting in a more organized process as well as the integration of more and new features.

It was established a strategy of resolution of the problem. In the broadest sense of the problem, the following block diagram was developed (Fig. 2).

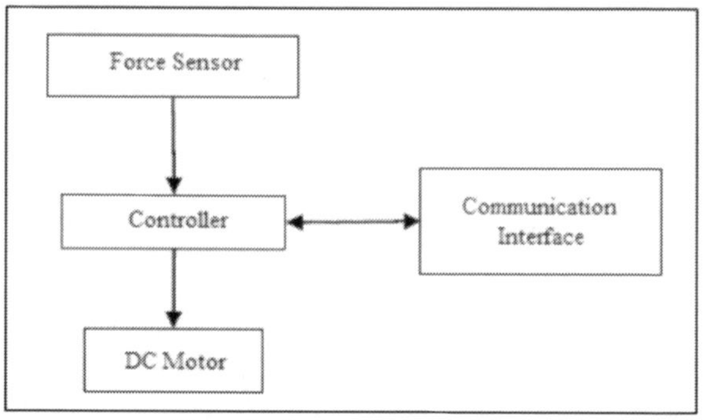

Figure 2. Project block diagram.

As presented in Fig. 2, the data provided by the sensor should be treated by the controller and sent to the interface; the motor which represents the motion of the sleeve, receives orders from the controller that can either be subsequent of sensor data or orders from the operator through the interface. In order to store the information of each tested segment as well to include the date of the tests, there was a need to integrate a database in the software application.

A. *System Design*

In a first approach to the project it was necessary and important to perform several manual diagnostic tests to understand the whole process from scratch. If the test is invalid, it is necessary to repair the sleeve by changing the spring or, in some cases, by cleaning the inside of the sleeve, which is enough to restore the correct functionality of the spring.

Once defined the resolution strategy it was crucial to begin the research about the sensor to use knowing that, it would be important to measure the force intensity applied in Newton (N) [5, 6].

After a research of existing sensors in the market that could supply this project needs, we considered the force sensor reference FSG015WNPB from Honeywell (Fig. 3) [6]. This sensor has a plunger area, a total volume of 916,16 mm^3, a measurement range between 0 to 15N, a value of 0,5% span relativity to linearity and 0,2% of span relativity to repeatability, in order to detect the small force oscillations of the sleeve during the test.

Figure 3. Force sensor [7].

The force sensor chosen is based on a Wheatstone bridge; by applying a force on the plunger of the sensor it will cause a symmetrical variation, however opposite, in the sensor outputs; as various forces represent variations of different voltage, it has a fundamental tension force ratio to determine the force applied. As a result of the information requested from the manufacturer along with this sensor, we also acquired an instrumentation amplifier (IA) [8, 9], with the reference INA122 from Texas Instruments [10].

The controller used was the Arduino UNO platform since the company already had one and it also can meet all the requirements necessary for the development of this project. With this controller it was possible to power up the circuit chosen.

To control the speed and direction of the DC motor, we used an Arduino module of the H bridge, as it allows to control both directions of the motor rotation. The module used is based on the IC L298 from ST, which is a dual H bridge [11]. The motor speed can be regulated through PWM (Pulse Width Modulation) being able to rotate at different speeds allowing faster/slower testing times. However, in order to get proper results, once the sleeve approaches the sensor, the motor speed should be as slow as possible, and in this case the possible slowest speed is manifested by the PWM value of 40, on a scale from 0 to 255. PWM values lower than 40 aren't enough to keep the motor in motion.

For position switches, we considered some roller switches as they are very affordable and of great efficiency.

Figure 4 presents the sensor output circuit designed [12, 13].

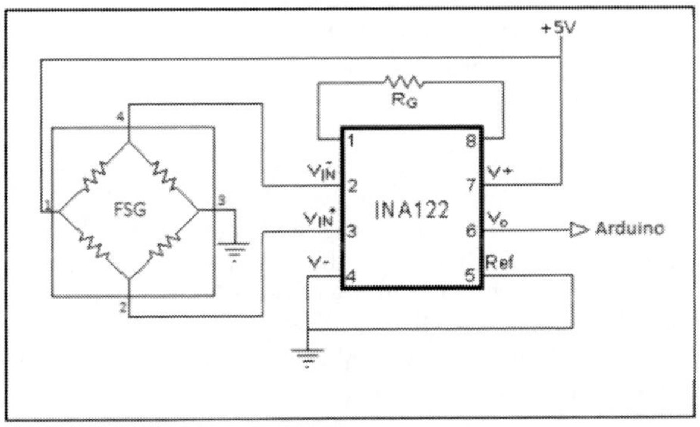

Figure 4. Circuit designed to read the sensor output.

Outlined the circuit, it was essential to scale the value of R_G (Fig. 4) being the gain (G) of the IA, $G = 5 + (200k/R_G)$. Since the circuit is powered from a 5V source it has to be ensured that the output does not exceed the 5V to force values up to 2.2 N, as it is the value of the maximum force applied to the spring of the sleeve. So, to calculate the gain, we defined as maximum value, hypothetically, applied to a weight of 308.8 g corresponding to an output of 0.038 V. For a maximum voltage of 4.8V, as a precaution, $G = 4.80/0.038 = 124$. Then, $R_G = 200k/(124-5) = 1.6k\Omega$.

In order to read the values from the sensor, we developed an application with the Arduino interface software (Fig. 5). The input considers an analogue port from the Arduino and depending on the ratio between the maximum and minimum values read there is a direct correspondence to the maximum and minimum values of the applied force value, respectively. Moreover, it is possible to make the mapping of values to get the current value of the force. This is only possible because the sensor features a linear behaviour.

So, verifying the minimum weight and the maximum weight that the Arduino can read, a relationship was established between the weight applied and the output voltage. Knowing the weight being applied, easily, it is then converted to Newton, multiplying it by 9.8 m/s^2 (acceleration due to gravity on Earth).

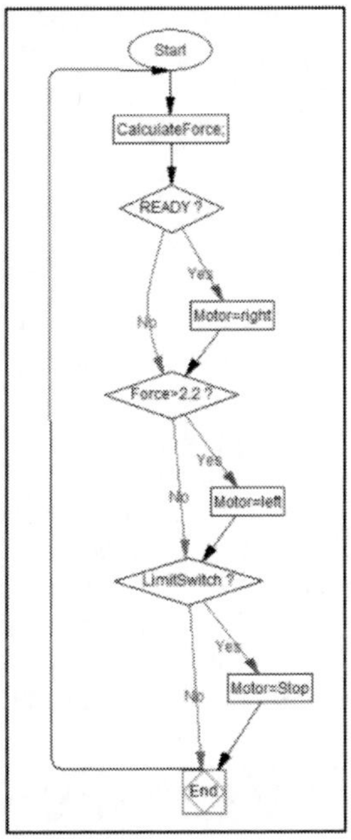

Figure 5. Flowchart of the Arduino interface code.

Following the flowchart (Fig. 5), the first step is to calculate the force in Newton; then if the operator chooses to begin the test, the motor will spin to the right, which means the sleeve will start to approach the sensor, if not, the motor does not spin.

Up next, if the applied force is higher than 2.2N, the motor will reverse its rotation, if not, the motor will keep his current configuration whether is stopped or is on the move.

If the limit switch is activated, it means that the sleeve is coming back, so the motor must stop, otherwise, the motor keeps the current configuration.

For security reasons, we implemented an emergency switch. This is a way to ensure control of the system, as once activated cuts off the system power. This switch should only be activated if the sleeve, for some reason, mechanical or by software, overload the sensor and reaches the switch.

If there were no security system implemented, certainly the mechanical components could be damaged.

The source code represented by the flowchart is executed every 5ms which represents a frequency of 200Hz, corresponding to a sensor output reading almost continuously, which allows to make nearly live decisions.

Once the Arduino code was completed, the code was implemented in C# programming language [14, 15], with the purpose of creating a user friendly interface that shows graphically the applied force value to the segment, transmitted through the application on Arduino.

It was imperative to establish a communication between the Arduino and the application [16]. With this purpose it was necessary to receive and send data through the serial port of the computer.

As this application uses several distinct features such as establish a connection by serial port or define a graph on the interface, it is essential to use delegate methods it allows updating the UI (user interface) thread, for getting or setting data.

To set the chart it was established that the Y-axis will represent the values of the force in mN and the X-axis will represent time in ms.

The chosen chart type is a line chart. For better perception of the maximum peak, a label is displayed in the interface with this information, as well as in any place of the chart it is displayed a tooltip with the coordinates.

Additionally, some other features were implemented in the application (Fig. 6), that result from the need to explore new concepts and offer different and contemplative solutions to the operator, such as the possibility of saving the chart to a file in JPG format, creation of a database (DB) [17] to store information regarding tests performed, or to print data and display it in a HTML page [18].

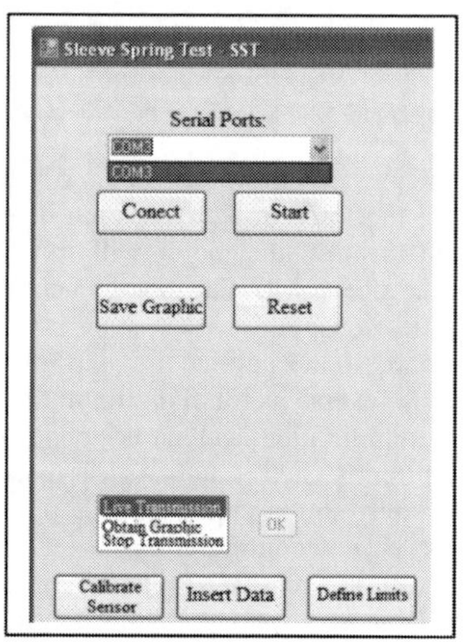

Figure 6. User interface.

B. *Hardware Implementation*

It was known beforehand that the device to develop should be robust. The idea was to create a system with a strap to allow the sleeve to move in the horizontal plane (Fig.7).

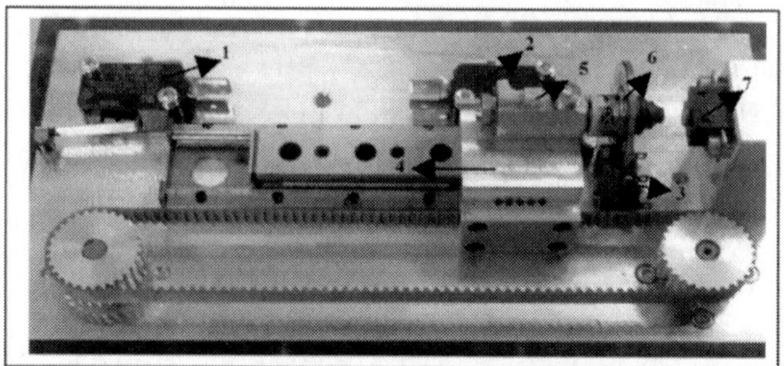

Figure 7. Motion system [1- position switch; 2- motor speed limit switch; 3- emergency switch; 4- movable part; 5-mechanical shirt; 6-sleeve/segment; 7- force sensor.]

Observing Fig. 7, the motor is connected to a pulley and, through a strap, this is linked to another pulley as well, as the movable part that carries the sleeve is attached to the belt, this will move horizontally. To give mobility to the movable part, this is attached to a bearing system, so when the belt moves, the movable part follows this movement. To put the sleeve to test in the movable part it was used a mechanical shirt that is permanently affixed to the movable part, so any sleeve can be tested as long as it is embedded in the mechanical shirt.

The electronic circuit was welded into a board allowing that all the components stay inside of the structure, thus protected from external disturbances.

The structure must guarantee that the test conditions are the same for all segments to be tested.

III. FINAL TESTS AND INSTALLATION

Once the software and the hardware were completed, the testing phase was undertaken. At first two sleeves were tested, one in a good state and another in a bad state, previously tested through the manual system. The results were very positive because we found large differences in the graphs obtained, so then only sleeves in good condition were tested for being able to establish parameters that identify the state of any sleeve (Fig. 8).

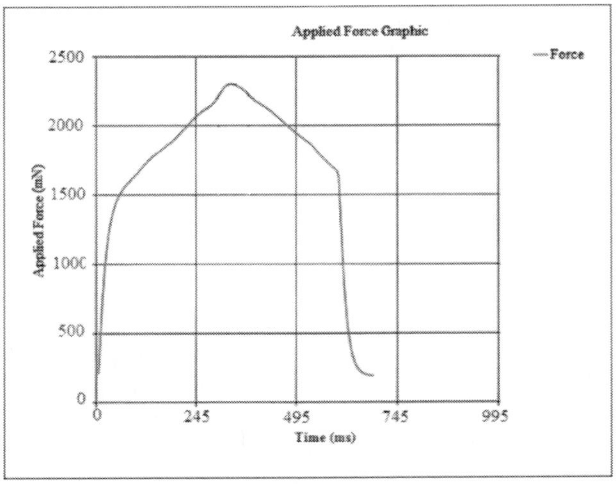

Figure 8. Sleeve in good condition.

On the basis of these tests, it was managed to check that if all the graphics of sleeves that show up in conditions of being used, approach the symmetry between the range 650ms and 800ms and the maximum number of force applied may not exceed the 2200mN.

By testing different sleeve states, we also verified distinct characteristics for each spring condition. Figures 9 and 10 are examples of graphs that represent the state of a loose spring (Fig. 9) and a stuck spring (Fig. 10).

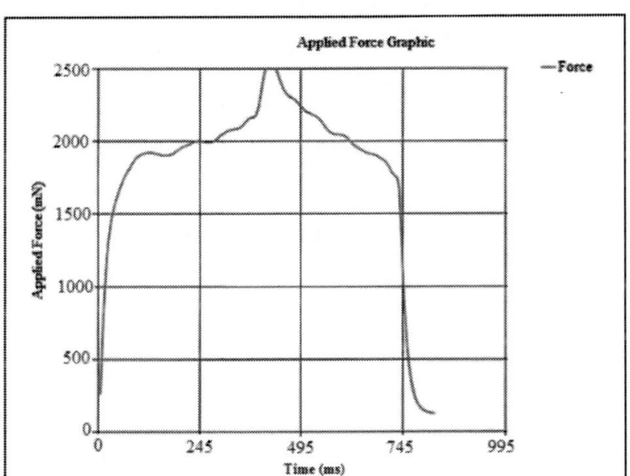

Figure 9. Sleeve with a loose spring.

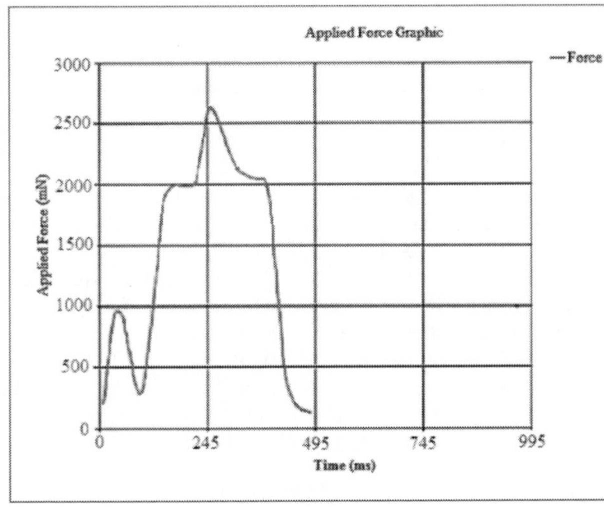

Figure 10. Sleeve with a stuck spring.

A loose spring does not offer as much resistance as a normal one so it takes longer time to achieve the maximum force. Moreover, when a stuck spring is tested the opposite is verified because the sensor captures the oscillations that a spring of this type causes - several peaks may result.

We performed several tests with segments in which it was previously knew the condition of them for validation. Afterwards, the device has been put to the test, and were carried out tests to about 50 segments, in which their condition was unknown. The application was able to successfully distinguish the sleeves that were ready to be used from sleeves that were in bad condition. Moreover, these results were later verified by the manual process and the results matched.

Furthermore, we implemented a functionality that allows to calibrate the sensor over time. The calibration procedure is accomplished by the same way as the method that is used to calculate the force, in other words is based on known masses. The relationship between the weight applied and the output voltage is recalculated given the new weights.

This calibration option is available, as seen, in the interface application and it is protected by password for security reasons.

The calibration, as previously referred, is performed using two weights, both of known masses, one which represents the minimum value and the other the maximum value. For that, simply it puts the weight on the sensor and depending on the value that the Arduino is receiving, a high or low value, it is regarded as a new value for the calculation of the force.

IV. CONCLUSION AND FUTURE WORK

This paper presents the development of a mechanical sleeve diagnosis system through a force sensor. The defined objectives for this project were achieved. Concerning the hardware, two weights, both of known masses all the test conditions to the sleeve. Regarding the software, we created a user interface for interaction with the operator in order to control and analyse the measures as well as represent them graphically, a DB was created for organization and storage of data. Additionally, it was implemented a sensor recalibration option as well as a function to define limits for analysis of the measures.

Based on the presented results and on the feedback from the operators, this new device shall allow the optimization of the performance and efficiency of the manufacturing unit. The developed product will have a great utility for the company in the way that it presents clear advantages compared with their previous manual method, among others, it saves time, enables better decision-making ability on the realized test, increasing the overall efficacy.

Furthermore, there are some ideas for future development, namely, to improve the user interface and to make the decision process of the sleeve state autonomous.

V. References

[1] Verhagen, W.; Vrught, B.; Schut, J.; Curran, R. (2015). A method for identification of automation potential through modelling of engineering processes and quantification of information waste. Advanced Engineering Informatics 29, P.307-321.

[2] Limoncelli, T. (2016). The "Leftover Principle" requires increasingly more highly skilled humans. Communications of the ACM, Vol.59, No 9.

[3] Luz, G.; Kuiawinski, D. (2006). Mecanização, Autonomação e Automação – Uma Revisão Conceitual e Crítica. XIII SIMPEP Bauru, SP, Brasil.

[4] Zuboft, S. (1994). Automatizar/ Informatizar: As Duas faces da Tecnologia Inteligente. Revista de Administração de Empresas. São Paulo, V.34, n.6, p.80-91.

[5] http://www.farnell.com/datasheets/1728715.pdf, <consulted in 14-02-2015>

[6] http://sigma.octopart.com/21314551/instruction_sheet/Honeywell-FSG015WNPB.pdf, <consulted in 16-02-2015>

[7] http://sensing.honeywell.com/honeywell-force-sensors-fsg-series-72dpi.jpg, <consulted in 16-02-2015>

[8] S. Franko, Design with Operational Amplifiers and Analog Integrated Circuits, McGraw–Hill.

[9] Ron Mancini (2002). OP Amps for everyone, Texas Instruments.

[10] http://www.ti.com/lit/ds/symlink/ina122.pdf, <consulted in 14-02-2015>

[11] http://www.instructables.com/id/Arduino-Modules-L298N-Dual-H-Bridge-Motor-Controll/?ALLSTEPS, <consulted in 05-03-2015>

[12] http://www.ti.com/lit/ds/symlink/ina122.pdf, <consulted in 15-02-2015>

[13] Louis Nashelsky, Robert L Boylestad, (2013), Dispositivos Eletrônicos e Teoria De Circuitos, Prentice Hall. (in portuguese).

[14] C# 3.5, Paulo Marques, Hernâni Pedroso e Ricardo Figueira, FCA editora, 2009. (in portuguese).

[15] Visual C# 2008 How to program (Third edition), P.J. Deitel & H.M. Deitel, Prentice Hall, 2009.

[16] http://www.embarcados.com.br/comunicacao-serial-c-arduino-parte-1/, <consulted in 12-03-2015>.

[17] http://www.macoratti.net/08/06/c_shp4.htm, <consulted in 02-03-2015>.

[18] https://ivanmeirelles.wordpress.com/2012/11/07/exportar-uma-datagridview-para-html-em-c/, <consulted in 16-05-2015>.

Measurement of Water in Oil for Active Bearing Performance Monitoring Using Optical Fiber Sensor System

Florin Tatar
Mechatronics/ERC
SKF
Nieuwegein, Netherlands
e-mail: florin.tatar@skf.com

Elfed Lewis / Gerard Dooly
Department of Electronic and Computer Engineering
University of Limerick
Limerick, Ireland
e-mail: elfed.lewis@ul.ie
e-mail: gerard.dooly@ul.ie

Abstract— **The utilization of an optical fiber sensor for the measurements of water in oil has been demonstrated. Absorption of light by water in oil in the near infra-red region (850 to 1650 nm) is measured with low noise level. Further, measurements of water contamination in oil with a minimum level of detection of around 0.002% were performed.**

Keywords-bearing; lubrication monitoring; oil; water; optical fiber.

I. INTRODUCTION

Measuring the quality of oil in real time, and suggesting corrective actions when needed constitutes real commercial market demand. In the past, several researches activities have been run regarding oil quality monitoring in bearings, to measure for example remaining lubricant life, the lubrication film thickness or investigating the capabilities of chemical or viscosity sensors [1-4]. Among all these parameters, one of the priorities of the lubrication experts is to measure the quantity of water in the oil and especially the percentage of water saturation of the oil. Indeed, water incursion into the oil can have a major impact on the lifespan of the bearings. In general, depending of the type of the lubricant, the water level accepted can be in a range of 200 ppm to 5000 ppm.

This article is focused on the development of a sensor system based on one immersible open path optical fiber sensor for measuring the concentration of water in oil. In Section 2, the sensor concept is introduced and the measurements results are presented. In Section 3, conclusions are summarized.

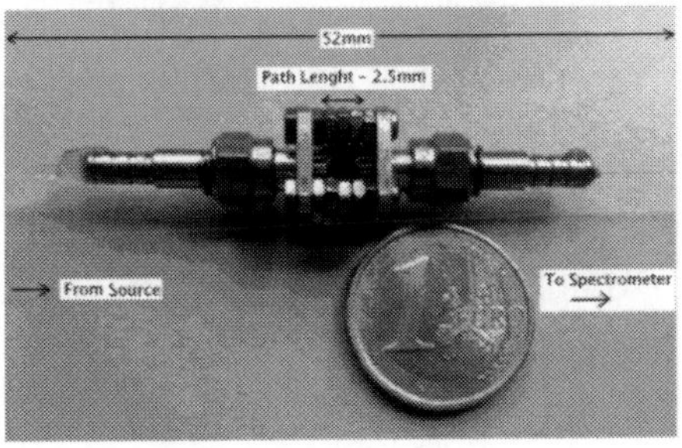

Figure1. Optical sensor

II. CONFIGURATION OF THE SENSOR

An open path configuration was chosen as the sensing element for delivering a high level of sensitivity. Optical fiber cable, capable of operating effectively within the range 850 nm – 1650 nm, was sourced and tested to ensure a significant level of transmission in this wavelength range. An standard fiber connector (SMA) based miniature coupling cell, fabricated out of brass and stainless steel, was configured to be used as the sensing element. A photograph of the sensing element is shown in Figure 1.

During the testing stages, the sensing element (Figure 1) was simply immersed in the oil sampling medium. Light from the Tungsten light source propagates through a 400 mm length of optical fiber before traversing across an open path space where it interacts with the sensing medium. The light is then coupled back into a second length (400 mm also) of optical fiber before being recorded by a spectrometer located at the receiving end.

The use of dedicated optical fiber and a small open path length resulted in a significant amount of light intensity being detected by the spectrometer. The choice of the length of open gap in turn resulted in a optimum accuracy of the absorption measurement through the S/N ratio.

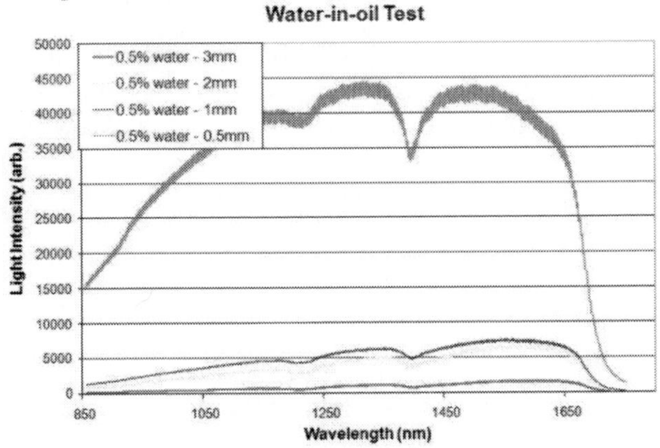

Figure 2. Light transmissions through 0.5% water in oil mixture depending of open path length 0.5, 1, 2, 3 mm

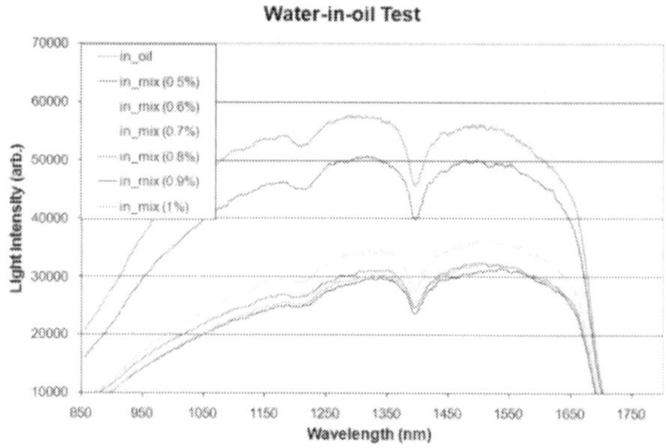

Figure 3. Light transmissions through different water in oil mixture samples

A. Path Length

Preliminary tests were taken to record the effects of the sensing system with regards to path length changes within the sensing element. For this a number of sensing elements were constructed (lengths 3 mm, 2 mm, 1 mm and 0.5 mm).

Significant sensitivity for water incursion was detected for each of the sensing element including the smallest one of 0.5 mm (see Figure 2). Therefore, taking the signal-to-noise ratio into consideration, the 0.5 mm sensing element was chosen for use within the sensor for the subsequent tests.

B. Measurements

1) Sensitivity Tests

Sensitivity testing comprised seven samples of testing liquids used during the testing stages; these were 0% and 0.5% through to 1% water content in oil (Cirkan C100). The samples were mixed using an ultrasonic bath. The resulting intensity spectra can be seen in Figure 3.

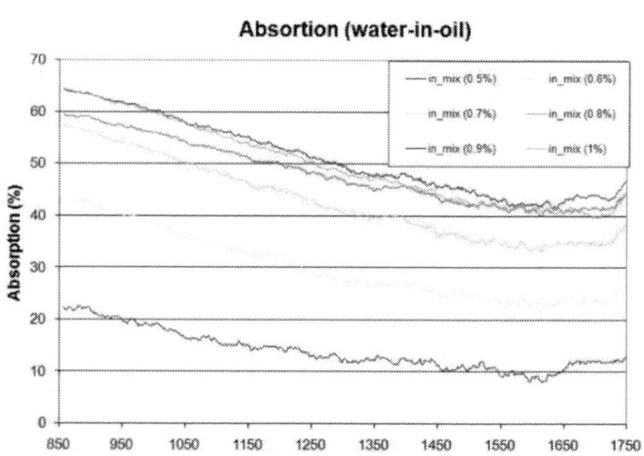

Figure 4. Light absorption for different water in oil mixture samples

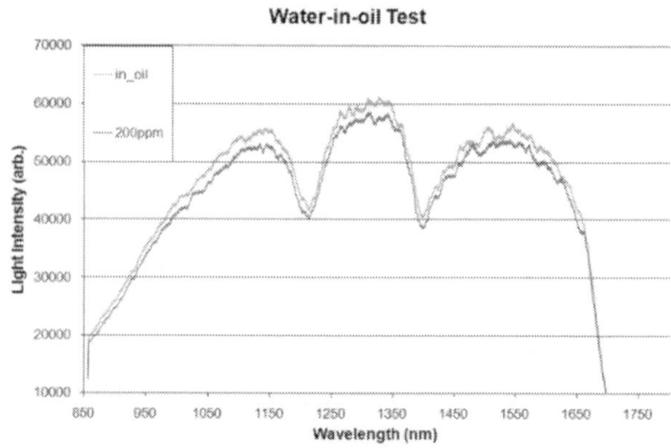

Figure 5. Light transmission spectrums showing a difference of 200ppm water in oil concentrations of two oil samples

The differences in the absorption percentages of the light recorded for mixed water in oil samples (0.5% to 1%) referenced to the light intensity recorded during the pure oil test was calculated and can be seen in Figure 4.

2) Lower-Detection-Limit

Recently, the lower detection limit of the sensor has become a major factor, with targets of 50 ppm water-in-oil. To achieve this accuracy in the mixing stage necessary mixing equipment such as a micropipette (capable of 2.5 um deliveries) were used.

Due to constrains in access to the experimental testing rig only one sampling experiment has been completed thus far (at least two of every experiment has been completed up to this stage – this was deemed necessary in order to correlate results in an accurate manner). In order to enhance sensitivity an increased path length of 2 mm was chosen.

Figure 6. The Hydac, Pal and optical SKF sensors measuring in parallel in a well controlled humidity chamber

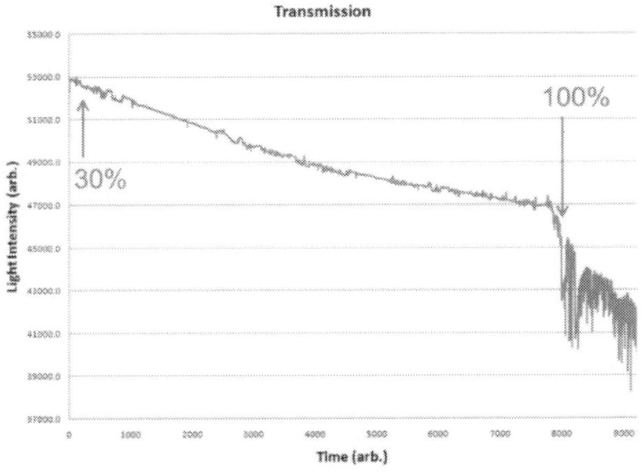

Figure 7. Light transmission variation (wavelenght of 1108 nm) for change of mineral oil saturation between 30-100%

The concentration chosen for this experiment test was 200 ppm and as can be seen from the result in Figure 5, a significant amount of absorption was recorded.

3) In-Situ Experiments

The sensing element was placed into a bath of mineral oil which in turn was placed into an environmental chamber where the humidity and temperature are very well controlled. The concentrations of the water within the sample were thus varied by accurately changing the temperature and humidity within the chamber.

The measurements were performed in parallel with one Hydac aqua sensor (type AS1008-C-000) and one Pall (type WS05S) water in oil commercially sensors for calibration purpose (see Figure 6).

The full spectrum was recorded over a number of hours during which the concentration of the water was gradually increased. The concentrations were increased steadily over a number of hours until saturation level in oil was reached (more precisely about 100% saturated).

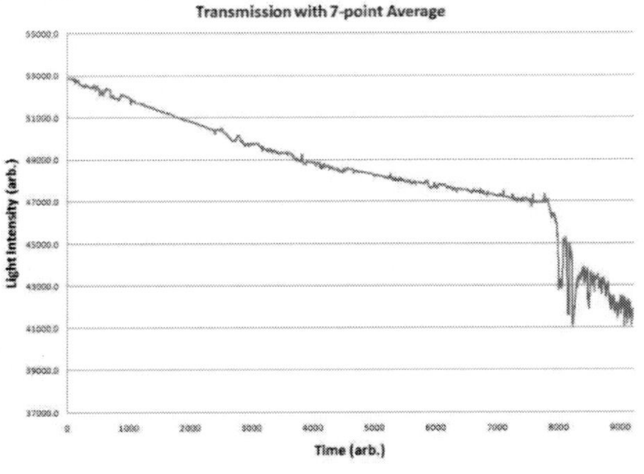

Figure 8. Averaged measurements for light transmission variation (wavelenght of 1108 nm) for change of mineral oil saturation between 30 - 100%

The measured optical transmission for the full experimental test recorded at a wavelength of 1108 nm is shown in Figure 7.

The results show a strong and stable response to the ever increasing levels of water content. However, when the sample reaches a level above saturation, the sensor records a significant increase in measured noise levels. The sampling frequency of the measurement was 2 Hz, and the measured noise level can be significantly reduced using digital filtering such as a moving point average (see Figure 8).

Although, this shows a reduction in the level of noise, it is expected that additional averaging and filtering will further reduce this. In fact for the response shown above and taking a signal-to-noise level of 1 into account, the lower detection limit of the sensor can be estimated to be below 20 ppm. The final graph (Figure 8) simply has shown the percentage absorption taken from the in-situ experimental results. These percentages also correlate to experimental results previously taken in the lab (specifically during the sensitivity testing stage).

An interesting conclusion is that after reaching 100% oil saturation, the measurements of the optical sensor become apparently instable due to the free water oil content. An important advantage of this is the possibility to autocalibrate the sensor for different types of oils. The 100% saturation limit can be detected very precisely.

One more observation was done for free water region. Based on averaging the measured signal the water content can be estimated. All these observations make the sensor unique.

These experimental results have shown that the sensor portrays a significant level of resolution of 20 ppm, a wide range of detection (20 ppm – 10000 ppm. In a future development, microspectroanalyzers or cheap LED's should be integrated in the readout measurement system for scaling down the price of the sensor unit.

III. Conclusions

The results of the experimental investigation of water content in oil using a novel optical fiber sensor system have resulted in the following successful outcomes:

- The saturation of water in oil (Circan 100cc) was measured
- Measurements were done in a range of 30-100% Relative Humidity (RH)
- The accuracy of measuring the water concentration is around 20 ppm (0.002%)
- The sensor shows good capabilities to measure also emulsified water and free water
- The sensor can be easily auto calibrated for 100% oil saturation

References

[1] R. E. Kauffman, "Rapid Determination of Remaining Useful Lubricant Life." Handbook of Lubrication and

Tribology, Volume III. E. Richard Booser, Editor. CRC Press, Boca Raton, Fla. 1994.

[2] A. Cameron, R. Gohar, "Theoretical and experimental studies of the oil film in lubricated point contact." Proc. R. Soc. A Math. Phys. Eng. Sci. 291, 520–536, 1991.

[3] H. Cen, P. M. Lugt, G. M. Espejel, "On the Film Thickness of Grease-Lubricated" Contacts at Low Speeds, Tribology Transactions, 57:4, 2004, 668-678, DOI: 10.1080/10402004.2014.897781.

[4] B. J. Hamrock, "Fundamentals of Fluid Film Lubrication," NASA RP-1255, 1991.

SAW Based Phononic Crystal Liquid Sensor with Integrated Periodic Microfluidic Channels

Aleksandr Oseev, Ralf Lucklum, Mikhail Zubtsov, Marc-Peter Schmidt
Institute of Micro and Sensor Systems (IMOS)
Otto-von-Guericke University Magdeburg
Magdeburg, Germany
aleksandar.oseev@ovgu.de
ralf.lucklum@ovgu.de
mikhail.zubtsov@ovgu.de
marc-peter.schmidt@ovgu.de

Soeren Hirsch
Department of Engineering
University of Applied Sciences Brandenburg
Brandenburg, Germany
soeren.hirsch@fh-brandenburg.de

***Abstract*— Phononic crystal sensors that have been developed in the last years proof being a promising sensor platform for different applications as liquid sensors. It has been already shown that the transmission spectrum of phononic structures depends on properties of liquids confined within a crystal. In comparison to known established sensor approaches, where sensors respond to near surface effects such as mass load, the distinguishing feature of proposed solutions is confining the liquid in resonant cavities of the phononic structure allowing determination of volumetric (bulk) properties of the liquid. Current contribution presents technological and experimental results of the surface acoustic wave (SAW) based phononic crystal liquid sensor research. The presented sensor concept integrates an array of periodical microfluidic channels into the SAW platform. Theoretical predictions underline strong demands regarding tolerances of phononic structure dimensions. As a result, the technological process of the sensor manufacturing had to be redesigned in a certain manner. Achieved results, technological challenges and solutions are described in current work.**

Keywords- phononic crystal sensor; liquid sensor; SAW sensor.

I. INTRODUCTION

Developed in recent years phononic crystal liquid sensors [1–4] vividly demonstrate advantages of this sensor approach. It is necessary to move the sensor to higher probing frequencies in order to achieve a higher sensitivity. The realization of the sensor in the frequency range of 100 MHz till several gigahertz requires application of different platforms for excitation and detection of acoustic waves. This frequency range is well developed with respect to surface acoustic waves (SAW) devices. The experimental verification of phononic crystal structures (PnC) in piezoelectric materials introduces well-known fabrication challenges. We are specifically interested in the development of SAW PnC liquid sensors. In comparison to well-established SAW sensor approaches, where the sensor effect is gained from surface effects (such as a surface mass load caused by absorption of analyte molecules in a recognition layer), the most promising feature of this high frequency sensor class is its capability to measure a sound velocity and a bulk viscosity of liquids with a precision superior to established instruments. It applies an acoustic signal amplification of a resonant liquid-filled cavity. The objectives of current research are the design of a SAW based phononic crystal sensor with at least one element being a liquid, and its fabrication with a high accuracy.

Originally, two different schemes were applied for building of the sensor, structures, i.e., holes and channels that are etched into the piezoelectric material and similar structures etched into an overlayer or a set of overlayers deposited onto the piezoelectric crystal.

Within the first approach, the etching of deep structures with steep sidewalls is required. This concept was initially developed towards SAW based phononic crystal sensor realization and was previously described in details [5]. Figure 1 shows an example of a manufactured regular phononic crystal in quartz.

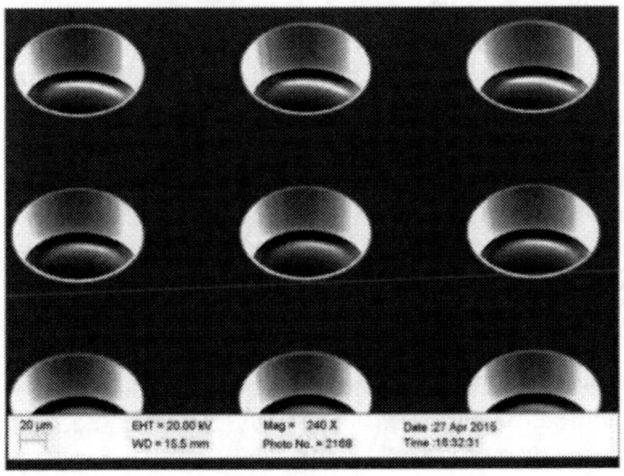

Figure 1. Etched periodical array of holes in ST-cut quartz.

Top edges and sidewalls allow for an idealization as a hole. The known limitation lies in complexity of structuring strong piezoelectric materials such as of lithium niobate ($LiNbO_3$) or lithium tantalate ($LiTaO_3$) substrate in a quality that is required to achieve an efficient structure. [5]

However, this approach requires a piezoelectric material that contrasts some sensor requirements. We report on the development of alternative sensor approaches. As a result, the sensor concept applies polymer based microelectromechanical systems (MEMS) technology with a specific attention to an exceptional tolerances control was developed. It utilizes the structure that has been fabricated in overlayers instead of etched into the substrate. This approach allows selecting a structure material independent on the substrate. The schematic representation of the sensor utilizing this concept is demonstrated in Figure 2.

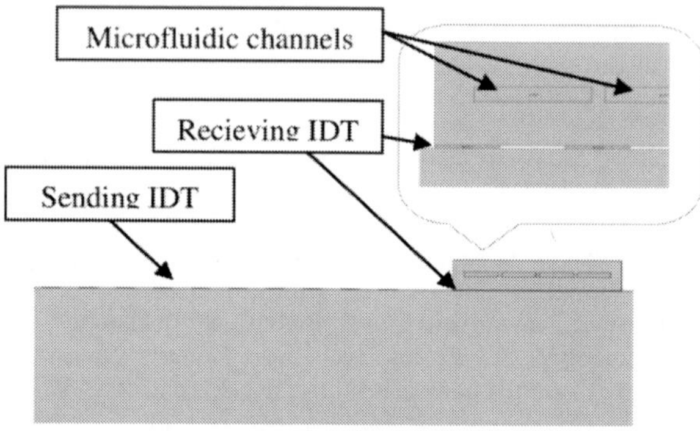

Figure 2. Schematic representation of sensor concept based on overlayer structures

The manufacture of designed structure can be completed within different approaches. The manufacturing processes can be split into a solid state based and a polymer based one. A technology based on a solid state approach introduces several advantages, such as a high long term mechanical stability, application of well-established processes etc. However, for the proposed sensor design this approach appeared to be complicated for a fabrication. On the other hand, the polymer based technological approach opens an opportunity for a rapid prototyping at a relatively low cost and allows to simplify the technological process in general. Among all possible technological processes that can be based on Polyimid, polydimethylsiloxane (PDMS), Poly(methyl methacrylate) (PMMA) or epoxy-based negative photoresist SU-8, the chosen approach must satisfy initial design demands. At the same time, the respective technology should be adjusted in a way to obtain an expected sensor structure performance.

The SU-8 negative photoresist is currently widely applied as a construction material for microfluidic devices, sensors and other applications. Due to number of advantages, such as chemical stability to most of fluids, controllable mechanical properties through the crosslinking process management, this photoresist can be applied for building of microfluidic structures for a variety of different applications [6].

Therefore, we have realized SU-8 based microfluidic structures integrated into a SAW device. A set of microfluidic channels acts as a liquid analyte container. They are periodically arranged as PnC. Several initial designs and influence of a phononic structure geometry on the sensor performance were previously discussed [7]. Despite the possibility of a further structure improvement, in current contribution we concentrate on the manufacture of designed structures.

In order to achieve a mechanical performance required for designed structures, technological parameters of SU-8 processing have to be reconsidered. Previously, an influence of technological parameters of SU-8 processing on mechanical properties of SU-8 layers have been studied [8–11]. It also was demonstrated that considering a certain application, SU-8 layer can be differently manufactured in order to fulfill defined requirements. Due to staged SU-8 processing, different improvements can be made by changing some of the conditions of certain technological steps. As it was shown in [10], the number of such technological parameters that directly influence on final SU-8 layer performance can exceed thirty. Thereby, it becomes evident that with the consideration of certain application of SU-8 structures, processing parameters have to be adjusted in order to obtain required performance.

The study of influencing of tensile properties of coated SU-8 layers has demonstrated that an increase of SU-8 curing temperature significantly changes mechanical properties of SU-8 layers [8]. It was shown that high temperature curing of SU-8 during a post exposure bake (PEB, 95 °C) and hard bake (HB, 200 °C) make layers much more fragile. Previously published results [9] have shown that changes in SU-8 processing can considerably influence following SU-8 crosslinking. It was demonstrated how a soft bake conditions, an exposure dose and a post exposure bake parameters influence on a resolution and crack formations of SU-8 layers because of inner SU-8 film stress accumulated during processing. In [10] was shown that at low soft bake temperature an exposed SU-8 polymerizes at faster rate with reduced stress. Completely crack free structures with aspect ratios of 10 and 8 for trench and ridge structures have been achieved with the soft bake temperature of 65 °C.

In order to complete closed microfluidic channels, the SU-8 adhesive bonding process should be performed. On the one hand, it is required to achieve well-defined structures. On the other hand, the fabrication process should be kept within several standard technological steps without necessity to implement complicated approaches. For this reason, the SU-8 bonding recipe has to be adjusted. In order to achieve a sufficient performance of bonding process, the polymer crosslinking reactions of bonding wafers should be taken under control. It was already shown that in order to achieve a sufficient bonding strength, it is necessary to apply the wafer with incompletely cross-linked SU-8 in order to perform a final mutual crosslinking step during the bonding process. At the same time, SU-8 should be sufficiently crosslinked to complete developing process.

In current contribution, the initial results of manufactured sensors assessment are presented. In section II, the technological description of sensor manufacturing process is provided in details. In section III, the information regarding the sensor experimental setup is described. Achieved experimental results and a future work are underlined in subsequent sections "Discussion" and "Conclusions".

II. TECHNOLOGY

For the fabrication of the sensor structure, following materials were utilized. Titanium and aluminum targets were used in physical vapor deposition (PVD) sputtering process and supplied by a local manufacturer. Structuring of metal layers was completed applying TI35ES positive photoresist in conjunction with TI Prime adhesive promoter that were supplied by MicroChemicals GmbH. AZ and AZ400K photoresist developers as well as acetone, isopropanol, aluminum etcher, 1-propanol and other supplies were ordered from Carl Roth GmbH and Sigma-Aldrich Chemie GmbH. Applied for structuring of microfluidic channels SU-8-50 photoresist and mr600Dev developer were supplied by Micro Resist Technology GmbH.

The deposition of metal layers was completed with LS 500 ES physical vapor deposition equipment. For photoresist spin coating, SUSS Labspin manufacturing line was utilized with SUSS_MA6_BA6 mask aligner. Processes of SU-8 adhesive bonding were conducted in SUSS SB6E substrate bonder. Manufactured SAW based phononic crystal sensors were analyzed with Zeiss EVO 50 scanning electron microscope and FTR MicroProf 300 profilometer.

The technological process of a SAW based phononic crystal liquid sensor manufacturing begins with fabrication and analysis of SAW structures. According to the sensor design, the lithium niobate ($LiNbO_3$) 128° Y-X cut wafers with X direction of the wave propagation were chosen as a substrate material. In order to excite and detect surface acoustic waves, the interdigitated transducers (IDTs) have been manufactured on the surface of the substrate.

The manufacture of phononic structure was completed atop of fabricated IDTs. The phononic structure represents a system of periodically placed microfluidic channels closed from the top and the bottom with another polymer structure. In current work, the microfluidic structure and covering (interfacial) layers were fabricated utilizing SU-8 polymer. The structure manufacturing process involves subsequent layer after layer processing. In order to complete the structure, the wafer should be processed with two structured SU-8 layers. Initially interfacial SU-8 layer has to be defined atop of the IDTs area and then the microfluidic channels should be structured atop.

An application of polymer based bonding technology was utilized for manufacturing of a covering layer. The covering layer was fabricated on a silicon wafer basis and then transferred to the structure. The omnicoat releasing layer was utilized to remove the handling wafer. SU-8 50 covering layer was then spin coated and soft baked at the temperature 65°C during 3 minutes. Thereafter, the temperature was ramped up to 85°C at which the wafer was baked another 10 minutes. At the completion of the soft bake, the wafer was cooled down back to the room temperature during 40 minutes. Then, fabricated SU-8 layer was exposed with an exposure dose of 160 mJ/cm^2 in SUSS_MA6_BA6 mask aligner. The post exposure bake of the covering layer was made at the temperature of 65°C during 2 minutes with following ramping up to 85°C where it was baked another 10 minutes and then cooled down to the room temperature during 40 minutes. After a completion of the covering layer, another thin layer of SU-8 5 that serve as an adhesive during bonding process was spin coated. As soon as the layer is pilled off, it was removed and rinsed in deionized water (DI-water). Afterwards, dried covering layer was applied for bonding process.

The bonding process starts with evacuating of the camera. During the preheating step at the temperature of 45°C during 3 minutes, the rest of the surface contaminations and SU-8 solvents supposed to be removed. After that, the structure was top loaded with a pressure of 1000 mBar and heated up to 50°C. At this temperature, the structure was bonded during 10 minutes and then slowly cooled down back to the room temperature. Thereafter, bonded with covering layer wafer was exposed with an exposure dose of 160 mJ/cm^2. Afterwards, it was post exposure baked at the temperature of 65°C during 2 minutes and 85°C for 10 minutes with following cooling down back to the room temperature during 40 minutes.

Completed example of SU-8 microfluidic channel is demonstrated in Figure 3.

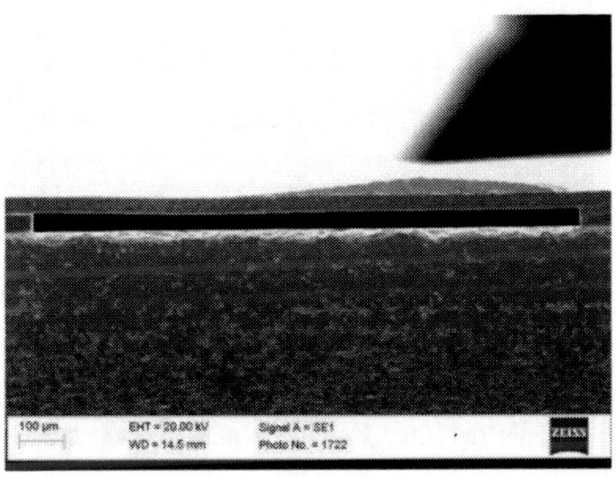

Figure 3. Cross section of the manufactured microfluidic channel.

III. EXPERIMENTAL

Experimental investigations of the manufactured sensor were completed with the help of probe station SUSS EP6 with high frequency probes, Figure 4. A complete 4" LiNbO3 128° Y-X cut wafer with IDTs and integrated microfluidic structures was placed on a probing table. High frequency probes (2 signal probes and 2 ground probes) were connected with a help of 50 Ohm up to 500 MHz coaxial cables with network analyzer in S-parameters measuring mode. The structure was connected as a standard 2-port SAW device. Analyzed liquid was manually placed in microfluidic structure with a micropipette. Transmission (S_{21} parameter) amplitude and phase response were measured with Agilent4395A together with an S-parameter test set Agilent 87511A (100 kHz–500 MHz). Several subsequent measurements were performed to reduce a measurement error. The repeatable sensor response was recorded for each measuring liquid mixture.

Figure 4. Experimental setup.

Measurements were conducted directly on the wafer (4" LiNbO3 128° Y-X cut wafer) with fabricated microfluidic phononic structures and IDTs.
Measurements were completed with binary mixtures of a deionized water and a 1-propanol in molar concentrations (X) range 0.23 – 0.507 that corresponds to the range of the most linear speed of sound dependence. The respective speed of sound and density data for water – 1-propanol mixtures are shown in Table 1.

TABLE I. PROPERTIES OF WATER AND 1-PROPANOL MIXTURES [12].

1-Propanol molar concentration, X	Density, kg/m^3	Speed of sound, m/s
Water	998	1483
0.158	933	1472
0.230	908	1421
0.347	881	1367
0.507	852	1322
1-propanol	804	1220

IV. RESULTS

As it can be seen, the amplitude and phase measurement results provide a distinct sensor response on different liquids that filled into the microfluidic channels Figure 5-6.

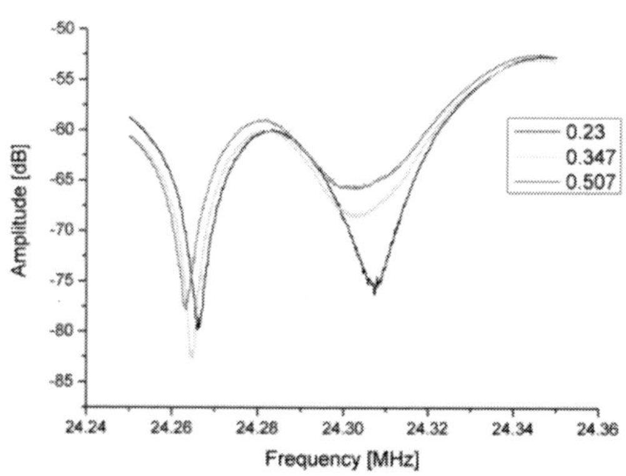

Figure 5. S_{21} parameter (transmission) amplitude response for binary mixtures of water and 1-propanol with molar concentration of 1-propanol X = 0.23; X = 0.347; X = 0.507

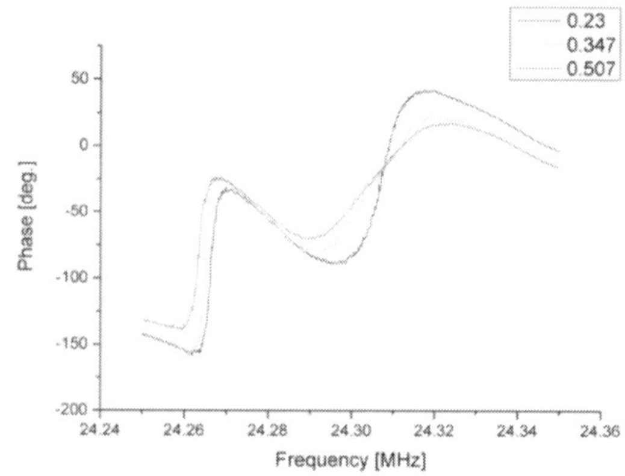

Figure 6. S21 parameter (transmission) phase response response for binary mixtures of water and 1-propanol with molar concentration of 1-propanol X = 0.23; X = 0.347; X = 0.507

The amplitude minima as well as the corresponding phase shift demonstrate a tendency to move in a direction of lower frequencies when the microfluidic channel is filled with a liquid with lower speed of sound. The dependence of phononic crystal sensor response on speed of sound of the liquid constituting the PnC or filling the defect (such as cavity) were previously demonstrated [2, 4, 13, 14]. It has been shown that frequency of corresponding transmission peak (or dip) depends mostly on changes in speed of sound of the liquid analyte rather than on changes in density or viscosity. However, in the reported case, it should be noted that transmission curves have two clear transmission minima that behave differently, Figure 5. The (local) transmission minimum frequencies depend on the molar ratio of 1-propanol in water in a similar manner; however, the band width of the second one is much broader than the first one. Both, band width and amplitude change considerably with molar ratio. As characteristic for a dissipation mechanism, bandwidth decreases with an increasing depth of the dip in the spectrum. We assume that the second minimum corresponds to a complex vibration of the polymer structure with different contributions from the microfluidic liquid resonator and overlayers and radiation or mode conversion losses.

The phase shift results match to the transmission amplitude response, Figure 6. It can be seen that the first phase shift corresponding to the first minimum is much sharper than the second one. Although we note a slight difference in slope we find a shift to a lower frequency when microfluidic channels are filled with liquids with decreasing speed of sound for the first transmission minima consistent with the amplitude findings. The phase corresponding to the broad band minima crosses at a frequency of about 24.31 MHz. However, this finding is also just a consequence of a change in wave attenuation.

The physical understanding is subject of ongoing research, specifically the analysis of the involvement of complex vibration mechanisms and their interaction with waves.

V. Conclusions

The alternative approach for phononic crystal based sensors has been demonstrated. The SAW sensor platform serves as a reliable sensor platform for frequencies of several tens megahertz with good perspectives in a range to several hundreds of megahertz and perhaps up to a few gigahertz, very much depending on accuracy issues in fabrication of the downscaled feature sizes. In comparison to traditional SAW sensors, the phononic crystal SAW sensor can be applied to liquids and is sensitive to volumetric material properties such as speed of sound of an analyte. Our alternative overlay technology approach can be considered as a replacement of the technologically challenging approach that is based on realization of PnC structures directly in piezoelectric substrates. The experimental results demonstrate the feasibility of described approach. It provides a distinct and predictable sensor response on speed of sound of binary mixture of water and 1-propanol.

Acknowledgment

The support by the German Research Foundation under grants LU 605/16-1 and HI 1261/5-1 are gratefully acknowledged.

References

[1] R. Lucklum and J. Li, "Phononic crystals for liquid sensor applications," Measurement Science and Technology, vol. 20, no. 12, p. 124014, 2009, doi: 10.1088/0957-0233/20/12/124014

[2] R. Lucklum, M. Ke, and M. Zubtsov, "Two-dimensional phononic crystal sensor based on a cavity mode," Sensors and Actuators B: Chemical, vol. 171, pp. 271–277, 2012, doi: 10.1016/j.snb.2012.03.063

[3] M. Zubtsov et al, "2D phononic crystal sensor with normal incidence of sound," Sensors and Actuators A: Physical, vol. 186, pp. 118–124, 2012, doi: 10.1016/j.sna.2012.03.017

[4] A. Oseev, M. Zubtsov, and R. Lucklum, "Gasoline properties determination with phononic crystal cavity sensor," Sensors and Actuators B: Chemical, vol. 189, pp. 208–212, 2013, doi: 10.1016/j.snb.2013.03.072

[5] M.-P. Schmidt, A. Oseev, R. Lucklum, M. Zubtsov, and S. Hirsch, "SAW based phononic crystal sensor, technological challenges and solutions," Microsystem Technologies, pp. 1–7, 2016, doi: 10.1007/s00542-015-2781-3

[6] A. Ezkerra, L. J. Fernandez, K. Mayora, and J. M. Ruano-Lopez, "Fabrication of SU-8 free-standing structures embedded in microchannels for microfluidic control," Journal of Micromechanics and Microengineering, vol. 17, no. 11, p. 2264, 2007, doi: 10.1088/0960-1317/17/11/013

[7] A. Oseev, M. P. Schmidt, R. Lucklum, M. Zubtsov, and S. Hirsch, "Phononic crystal based liquid sensor governed by localized defect resonances," Ultrasonics Symposium (IUS), 2015 IEEE International, 2015, doi: 10.1109/ULTSYM.2015.0053

[8] R. Feng and R. J. Farris, "Influence of processing conditions on the thermal and mechanical properties of SU8 negative photoresist coatings," Journal of Micromechanics and Microengineering, vol. 13, no. 1, p. 80, 2002 doi: 10.1088/0960-1317/13/1/312

[9] S. Keller, G. Blagoi, M. Lillemose, D. Haefliger, and A. Boisen, "Processing of thin SU-8 films," Journal of Micromechanics and Microengineering, vol. 18, no. 12, p. 125020, 2008 doi: 10.1088/0960-1317/18/12/125020

[10] T. A. Anhoj, A. M. Jorgensen, D. A. Zauner, and J. Hübner, "The effect of soft bake temperature on the polymerization of SU-8 photoresist," Journal of Micromechanics and Microengineering, vol. 16, no. 9, p. 1819, 2006 doi: 10.1088/0960-1317/16/9/009

[11] B. Bohl, R. Steger, R. Zengerle, and P. Koltay, "Multi-layer SU-8 lift-off technology for microfluidic devices," Journal of Micromechanics and Microengineering, vol. 15, no. 6, p. 1125, 2005 doi: 10.1088/0960-1317/15/6/002

[12] W. Schaaffs, K.-H. Hellwege, and A. M. Hellwege, Molecular acoustics: Springer-Verlag, 1967.

[13] A. Oseev, M. Zubtsov, and R. Lucklum, "Octane number determination of gasoline with a phononic crystal sensor," Procedia Engineering, vol. 47, pp. 1382–1385, 2012, doi: 10.1016/j.proeng.2012.09.414

[14] A. Oseev, R. Lucklum, M. Ke, M. Zubtsov, R. Grundmann, Eds, "Phononic crystal sensor for liquid property determination," International Society for Optics and Photonics, 2012, doi: 10.1117/12.914783

High Speed Magneto–Optical Sensor for Magnetic Stripe Readout

Johannes Egger
Johannes Kepler University, Linz, Austria
Email: johannes.egger@jku.at

Bernhard Zagar
Johannes Kepler University, Linz, Austria
Email: bernhard.zagar@jku.at

Abstract—**We report on a Faraday–sensor to read out optically test pattern recorded to magnetic stripes on smart cards in a non–contacting way at scanning speeds of several meters per second. The pattern densities of several bits per millimeter can be resolved properly. The sensor employs a magneto–optical crystal of iron doped Yttrium–Aluminum–Garnet known to exhibit one of the highest known Verdet–constants ($\approx$ 130 rad/Tm). It is epitaxially grown to a rather small thickness of approximately 50μm, a small thickness that on the one hand reduces the overall sensitivity dramatically but on the other hand allows for a very fine pitched spatial resolution to image the normal component of the magnetic flux density. The to be tested specimen in the production line is moving at a rather high speed so the optical system and the readout electronics is geared toward rapid scan and to maintain a rather high sustained data streaming rate onto a solid state disk for archival purposes. Scan rates exceeding 50.000 scans per second (@ 128 pixels per scan) were attained and the camera still is sufficiently exposed to attain a fair signal to noise ratio.**

Keywords–Faraday effect; magnetic field sensor; magnetic field imaging; magnetic tape; quality control

I. INTRODUCTION

For compatibility reasons, most smart cards still have a magnetic stripe to store some basic information that typically is not cryptographically secured from inadvertent access. At the end of the production line of such cards it is necessary to also check with high speed scanners the successful magnetic recording of a test pattern, which ultimately is erased again. The characterization of these magnetic stripes that ultimately be attachted to the back of, e.g., credit cards or smart cards is necessary for the in–line quality control of the production line [1]. Typical feed rates are in the several meters per second range and the finest period of the recorded magnetic pattern is in the tens μm–range. The magnetic sensor to be employed needs to operate contact–free to avoid mechanical damages and must be able to also resolve any transversal (error–) pattern to check for cross–sectional evenness. This requirement prevents the usage of very well known and cheap magnetic tape readout heads, since those provide information about the magnetic flux (actually the time derivative of the magnetic flux) as an integral measure only.

The contribution is organized as follows. In section II the theory on the sensing effect is detailed. Section III details the chosen optical set–up and the problems encountered designing the illumination unit. This is followed in section IV by the description of the signal processing necessary to attain a sustained data and streaming rate in excess of 10 Mbytes/s. In the results section preliminary measurement results are presented followed by a short conclusion.

II. FARADAY–EFFECT

We developed a sensor system using the Faraday–effect [2], which is a magneto–optical effect rotating the plane of polarized light dependent on the magnetic flux density component parallel to the incident light. It's operating principle is depicted in Figure 1. Polarized collimated light that can be seen as the superposition of a right– and a left–circularly polarized light enters the medium exhibiting the Faraday–effect [3]. The magnetic field in matter can be seen as the effect of spinning or circularly moving charges. For the direction of the B–field indicated in Figure 1, the two superimposed rotating (circularly polarized) electric field vectors will affect differently co– or counterrotating charges thus the net B–field is diminished or enhanced in one direction or the other. Thus effectively the direction of polarization is rotated slightly ones superimposed again. This effect is seen in any matter to a rather small degree. There are, however, a few materials, in particular Yttrium-Iron-Garnet (YIG), that exhibit rather strong effects (show a rather large so–called Verdet constant that can go up — for near infrared light — to 130 rad/Tm).

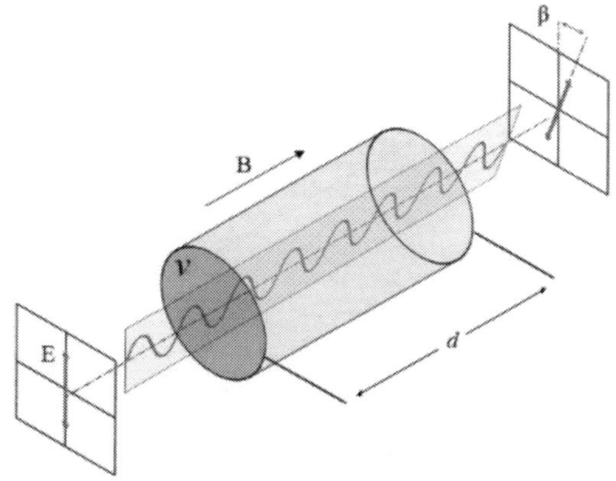

Figure 1. Faraday effect effectively rotating the plane of linearly polarized light (represented by its electric field vector E) dependent on the magnetic flux density B in direction of light propagation [4].

In a sensor type application the YIG–crystal typically has one face mirrored so the light traverses the crystal twice thus effectively doubling the sensitivity and also giving spatial access for placing the mirrored surface in close proximity to a magnetized object to be measured.

To mathematically describe this phenomenon the permeability μ needs to be treated as a non–diagonal tensor as can be seen from (1) [5].

$$B(\omega) = \begin{vmatrix} \mu_1 & -j\mu_2 & 0 \\ j\mu_2 & \mu_1 & 0 \\ 0 & 0 & \mu_2 \end{vmatrix} \cdot H(\omega) \qquad (1)$$

with:

B	T	vector of magnetic flux density
H	A/m	vector of magnetic field strength
μ_x	Vs/Am	components of permeability tensor
ω	rad/s	angular frequency of light

The net effect of (1) can by summed into a constant V, the Verdet–constant (which is a function of the frequency ω of the light used). It turns out that the largest sensitivity is seen for light in the infrared region of the spectrum. The angle of rotation β can then be written as:

$$\beta = \int_{x=0}^{d} V(x) \cdot B_n(x) \cdot dx \qquad (2)$$

with:

β	radians	angle of rotation
$B_n(x)$	T	magnetic flux density in the direction of light propagation as a function of position x
$V(x) = V$	rad/Tm	Verdet constant
d	m	interacting distance

With typical values of the Verdet–constant for the material YIG in the range of 100 rad/Tm.

The Farady–sensor yields a rotation angle of the polarization that, according to (2), is averaging the normal component of the magnetic flux density over the thickness of the crystal d. Thus the thickness of the YIG disk must be rather thin (here on the order of a few tens of μm) to measure very locally. Furthermore, one is interested to measure the magnetic flux density in a non–contacting way right at the surface of the magnetic tape. So the distance of the crystal with respect to the tape surface has to be kept constant and in close proximity to the tape. This will be accomplished in the final version of the sensor by an appropriate aerodynamic design.

The overall rotation of the polarization that can be attained while still maintaining a sufficient spatial resolution while realizing a non–contact measurement action is very limited as the example shows:

For typical magnetic stripes, two coercitivities are used (HiCo with approx. 275 to 400 mT and LoCo with 30 mT of remanence). Given these parameters and considering the mirror action close to the specimen effectively doubling the thickness of $d = 50\mu$m one can estimate the maximum rotation β for the lower remanence ($B = 0.03$ T) zu be

$$\beta_{\max} = 2 \cdot 100 \cdot 0.03 \cdot 50 \cdot 10^{-6} = 0.15 \text{ mrad} . \qquad (3)$$

This rotation is barely detectable with the used low cost (foil–) polarizers resulting in an intensity modulation following the typical $\cos^2$–rule for the recorded intensity at the camera (Malus'–law [6]). In the presented sensor system we didn't aim to and probably wouldn't be able to quantitatively measure the locally averaged magnetic flux density but were only interested in visualizing the presence of magnetizable domains of similar magnetization strenghts to check for error patterns that might be present.

III. Optical Set–up

The major problem encountered while developing this magnetic field sensor was the required scan rate of more than 50,000 scans per second, which is necessary in order to accomodate the spatial resolution along the stripe direction and realizing approximately 100 pixels perpendicular to the stripe direction using a line–scan camera with sufficient resolution. While there are line–scan cameras available to cope with those requirements the problem of properly exposing them isn't trivial since the Faraday–cell readout requires crossed polarizers thereby diminishing greatly any light intensity used for illumination. Even foil polarizers attain so–called extinction ratios greater than 1:1000, transmitting only light according to Malus'–law (4).

$$I(\beta) = I_0 \cdot \cos^2(\pi/2 - \beta) . \qquad (4)$$

In (4), I_0 is the incident intensity of light to the crossed pair of polarizers and β is the angle of rotation due to the magnetic field in the setup.

We chose a Hamamatsu camera (type S11106-10) that has a pixel size of $63.5\mu\text{m}\times 63.5\mu\text{m}$ and offers a spatial resolution of 128 pixels. It allows for a sustained data rate of 10 Msamples/s, which is equivalent to approximately 64,000 scan lines per second. In order to properly expose this camera (to a maximum of 80% of saturation value) at its spectral peak sensitivity (80 V/(lx s) @ 700 nm wavelength) very intensive light for illumination is necessary as can be seen from (5) considering the fact that the exposure time T has to be lower than $20\mu s$ for the intended scan rates above 50.000 lines per second.

$$I_{CCD} = \frac{U_v}{E \cdot T} \qquad (5)$$

with:

U_v	V	analog out of camera (0.8 V max.)
E	V/(lx s)	photosensitivity (here 80 V/(lx s))
T	s	exposure time (here < $20\mu s$)
I_{CCD}		illuminance at face plate

For the parameters given above and an exposure time $T = 20 \cdot 10^{-6}$s aiming for 80% of saturation voltage one requires — at the cameras face plate 400 lx. The objective lens is designed to yield an optical magnification of unity which, given optical principles [6] reduces the effective aperture by two stops. Given an objective lens with a numerical aperture of $f/2.8$ becoming an $f/5.6$ lens thus requires an intensity of $400 \cdot 5.6^2 \approx 12800$ lx from the object, which is rather much. Using a LED illumination able to supply (at maximum) 40 lumens and employing an appropriate condenser optics this requirements can be met, however.

Figure 2 shows the devised first prototype of the scanning–system built using standard optical components (Linos Photonics [7]). It consists of a high power LED illumination system

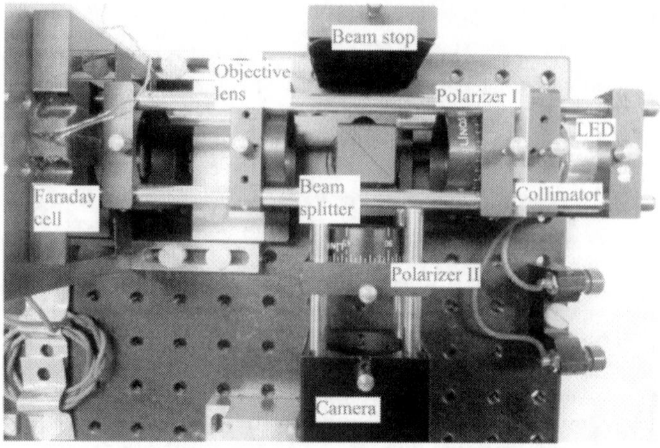

Figure 2. Optical set–up of the experimental Faraday–sensor.

Figure 3. Photo of the thin–sheet Faraday cell.

(manufacturer Cree, type XRCRED-L1) delivering a luminous flux of 40 lm at 620 nm wavelength, a high numerical aperture collimating optics (free diameter 21.4 mm, focal length 16 mm), which collimates the emitted light into a beam of approx 12 mm diameter, the polarizer I (Linos sheet polarizer with an extinction ratio of 1:3500 at 42% transmission for randomly polarized white light), followed by a non–polarizing beam–splitter that allows for a perpendicular viewing direction with the camera path in the second arm, and a beam stop for spurious reflections off the illuminating path. On the return path an objective lens (free aperture f/2.8) is used to project a focussed image (optical magnification 1:1) of the magnetic field via the second polarizer onto the camera's face plate. The camera is a Hamamatsu S11106-10 camera with 128 square pixels ($63.5 \times 63.5 \mu m^2$).

Figure 3 shows a view onto the mirrored face plate of the Faraday crystal. The YIG–crystal is approximately 50 μm thin and is traversed twice by light thus doubling its effective rotation. To protected it from abrasion it is coated by a highly reflective and scratch–resistant layer of chemical vapor deposited nano–crystalline diamond giving it this golden color observed.

IV. Signal processing

A position encoder is used to meter the feed rate of the stripe. This encoder via a phase locked loop circuit synchronizes the camera clock signals appropriately thus allowing a bit–synchronized optical scanning of the magnetic pattern by the camera. The analog video signal is digitized via a video AD–converter (Analog Devices type AD9057) and stored into a 4kB dual–ported RAM (type IDT72240). This RAM type allows for non–synchronized writing and reading processes to take place concurrently. By avoiding byte–by–byte memory access and reading at least 4089 (full–minus–7–byte flag asserted) the overhead of a single PC interrupt is split upon more than 4000 read bytes. This allows a sustained data rate of 10 Mbytes/s even with a medium performance Raspberry Pi unit.

Each scan–line is analyzed for mean, maximum and minimum values of the magnetization and an error is flagged (a single bit per unit length) if set thresholds are exceeded.

V. Results

Preliminary results are shown in Figure 4 where 150 scan lines with 128 pixels each are displayed. The figure shows the normal component (out of plane direction) of the magnetic flux density at an estimated distance of approximately 60μm from the magnetic tape surface. One can clearly observe that the system is able to image with the designed scan density, although the finer pitched structures on the right hand side seem to exhibit some problems that might be attributed to aliasing effects [8] stemming from a still too low spatial sampling rate for that particular testing pattern density. The depicted result was obtained with the still experimental unit depicted in Figure 2. The optical field imaged has a width of approximately 12 mm, the acquisition rate was reduced to only 1000 lines per second and the video signal was acquired using a digital storage oscilloscope.

Unfortunately it isn't possible to ascribe numerical values to the imaged magnetic flux density. It would be possible to do so if the rotation angle β were measured via a fast acting compensation scheme sweeping over all possible rotation angles of the local polarization, but this would require a totally different concept to be realized. For the quality control purpose it is sufficient to simply show the presence of magnetizable domains and not so much their actual magnetization, since that is only dependent on the material used and wouldn't change along the stripe.

VI. Conclusion

We reported on the first version of a high scanning speed magneto–optical system able to image and process up to (and beyond) 50.000 scan lines (at a resolution of 128 pixels) per second of magnetic test patterns recorded on a magnetic stripe film. This system is designed to be included for the in–line inspection and quality control at the production line up to feed rates of approximately 3 meters per second (considering necessary at least two scans per bit length at the highest magnetic pattern density).

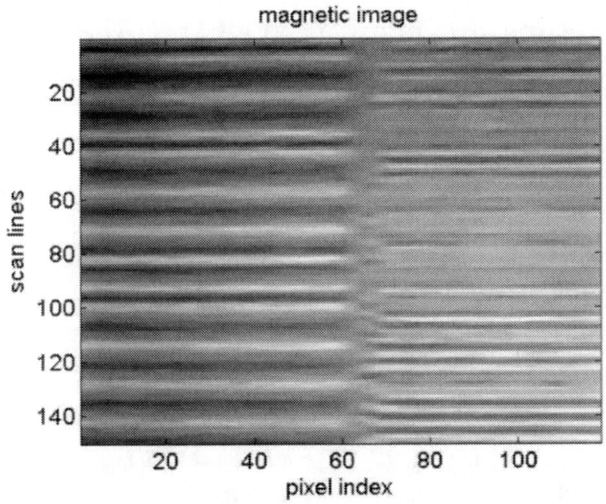

Figure 4. Image (120 pixels wide) of the magnetization of a credit card. Clearly discernible are two tracks the right one recorded with a typically density of 210 bits per inch (8.27 bits per mm), while the left track typically has a recording density of 75 bits per inch (2.95 bits per mm). Currently the magnetic flux density can only be visualized qualitatively. To ascribe numerical values of B to image intenisty values had proven to be rather difficult.

The attached Linux–based PC (a Raspberry Pi/2 model B) is streaming the scanned image data via a FIFO–memory unit at a sustained rate of 10 MB/s onto a solid state disk for archival purposes. It is further planned to have a fully operational system by the end of this year. Improvements to be made include a better synchronization of the camera clocks to the position encoder signals to avoid smearing effects, a more compact optical arrangement less prone to vibrations, a better digital signal processing scheme, allowing to scan for additional quality measures to still be discussed and overall a more thourough qualification test of the complete system. Furthermore, research has to be put into the question of assigning quantitative flux denisty values to intensity values recorded by the camera. Here a standardized calibration procedure is definitely needed, and will be worked upon.

ACKNOWLEDGMENT

This work has been carried out at LCM GmbH as part of a K2 project. K2 projects are financed using funding from the Austrian COMET K2 programme. The COMET K2 projects at LCM are supported by the Austrian federal government, the federal state of Upper Austria, the Johannes Kepler University and all of the scientific partners, which form part of the COMET K2 Consortium. Furthermore, the authors gratefully acknowledge the partial financial support of this work by the Austrian Research Promotion Agency under grant 838515.

REFERENCES

[1] J.J. Blackwell, K. O'Grady, N.K. Nelson, M.P. Sharrock, The characterisation of magnetic pigment dispersions using pulsed magnetic fields, J. Magnetism and Magnetic Materials, 266, 2003, pp. 119–130

[2] M. von Ardenne, G. Mussiol, S. Reball, Effekte der Physik, Harri Deutsch, 1997

[3] P. F. Kelly, Electricity and Magnetism, CRC–Press, Boca Raton, 2014

[4] http://www.matesy.de/ [retrieved: May, 2016]

[5] P. Ripka ed., Magnetic Sensors and Magnetometers, Artech House, Boston, 2001

[6] E. Hecht, Optics, Prentice Hall International, 2016

[7] http://www.qioptiq-shop.com/en/Precision-Optics [retrieved: May, 2016]

[8] A. V. Oppenheim and R. W. Schafer, Discrete–Time Signal Processing, Prentice Hall International, 2015

Progress in Design and Fabrication of Resonator Quantum Well Infrared Photodetectors (R-QWIP)

Jason Sun, K. K. Choi, K. Olver and Rich Fu
Electro-Optics and Photonics Division
U.S. Army Research Laboratory
Adelphi, MD 20783, USA
E-mail: guifu.n.sun.civ@mail.mil; kwong.k.choi.civ@mail.mil; kimberley.a.olver.civ@mail.mil; richard.x.fu.civ@mail.mil

***Abstract*—Resonator-Quantum Well Infrared Photo detectors (R-QWIPs) are the next generation of QWIP detectors that use resonances to increase the quantum efficiency (QE). Collaborating with L-3 Communications - Cincinnati Electronics, recently we explore R-QWIPs for long wavelength applications. By using our two optimized inductively coupled plasma (ICP) etching processes, two format (1Kx1K and 40x40) R-QWIP detectors were fabricated successfully. We achieved a quantum efficiency of 37% for 19 quantum wells and 35% for 8 quantum wells under a doping density of 0.5 × 10^{18} cm^{-3}. The cutoff wavelength and bandwidth of both detectors are 10.5 μm and 2 μm respectively. The thermal sensitivity of the large format FPA is 27.2 mK at half well-fill (Nw/2) of 8.85 M electrons and intergration time of 4.46 ms under F/2.5 optics.**

Keywords-QWIP; resonance; FPA; electromagnetic modeling; quantum efficiency; inductively coupled plasma (ICP) etching; GaAs substrate removal.

I. INTRODUCTION

We established a highly reliable electromagnetic (EM) model to calculate the quantum efficiency (QE) of an infrared detector [1]. We subsequently applied it to design a new detector structure, which is referred to as the resonator-QWIP (R-QWIP) [2]. An R-QWIP consists of an active quantum well (QW) layer, a GaAs bottom contact layer, and a top GaAs contact layer. On the top contact layer, there is an array of diffractive elements (DEs) that are covered with ohmic metal and gold layers. The ohmic metal consists of Pd/Ge/Au layers. The mesa is surrounded by a low index material, such as epoxy, and the substrate underneath the ground contact layer is completely removed.

When light is incident from the bottom side of the detector, it is scattered by the DEs back to the detector volume, and the subsequent angles of incidence are larger than the critical angles for total internal reflection at all detector boundaries. The light is therefore trapped inside the pixel. By designing a properly sized detector volume, the trapped light forms a constructive interference pattern, with which the internal optical intensity is greatly increased, thereby yielding a large QE. To achieve the expected performance, the height of the DE and the thickness of the active resonator must be uniformly and accurately realized to within 0.05 μm accuracy and the substrates of the detectors have to be removed totally to prevent the escape of unabsorbed light in the detectors. To achieve these specifications, an inductively coupled plasma (ICP) etching tool is used to fabricate a good number of test detectors and

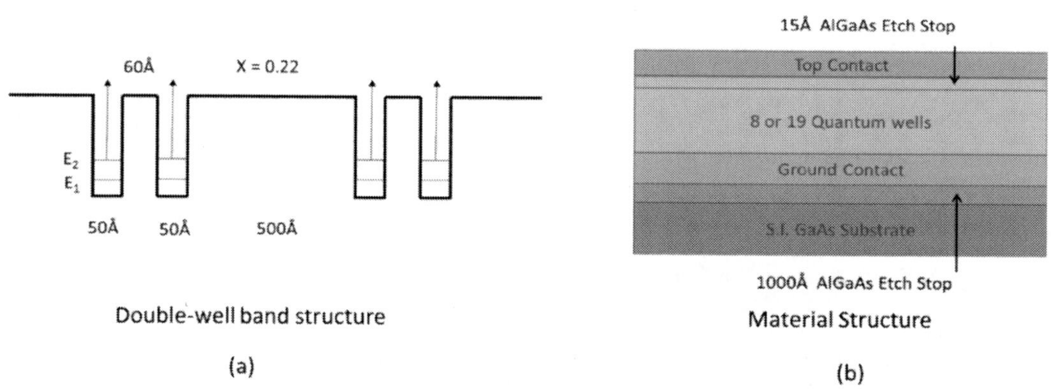

Figure 1. (a) The band structure of double-well QWIP material design. (b) The material layer structure.

FPAs. In an inductively coupled plasma (ICP) system, ion density is controlled by ICP source power alone. Increasing ICP source power increases ion density. Meanwhile, ion energy is affected by both ICP source power and RF chuck power. Increasing ICP power decreases induced dc bias. On the contrary, increasing RF chuck power raises dc bias on the chuck. Since an ICP system provides one more process parameter than a reactive ion etching (RIE) system for plasma control, it is more flexible to use ICP to optimize different etching processes, such as selective (etching GaAs over AlxGa1-xAs stop etching layer) versus non-selective etching, or isotropic versus vertical etching [3-7]. We thus adopted ICP etching (selective and non-selective) over reactive ion etching (RIE) for the fabrication of test detectors and FPAs. Our selective ICP etching process can yield a very high selectivity (>5000:1) and a fast GaAs etching rate (2700Å/min). The etching surface was perfectly smooth and mirror-like after processing. In addition to high selectivity and smooth etching surface, the process is also highly reproducible and shows no damage to the detector material [8-11].

In this work, we designed an R-QWIP with a broad resonance. When it couples to a broadband material, which has a cutoff wavelength at 10.5 µm, infrared radiation between 7.5 – 10.5 µm within the long wavelength infrared (LWIR) window can be efficiently detected. Two format R-QWIP detectors were fabricated (1K x 1K and 40 x 40). The pixel pitch size are 20 µm and 25 µm respectively. In this article, we will describe the material and geometry design, fabrication and test results.

II. 10.5 µM CUTOFF R-QWIP DESIGN

To design a broadband R-QWIP with 10.5 µm cutoff, we use a double-well structure to broaden the spectral bandwidth of the QWIP material. In the design, each quantum well (QW) period contains a 50-Å GaAs QW, a thin 60-Å $Al_{0.22}Ga_{0.78}As$ barrier, another 50-Å GaAs QW, followed by a thick 500-Å $Al_{0.22}Ga_{0.78}As$ barrier. To reduce the dark current level in this long wavelength detector, a moderate doping density N_D of 0.5×10^{18} cm^{-3} is adopted for each QW. If the two GaAs QWs are coupled through the thin barrier, its bandwidth is broadened from ~1 µm to ~3 µm. Figure 1 (a) shows the band structures of the design. Figure 1 (b) shows the material layer structure. Two types of wafer materials are subsequently grown, 19 QW periods and 8 QW periods. They are labeled as DX1 and DX2. The active layer thickness of DX1 and DX2 are 1.3 µm, and 0.6 µm respectively.

Figure 2(a) shows the R-QWIP geometry design. Each pixel consists of 9 GaAs rings as diffractive elements (DEs) that covered with ohmic metal and gold. The pixel size is 20 × 20 µm² with a 25-µm pixel pitch. In this structure, the incident light is diffracted by the DEs and reflected back to the active layer as shown in Figure 2(b) where it is trapped and circulated inside the pixel until it is absorbed eventually.

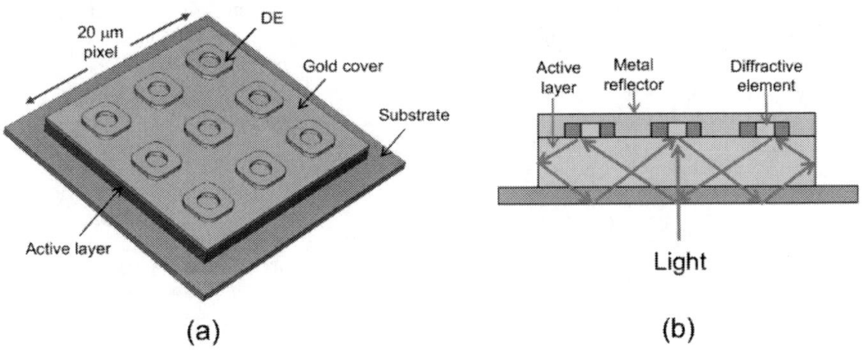

Figure 2. (a) The optimized R-QWIP geometry for the 7.7 – 10.5 µm band. (b) The schematic light path inside the detector.

III. R-QWIP FABRICATION

R-QWIP focal plane array (FPA) and test detector fabrication process involves five masks. We use the first mask to create an array of rings as DEs. By using an EVG 120 Resist Processing Cluster, 1.8µm thick AZ5214 photoresist was coated on the wafers. The resist was baked at 110C° for one minute in the system. Karl Suss MA/BA6 Contact Aligner was used to expose photoresist and align patterns over layers. The DEs were formed by using our optimized selective ICP etching process to etch down to the 15 Å etch-stop layer, which is shown in picture 1(b). The optimized etching parameters were: BCl3 = 20 sccm, SF6 = 10 sccm, Ar = 10 sccm; pressure = 0.5 mTorr; RF Power = 0 W; ICP Power = 200W; and substrate temperature = 25°C. Before the ICP etching, one minute oxygen plasma was used to clean the etching surface. The etching process was conducted in a Unaxis VLR 700 Etch System. Since the selective etching process has a very high selectivity (greater than 5000:1 for $Al_{0.4}Ga_{0.6}As$), 15-Å thick stop etching layer is sufficient to define the DE height. The etch-stop layer is also important to maintain a uniform height across the wafer as the etching rate is higher near the wafer edge. Figure 3 shows a microscope pictures that was taken after DE etching.

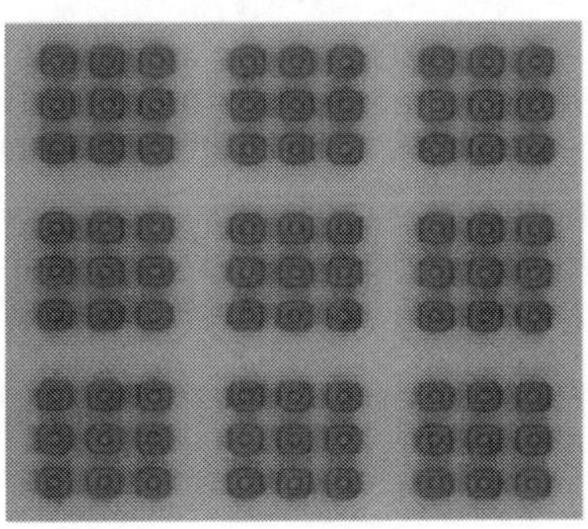

Figure 3. A microscope picture taken after DE etching.

We use second mask to delineate the ground contact area located outside the detector area. Optimized non-selective ICP etching recipe was used to touch the ground contact layer. The etching parameters were: BCl3 = 50 sccm, Ar = 10 sccm; pressure = 5 mTorr; RF Power = 80 W; ICP Power = 800W; and substrate temperature = 25°C. In this etching, we apply a finite RF power to form a vertical sidewall. Since The RF power also induces a DC voltage on the chuck, which accelerates the ions toward the etching material, we minimized the RF power to avoid the possible plasma damage.

In metallization step, instead of negative photoresist, we use positive photoresist to create a favorable undercut for metal lift-off. In our case, the DE elements scatter UV light during exposure, which results in the undercut. The metal layer consists of five layers of materials, and they are: Pd(50Å)/ Ge(200Å)/ Au(300Å)/ Pd(50Å)/ Au(5000Å). After lift-off, the wafer was annealed in a tube furnace at 350C for 25 minutes.

The fourth mask was used to define the pixels. We opened the pixel areas while other areas were covered with photoresist. In the pixel areas, the metal pads were used as etching masks, and non-selective ICP etching was utilized to create individual pixels. The fifth mask is indium bump mask. We coated 9 µm-thick positive photoresist (AZ9245) and deposited 5 µm-tall indium bumps on the wafer using a thermal evaporator. Figure 4. Shows a microscope picture taken after indium bump deposition. The wafer was then diced into FPAs and test detectors and candidates were bump bonded to readout and fanout circuits. The backsides of the detectors were then filled with low viscosity epoxy.

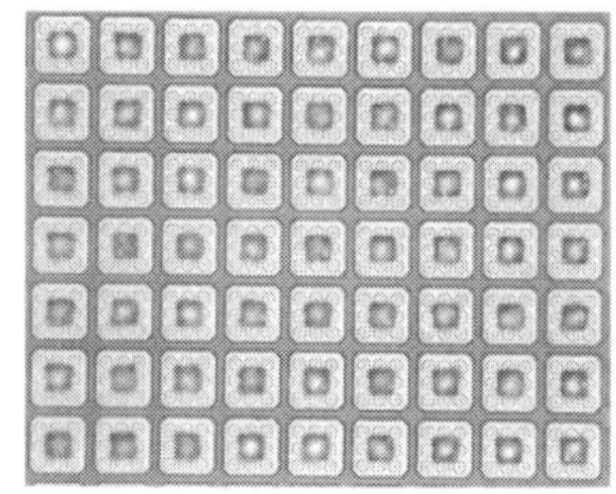

Figure 4. A microscope picture taken after indium bump deposition (1K x 1K format and 25 µm pixel pitch size).

One of the most important process step is substrate removal. Thinned QWIP FPAs offers several advantages over un-thinned detector FPAs. Besides other general benefits, substrate removal is specifically important for R-QWIP. The thinned R-QWIP FPAs and test detectors enhance the resonant effects, and the QE can rise by a factor of 3 - 5 according to EM modeling. To remove the substrate of FPAs and test devices, we need to mechanically lap the substrates to within 50 µm. Our optimized selective etching process was then use to totally remove the substrates. The surface of the dies is uniform, smooth and mirror-like after etching.[8]

IV. DX1 (19 QWs) R-QWIP CHARACTERISTICS

The test detector of DX1 R-QWIPs are fabricated into groups of 40 × 40 pixel elements and they are hybridized to fanout circuits. The fabricated pixel is shown in the insert of figure 5(b). After backfilling with epoxy, the substrate was removed completely. The conversion efficiency (CE) is measured at different substrate bias v at the operating temperature t = 10 K. The light source is a globar monochromator. Next, the gain of the detector is deduced from the noise measurements. From the values of CE and g, the QE spectrum can be obtained and it is shown in figure 5(b). The maximum QE at 2 v is 36.5%. Figure 5(a) shows the expected QE spectrum for the present detector material and structural designs. If we assume a planar wave front as in normal incidence, the peak at 9.7 µm will have a QE of 43%. On the other hand, if we assume a spherical wave front as in f/2.5 optics, the main peak will be slightly

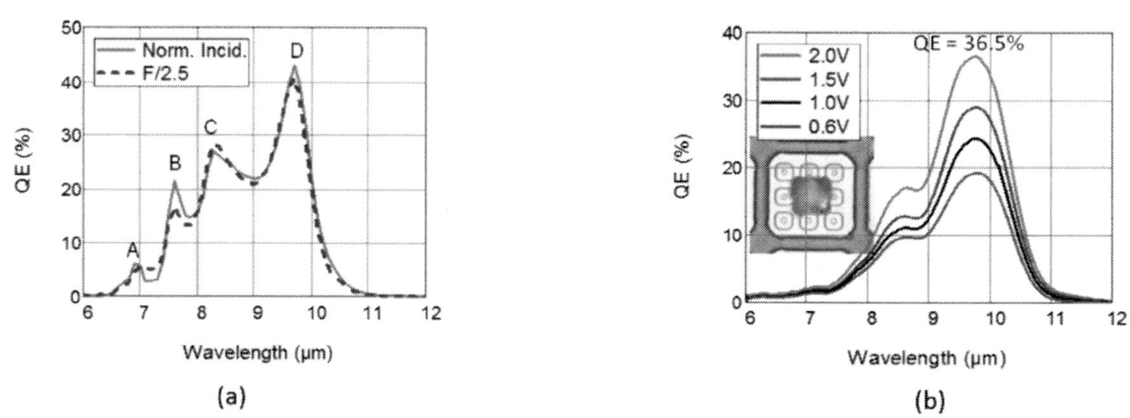

Figure 5. The calculated (a) and observed (b) QE of DX1 R-QWIP under positive substrate bias at T = 10 K. The insert shows the realized geometry, which is partly masked by an indium bump contact at the center.

reduced to 38%. The overall detection lineshape however remains almost the same. Comparing the calculated and

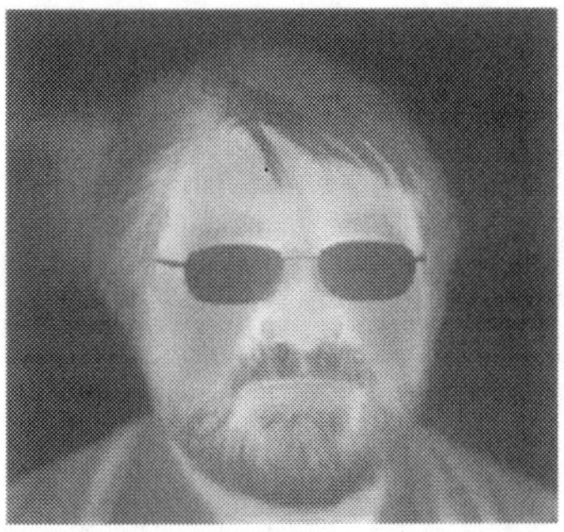

(a)

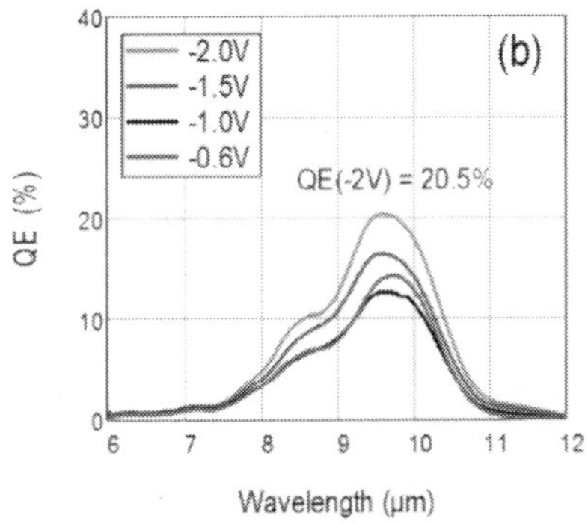

Figure 6(a) The IR image taken by the DX1 FPA. (b) The deduced QE of DX1 under negative substrate bias at T = 10 K.

observed QE spectrum in Figure 5(a) and (b), the observed peaks are broader. These broader peaks may help to explain the slightly lower averaged peak value from the theoretical expectations. Even with the broadened peaks, the individual peaks from A to D are still visible at the calculated wavelengths, although the magnitudes of A and B peaks are smaller than predicted. We attribute this peak suppression to the processing imperfections and nonuniformity. Since A and B are higher order resonances in the shorter wavelengths, their vertical electric polarization distributions have higher spatial frequencies and thus will be more sensitive to the fidelity of the global detector geometry. As seen in figure 4 and in the insert of figure 5(b), the fabricated pixel has rounded corners and the rings are slightly displaced from the pixel center, both are deviated from the EM model. These imperfections may be the causes for the lower peaks.

Although QE under positive substrate bias is consistent with EM modeling, QE under negative bias is substantially smaller, and it is shown in Figure 6(b). Under negative bias, QE at -2 V are 20.5%. It is nearly a factor of 2 less than that under positive bias. The same situation was also observed in three separate wafer materials in earlier studies. We attribute this polarity asymmetry to the fact that the resonant optical intensity is highly localized along the z axis. The value of vertical optical intensity decreases exponentially from the maximum at the top of the active layer to zero at the bottom of the ground contact layer. This highly localized intensity makes the creation of photocurrent sensitive to the internal potential drop across the QWs. It is known that the potential drop inside a QWIP is not linear but larger at the cathode than at the anode. The photoelectrons generated at the cathode are then more likely to drift out of the well and contribute to the photocurrent. The photoelectrons at the anode, on the other hand, are prone to recombine in the same well and do not create a photocurrent. Therefore, when the cathode is at the top of the QW layer under positive substrate bias, almost all optical absorptions generate photocurrent and thus the detection QE is closer to the absorption QE. Conversely, under negative substrate bias, the anode situates in the high intensity region where the QWs are less active. The detection QE is thus reduced.

In addition to the fanout circuits, we also produced a DX1 focal plane array with the same pixel size and pitch in a 1-megapixel format. The FPA was first characterized in an experimental dewar using a globar monochormator. Figure 6(a) shows an infrared image taken in this experimental dewar. The FPA operating condition is: T = 61 K, V ~ -1.1 V, F/# = 2.5, integration time τ_{int} = 3.06 ms, and signal processing = 1-point background subtraction. Under this operating condition, the pixel operability is 99.5% and thermal sensitivity (NEΔT) is 45 mK. After this measurement, the FPA was integrated into a camera that can operate at a lower T. With a F/2.5 lens, 300 K background, 55 K cold stage T, and a lower bias of ~ -0.5 V, the measured NEΔT is 27.2 mK at half well-fill ($N_{w/2}$) of 8.85 Me^- and integration time (τ_{int}) of 4.46 ms.

V. DX2 (8 QWs) R-QWIP CHARACTERISTICS

To confirm the explanation of the polarity asymmetry, we adopted the DX2 material structure, which has fewer QWs (8 QWs instead of 19 QWs) but has the same total thickness as DX1 so that they have the same resonant structure. In DX2, the original 1.3-μm thick active layer is divided into two material layers: a 0.6-μm thick active layer at the top and a 0.7-μm contact layer at the bottom.

Figure 7(a) shows QE of DX2 R-QWIP under positive bias. At 0.8 V, QE are 34.7%, which is only slightly less than the 36.5% for DX1. The similar QEs thus confirm that the vast majority of IR absorption indeed occurs within a very thin layer (< 0.6 μm) next to the diffractive elements. The nearly equal QE for different active thicknesses was predicted in a previous study[12] and is confirmed in this experiment. The photons cycle more times in less absorbing layers, thus yielding similar QE. Furthermore, the DX2 QE at negative bias of -0.8 V, shown in Fig. 7(b), is 33.8%, respectively. They are almost the same as that under positive bias, which again confirms that all DX2 QWs are in the high intensity region.

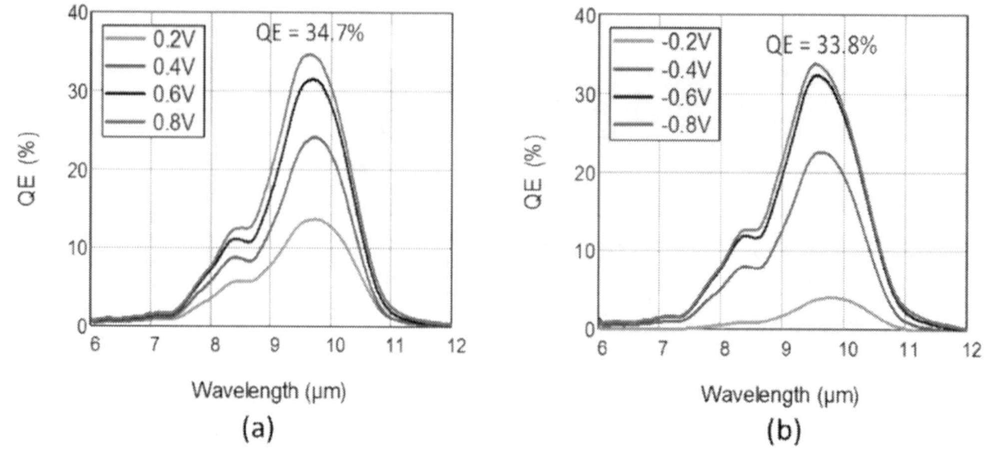

Figure 7 The QE spectra of the DX2 R-QWIP under positive substrate bias (a) and under negative substrate bias (b).

VI. CONCLUSION

We designed a broadband long wavelength R-QWIP detector. With the help of our two optimized ICP etching processes, we fabricated a good number of FPAs and test detectors. Using a moderate 0.5×10^{18} cm^{-3} doping, we achieved 37% QE in a 19-QW detector and 35% in an 8-QW detector at a large positive substrate bias. Similar QE can also be obtained under negative bias in the 8-QW detector. Despite the fact that the present readout circuit operates on negative bias, the DX1 FPA shows a thermal sensitivity of 27.2mK with 99.5% operability at 55 K under F/2.5 optics and 4.46 ms integration time. Higher sensitivity, shorter integration time, and higher operating temperature are expected at positive bias. With nearly double QE of DX2 relative to DX1 at negative bias, higher performance will also be expected from the DX2 FPA. To yield better R-QWIP performance under various operating conditions, we are studying single-well designs with different doping densities. Since contact mask allgner creates some pattern defects and non-uniformity, we are using a Step and Repeat (Stepper) Projection System to expose and align wafers, which will yield better resolution and more accurate alignment. The result will be reported elsewhere.

ACKNOWLEDGMENT

The authors would like to thank the support of FPA processing, testing, and demonstration at L-3 Cincinnati Electronics.

REFERENCES

[1] K. K. Choi et al., "Electromagnetic modeling and design of quantum well infrared photodetectors," IEEE J. Sel. Top. Quantum. Electron., vol. 19, pp.3800310(1)–3800310(10), 2013.

[2] K. K. Choi et al., "Resonator-quantum well infrared photodetectors," Appl. Phys. Lett., vol. 103, 201113(1)–201113(4), 2013.

[3] A. Mitchell, R. A. Gottscho, S. J. Pearton, and G. R. Schetler, "Real-time, in situ monitoring of GaAs and AlGaAs photoluminescence during plasma processing", Appl. Phys. Lett., vol. 56 (9), pp.821–823, 1990.

[4] C. M. Knoedler, L. Osterling, and H. Shtikman, "Reactive ion etching damage to GaAs Layers with etch stops," J. Vac. Sci. Technol., vol. B6, pp.1573-1576, 1988.

[5] S. J. Pearton et al., "Reactive ion etching of GaAs with CCl2F2:O2: Etch rates, surface chemistry, and residual damage," J. Appl. Phys., vol. 65, pp.1281-1292, 1989.

[6] T. R. Hayes, U. K. Chakrabarti, F. A. Baiocchi, and A. B. Emerson, "Damage to InP and InGaAsP surfaces resulting from CH4/H2 reactive ion etching", J. Appl. Phys., vol. 68, pp.785-792, 1990.

[7] J. W. Lee, M. W. Devre, B. H. Reelfs, D. Johnson, and J. N. Sasserath, "Advanced selective dry etching of GaAs /AlGaAs in high density inductively coupled plasmas", J. Vac. Sci. Technol., vol. A18, pp.1220-1224, 2000.

[8] J. Sun and K. K. Choi, M. D. Jhabvala, and C. Jhabvala, "Advanced Substrate Thinning Process for GaAs-Based Devices", J. Micro/Nanolith. MEMS MOEMS, vol.10(2), pp.023004(1)-023004(4), Apr–Jun 2011.

[9] Jason Sun, K. K. Choi, and Unchul Lee, "Fabrication of Pyramidal corrugated quantum well infrared photodetector focal plane arrays by inductively coupled plasma etching with BCl3/Ar", Journal of Micro/Nanolithography, MEMS, and MOEMS, vol.11(4), pp.043003(1)–044003(4), Oct–Dec 2012.

[10] Jason Sun, K. K. Choi, and K. Olver, "Fabrication of Resonator-quantum well infrared photodetector test devices", SPIE Journal of Micro/Nanolithography, MEMS, and MOEMS, Vol. 11(1), pp.013004(1)-013004(4), January 2014.

[11] Jason Sun, K. K. Choi, M. D. Jhabvala, C. A. Jhabvala, A. Waczynski and K. Olver, "Advanced Inductively Coupled Plasma Etching Processes for Fabrication of Resonator-Quantum Well Infrared Photodetector", Infrared Phys. Technol., Vol. 70, pp. 25–29, May 2015

A Device for Self-monitoring Breath Analysis

Danila Germanese*, Marco Righi*, Massimo Guidi‡, Massimo Magrini*, Mario D'Acunto*, Ovidio Salvetti*
*Institute of Information Science and Technology
National Research Council, Pisa, Italy
Email: name.surname@isti.cnr.it
†Institute of Science of Matter
National Research Council, Rome, Italy
Email: mario.dacunto@ism.cnr.it
‡Institute of Geo-sciences and Earth Resources
National Research Council, Pisa, Italy

Abstract—**Let's think about the numerous diagnostic screening methods. How many of them are invasive? How many of them present side effects? How many of them are expensive? We can affirm that the majority of the regular prophylactic checkups are sufficiently invasive, expensive and, sometimes, painful to discourage the subjects from participating in preemptive diagnostic procedures. As a consequence, in recent years, the need for the development of low cost, non invasive, rapid tools for the monitoring of metabolic processes has been increased. Breath analysis, performed by means of gas sensor array, may be an example of this kind of tools. In this paper, we will present the development of a portable, low cost, easy to use device for breath analysis, based on commercial semiconductor-based gas sensor array. We will describe its design, both from a hardware and software point of view. In addition, by describing the functionality tests of the device and the experimental results, we will highlight the pros and cons that come from the use of such type of low cost adopted technology to analyze breath molecules.**

Keywords–Breath analysis; Semiconductor gas sensors; Data analysis; Low cost technology; E-noses.

I. INTRODUCTION

Many of us frequently avoid classical diagnostic procedures (gastroscopy, colonscopy, X-rays, blood samples, magnetic resonance (RM), etc.) because of their costs, or because often they are invasive, and sometimes painful, too. As a consequence, the need for simpler, cheaper, less invasive methods of screening is becoming more and more considerable.

Many studies have been addressed to investigate the metabolic pathways of breath molecules in order to exploit breath analysis to monitor the metabolic processes that occur in human body in a non invasive way [1][2][3]. For instance, according to [4], kidney diseases may be investigated by analyzing the concentration of ammonia in exhaled breath; ethane and pentane may derive from lipid per-oxygenation in case of oxidative stress ([5]); acetone has been investigated as a biomarker for diabetes, as it seems to be correlated with blood glucose level ([6]).

Such studies were conducted by using chemical analysis technologies and methodologies: selected ion flow tube mass spectrometry, for instance, or proton transfer reaction mass spectrometry, or gas chromatography- mass spectrometry. All these techniques are the gold standard for gas analysis, being very sensitive and accurate. On the other hand, they are very expensive and time consuming; moreover, the results can be analyzed only by specialized personnel.

As a consequence, in recent years, the idea of exploiting gas sensor array to analyze breath molecules [7] has been arisen. E-noses, quicker than a gas chromatograph, are able to follow the trend in time of breath molecules. In many studies, they have been employed to monitor volatile biomarkers related to cancer [8], or microbial infection [9], or asthma [10]. Toshiba's recent research prototype "Breathalyzer" [11] is able to monitor breath acetone. Bedfont [12] Smokerlyzer detects high concentrations of carbon monoxide present in smoker's breath.

Nonetheless, the technology used by the majority of such e-noses is expensive [13] or requires complex circuitry [14][15]. Moreover, often the existing e-noses used for monitoring breath biomarkers are not purposely designed for clinical field. In this paper, we present the development of a device, so called Wize Sniffer (WS) [16], able to monitor in real time a set of breath biomarkers. In particular, the aim of our work was to develop a device which was:

- able to analyse breath gases in real time;
- portable;
- based on low-cost technology, to foster its purchase and use;
- easy-to-use also for non-specialized personnel, to promote its use also in home environment.

In particular, Section II lists the molecules detected by the WS and describes the device's general architecture; Section III explains the WS functionality tests and the experimental results, later discussed in Section IV.

II. THE WIZE SNIFFER, HARDWARE AND SOFTWARE

The idea of the Wize Sniffer was born in the framework of European SEMEOTICONS (SEMEiotic Oriented Technology for Individual's CardiOmetabolic risk self-assessmeNt and Self-monitoring) Project. SEMEOTICONS aims at developing a multi-sensory platform, with the appearance of a mirror, the so called "Wize Mirror", which is able to detect, in human face, all those "signs" related to cardio-metabolic risk. The Wize Sniffer will be integrated in the Wize Mirror, detecting all those molecules present in human exhaled breath related to the noxious habits for cardio-metabolic risk (smoking, alcohol intake, metabolic disorders).

Nonetheless, the modular configuration of the Wize Sniffer allows for changing the gas sensors according to the molecules to be detected, and, in addition, for using the Wize

Sniffer also as a stand-alone device.

A. Molecules detected by the the WS

In this section we describe briefly the breath molecules detected by the Wize Sniffer and how they are related to those noxious habits for cardio-metabolic risk: metabolic disorders, alcohol intake, smoking.

- **Carbon Monoxide (CO)**: it is present in cigarette smoke, very dangerous for cardio-metabolic risk. Its baseline value for a non-smoker subject is round about 3.5ppm, and it reaches 14-30ppm in smokers;
- **Oxygen and Carbon Dioxide** ($O_2 and CO_2$): Their variations show how much O2 is retained in the body, and how much CO_2 is produced as a by-product of cellular metabolism. Breathing rate influences the level of CO_2 in the blood: slow breathing rates cause Respiratory Acidosis (i.e., increase of blood CO_2 partial pressure, which may stimulate hypertension or heart rate acceleration); Too rapid breathing rate (hyperventilation) may provoke Respiratory Alkalosis (i.e., decrease of CO_2 concentration in blood, it no longer fits its role of vasodilator, leading to possible arrhythmia or heart trouble). Their baseline values are round about 40000ppm for CO_2 and 13-15% for O_2;
- **Hydrogen** (H_2): it derives from the breakdown of the carbohydrates in the intestine and in the oral cavity by anaerobic bacteria. Its baseline value is round about 9.1ppm;
- **Ethanol** (C_2H_6O): Ethanol derives from alcoholic drink. It is recognized that ethanol breakdown leads to an accumulation of free radicals into the cells, a clear example of oxidative stress. Ethanol may cause arrhythmias and depresses the contractility of cardiac muscle. Its baseline value is round about 0.62ppm;
- **Hydrogen Sulfide** (H_2S): it is a vascular relaxant agent, and has a therapeutic effect in various cardio-vascular diseases (myocardial injury, hypertension). Its baseline value is round about 0.33ppm.

B. Hardware and Software

In Figure 1, the Wize Sniffer first prototype's structure is shown. The acquiring system is based on a gas sampling box (of 600ml according to the tidal volume [17] and made up of (ABS) and Delrin) where six gas sensors are placed, and a micro-controller board. Other two gas sensors work in flowing-regime by means of a sampling pump. A heat and moisture exchanger (HME) filter is placed at the beginning of a corrugated tube to absorb the water vapor present in the breath. A flow-meter monitors the exhaled breath volume. A flushing pump purges the chamber to recovery the sensors' steady state between two consecutive measures.

As outlined before, our first aim was to develop a device based on low cost technology. Indeed, we used a widely employed opensource micro controller board to read, collect and analyze gas sensors' data: an Arduino Mega2560 with Ethernet module.

Regarding the gas sensor array, optical, carbon nano fiber (CNF), quartz crystal microbalance (QCM), metal oxide semiconductors (MOS), conducting polymers (CP), and surface acoustic wave (SAW), are the most common gas sensor types employed in e-noses [7]. Although very sensitive and able to detect concentrations lower than 10ppb, optical gas sensors are expensive and often they cannot be miniaturized. Also CNF-based gas sensors are expensive, especially for their fabrication and manufacturing, too. SAW and QCM-based gas sensors have very high sensitivity but they need complex circuitry and, in the case of QCM-based gas sensors, they have a poor signal-to-noise ratio.

Figure 1. a) Wize Sniffer first prototype's hardware. b) and c) show its internal configuration.

Then, our choice was to employ MOS-based gas sensors. They have long life, strong sensitivity, rapid recovery; in addition, they are low cost and easy to be integrated in the circuitry. Unfortunately, humidity strongly affects their behavior, as well as cross-sensitivity [18]. To reduce the water vapor present in exhaled breath from 90% up to 60% a HME filter is used. In addition, humidity (as well as temperature) is monitored within the gases store chamber (by means of a Sensirion SHT11). Cross-sensitivity makes these sensors be non-selective. This may be a problem for data processing (see Section III). In Table I, all the used gas sensors are listed, as well as the detected breath molecules.

TABLE I. SENSORS INTEGRATED IN THE WIZE SNIFFER'S ACQUIRING SYSTEM

Detected molecule	*Sensor*	*Best detection range*
Carbon monoxide	TGS2442	50-1000ppm
	MQ7	20-200ppm
	TGS2620	50-5000ppm
Ethanol	TGS2602	1-10ppm
	TGS2620	50-5000ppm
Carbon dioxide	TGS4161	0-40000ppm
Oxygen	MOX20	0-16%
Hydrogen sulfide	TGS2602	1-10ppm
Hydrogen	TGS821	10-5000ppm
	TGS2602	1-10ppm
	TGS2620	50-5000ppm
	MQ7	20-200ppm

In a second step of our work, we will try to develop CP-based gas sensors. Such type of sensors present the same MOS-based gas sensors' pros and cons, but they are highly adaptable and they can be configured in several ad-hoc solutions. In particular, we will try to exploit Polyaniline sensitivity to detect Nitric Oxide, a well-known marker for endothelial function [19].

As outlined in the previous sections, we aimed to develop a device which could be used not only in medical centers, but also in home environment. Indeed, a client-server architecture is implemented in order to send breath test results also to a remote Personal Computer: the user, after running a test, can forward the results to the family doctor, for instance (see Figure 2).

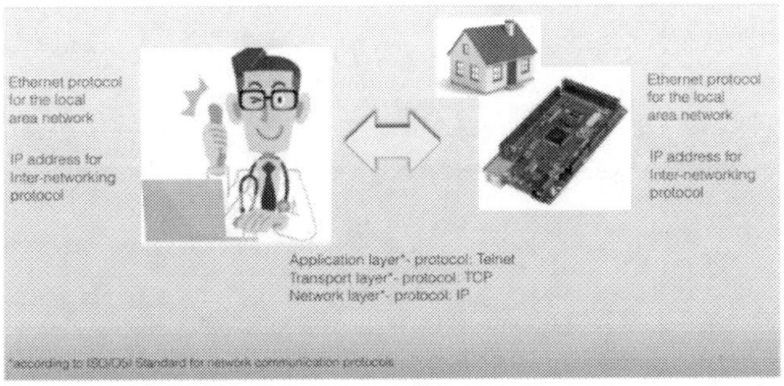

Figure 2. Client- server architecture including Wize Sniffer

It means that Arduino Mega2560 is programmed to process sensors' raw data and to execute a daemon on port 23. It waits a command line from the remote PC and provides the data. A measure is considered valid if the user's exhaled volume equals at least 600ml (store chamber's volume, see Figure 1). The next section describes how the WS microcontroller board analyzes row data.

III. Experimental Tests and Data Analysis

As described in Section II-B, semiconductor-based gas sensors are, on one side, very low cost, very easy to be integrated in the circuitry and very sensitive; on the other side, they are not selective, because of cross-sensitivity, and their behavior is strongly dependent on humidity.

Starting from raw data (see Figure 3), our aim is to calculate, as accurately as possible, the concentrations of the molecules present in exhaled breath and to be detected by the Wize Sniffer. It is understandable how the cross-sensitivity makes this aim a challenge, since there is not a single sensor for each breath compound. Moreover, we deal with something extremely variable: breath gases. Exhaled breath composition is strongly influenced by factors such as heart rate, breath flow rate [20], posture [21], ambient air [22], lung volume [23], breath sampling [24]. Consequently, breath composition may exhibit not only a strong inter-variability (among different subjects), but also a marked intra-variability (relative to the same subject). As a consequence, we have to face, on one hand, with an uncertainty of measure which derives from all those factors that affect the gas sensors' behavior; on the other hand, we have un uncertainty due to all the physiological conditions that may influence the breath composition. This is summarized in Figure 4. Note that, in our case, also factors such as BMI, sex, age, subject's lifestyle may influence the breath composition: for example, alcohol disposal in men is different than the one in women, and, in addition, it depends on body mass index (BMI), as well.

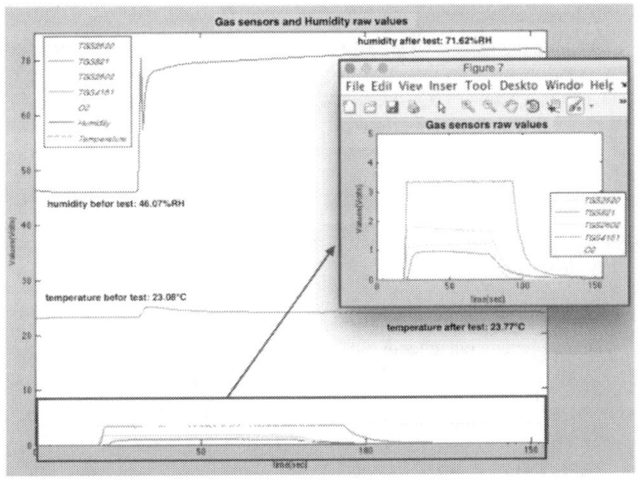

Figure 3. Raw breath curves. Also temperature and humidity trends are plotted.

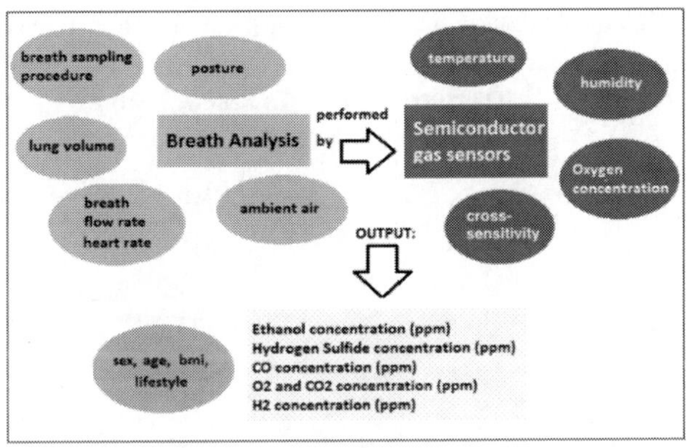

Figure 4. Breath analysis performed by semiconductor-based gas sensors. In the circles, all the influencing factors, both for breath analysis and gas sensors' behavior.

For these purposes, these are the experimental steps we are following:

- to investigate the behavior of semiconductor-based gas sensors in our measurement conditions: 30C+/-7% and 70%RH+/-5%, that are the ones that occur in the store chamber when a breath analysis is performed (see Figure 3);
- to investigate how the cross sensitivity affects their output, that means, how the several molecules influence each other in the chemical interaction with the sensors' sensing element;
- all this knowledge about gas sensors has to be exploited and applied to perform breath analysis and calculate molecules' concentrations.

A. Gas Sensors' Behavior Data Analysis

The aim of this phase of the work is to understand gas sensors' behavior under our measurement conditions: 30C+/-

7% and 70%RH+/-5%. In particular, we want to study not only their response to a well-known gas concentration, but also their behavior when humidity increases, due to the exhaled breath. In addition, in this phase, also the cross sensitivity has to be addressed.

In Figure 5, the MQ7 (CO sensor) output is plotted as a function of the humidity. The relationship between the humidity and MQ7 output can be fitted with a power model.

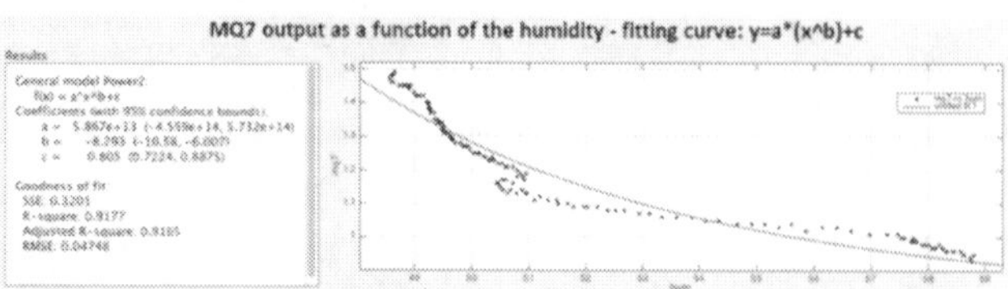

Figure 5. The relationship between MQ7 sensor and humidity is plotted. A power model is used for fitting curve.

It can be easily noted how the humidity strongly affects such type of gas sensors; as a consequence, also the gas flow rate indirectly influences gas sensors' behavior: a high flow-rate leads to a decrease in humidity, which causes (as shown in Figure 5), an increase in sensor's output. Keeping the humidity constant, sensor's output will depend on the gas concentration (CO concentration, in this case) only (as shown in Figure 6).

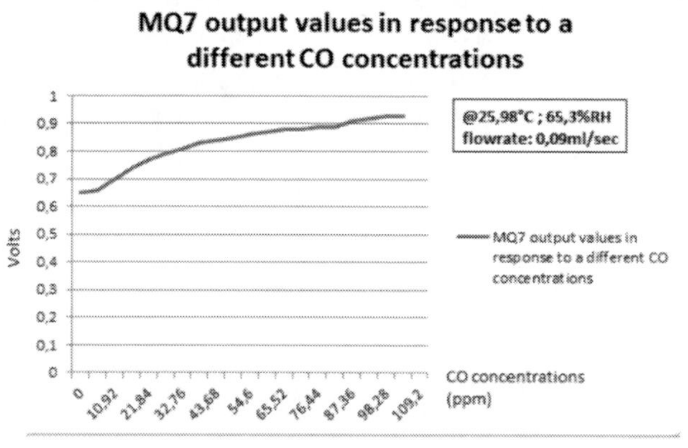

Figure 6. MQ7 sensor output as a function of different carbon monoxide concentrations. Measurement conditions: 25.98C, 65.3%RH

Unfortunately, when a breath analysis is performed, breath flow-rate may be kept low and constant, but the humidity inevitably rises in value. Figure 7 shows the relationship (modeled by a power law) between MQ7 sensor's output and different CO concentrations.

The cross sensitivity is investigated by keeping the humidity constant, of course, and by injecting in the test chamber, where the gas sensor under investigation is placed, well-known mixed gases concentrations (the experimental set-up is shown in Figure 9). In this way, how the different compounds add together and influence gas sensors' output can be understood. In Figure 8, the contributions of well-known carbon monoxide and hydrogen gaseous mixes on TGS2620 sensor's output are shown. TGS2620, as reported in Table I, is sensitive to ethanol, carbon monoxide and hydrogen. When, for instance, the sensor is exposed to a gaseous mix of 100ppm of carbon monoxide and 20ppm of hydrogen, its output (at about 28C, 61%RH) will be 1,01V. By investigating such behavior of semiconductor gas sensors, the "weight" of each compound on the output can be addressed. A simple model able to describe this phenomenon can be based on a linear regression.

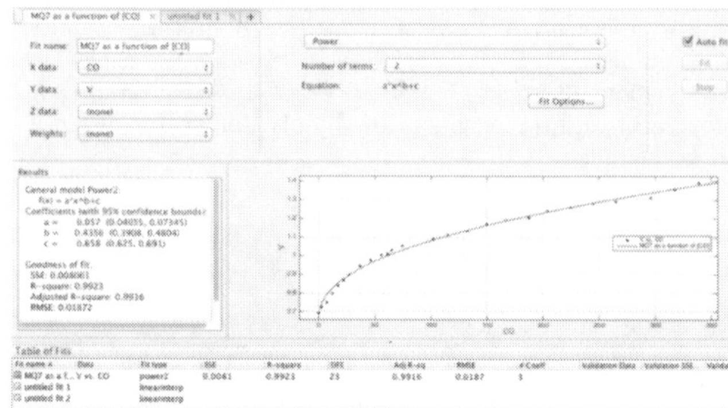

Figure 7. The relationship between MQ7 sensor's output and well-known CO concentrations is plotted. A power model is used for fitting curve. Measurement conditions: 25.98C, 65.3%RH

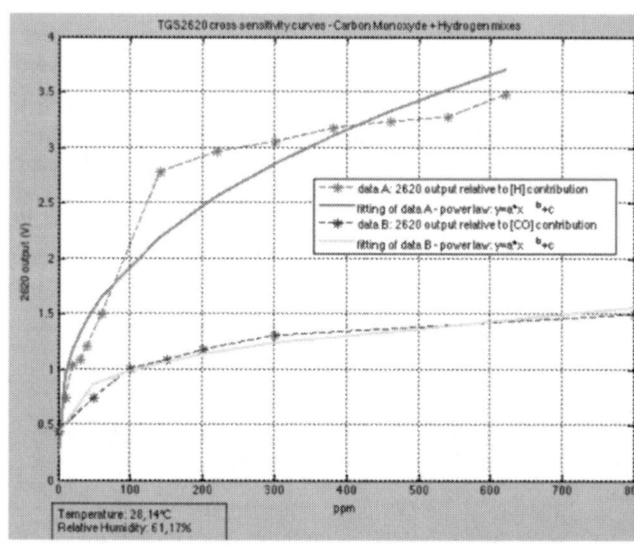

Figure 8. The contributions of well-known carbon monoxide and hydrogen gaseous mixes on TGS2620 sensor's output. It can be noted that such sensor is much sensitive to hydrogen than to carbon monoxide, especially at lower concentrations.

Finally, as already reported in Figure 4, the knowledge about sensors' behavior must be applied to breath analysis field: breath analysis, performed by semiconductor-based gas sensors, will have to take into account also the model which describe such type of gas sensors' behavior.

B. Breath Test Analysis

Our aim is to develop a model in order to calculate, as accurately as possible, the concentration of breath molecules to be detected by the WS, in order to compare such concentrations with the reference ones (see Subsection II-A). This

Figure 9. a) Experimental setup for gas sensors tests. b)The humidity is kept constant by means of a saturated solution of NaCl placed on the bottom of the vial. c) The data stream from sensors is read by an Arduino board.

model should be based on the data regarding the gas sensors' behavior (see Subsection III-A), but it also has to take into account other parameters (see Figure 4) that can influence breath composition.

We are developing such model by using a statistical approach. Meanwhile, we are also exploiting another approach for data analysis, more classical, based on Principal Component Analysis and K-nearest neighbor (KNN) classification algorithm. In Figure IV, we can see how this approach works.

For this purpose, a measurement protocol was draft and it involved a population of 26 healthy individuals, with different age (range 30-60 years old), habits, lifestyles, body type. We choose healthy individuals because, in this case, we are detecting those breath molecules related to cardio- metabolic risk. As a consequence, the Wize Sniffer does not make a diagnosis, but it only should help the user to monitor his/her well-being and lifestyle. For the measuring protocol, the methodological issues about breath sampling procedure had been taken into account [24], since (as shown in Figure 4) the breath sampling may strongly influence the breath composition. Actually, there is not a standardized procedure to sample the breath. The most common methods of sampling are three: "alveolar sampling" (it is used if only systemic volatile biomarkers are to be assessed), "mixed expiratory air sampling" (which corresponds to a whole breath sample), "time-controlled sampling" (which corresponds to a part of exhaled air sampled after the start of expiration, but this method shows large variations of samples compositions). For our purposes, mixed expiratory air sampling method was chosen, since our interest was focused on both endogenous and exogenous biomarkers. The individuals took a deep breath in, held the breath for 10sec., and then exhaled once into the corrugated tube trying to keep the expiratory flow constant and to completely empty their lungs. The study was approved by the Ethical Committee of the "Azienda Ospedaliera Universitaria Pisana", protocol n.213/2014 approved on September 25th, 2014; all patients provided a signed informed consent before enrollment.

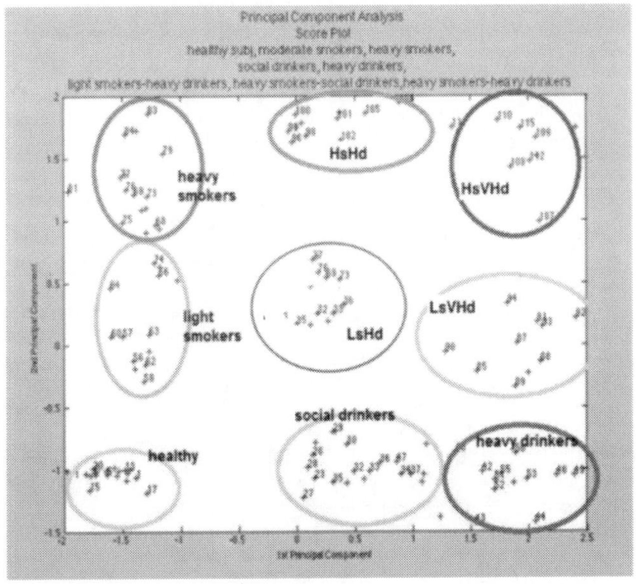

Figure 10. Score plot of the data analysed by Principal Component Analysis.

The raw data can be divided into 9 clusters according to subjects' habits: "Healthy" (that means subjects with low cardio-metabolic risk), "Light Smoker", "Social Drinker", "LsHd" (that means Light Smokers, heavy drinkers), "LsVHd" (that means Light Smokers, very heavy drinkers), "HsHd" (that means Heavy Smokers, heavy drinkers), "HsVHd" (that means Heavy Smokers, very heavy drinkers). The KNN classifier is able to correctly classify in 85,96% of cases.

It is important to highlight that while an alcohol consumption up to 1-2 Alcohol unit/ day is often considered not dangerous (in healthy subjects), smoking is considered very noxious in any case.

IV. Conclusion

In this paper, we described the development of a portable, easy-to-use device for breath analysis based on low-cost technology. In particular, the device makes use of an array of low-cost, semiconductor-based gas sensor array.

Such type of gas sensors are, of course, very robust, sensitive and easy to be integrated in the circuitry. That allows for having a modular configuration for the acquiring system and then for changing the gas sensors according to the molecules to be detected. On the other hand, semiconductor-based gas sensors require a very robust data post-processing in order to take into account all the influencing factors. In the case of breath analysis, the humidity plays an important role in that sense, as well as the cross sensitivity.

In addition, standardized procedures for breath sampling should be defined.

Thus, we retain that a big effort in this direction should be devoted. Having something low-cost, portable, easy to use, affordable to maintain, and so exploiting the great potential of breath analysis, may allow for a non-invasive daily monitoring that, even if without a real current diagnostic meaning, could represent a pre-screening in any case.

ACKNOWLEDGMENT

This work was funded in the framework of the Collaborative European Project SEMEOTICONS (SEMEiotic Oriented Technology for Individuals CardiOmetabolic risk self-assessmeNt and Self- monitoring), grant N. 611516. Paolo Paradisi and COSMED s.r.l. are warmly acknowledged for useful support.

REFERENCES

[1] C. Lourenco and C. Turner, "Breath analysis in disease diagnosis: methodological considerations and applications," Metabolites, vol. 4, 2014, pp. 465–498.

[2] F. DiFrancesco, R. Fuoco, M. Trivella, and A. Ceccarini, "Breath analysis: trends in techniques and clinical applications," Microchemical Journal, vol. 79, 2005, pp. 405–10.

[3] W. Miekisch, J. Schubert, and G. Noeldge-Schomburg, "Diagnostic potential of breath analysis- focus on volatile organic compounds," Clinica Chimica Acta, vol. 347, 2004, pp. 25–39.

[4] I. Essiet, "Diagnosis of kidney failure by analysis of the concentration of ammonia in exhaled breath," Jo. of Emerg. Trends Eng. Appl., Science, vol. 6, 2013, pp. 859–862.

[5] M. Phillips, R. Cataneo, J. Greenberg, R. Grodman, and M. Salasar, "Breath markers in oxidative stress in patients with unstable angina," Heart Disease, vol. 5, 2003, pp. 95–99.

[6] Z. Wang and C. Wang, "Is breath acetone a biomarker of diabetes? a historical review on breath acetone measurements," J. of Breath Research, 2013, p. 037109.

[7] A. Wilson, "Recent progress in the design and clinical development of electronic-nose technologies," Nanobiosensors in Disease Diagnosis, 2016, pp. 15–27.

[8] T. de Meij, I. Larb, M. van der Schee, and et al., "Electronic nose can discriminate colorectal carcinoma and advanced adenomas by fecal volatile biomarker analysis: proof of principle study," Int. J. Cancer, 2014, pp. 1132–1138.

[9] N. Yusuf and al., "In-vitro diagnosis of single and poly microbial species targeted for diabetic foot infection using e-nose technology," BMC Bionformatics, 2015, pp. 158–169.

[10] P. Montuschi, N. Mores, A. Trov, C. Mondino, and P. Barnes, "The electronic nose in respiratory medicine," Respiration, 2013, pp. 72–84.

[11] "www.toshiba.co.jp/about/press."

[12] "www.bedfont.com."

[13] D. Walt and al., "Optical sensor array for odor recognition," Biosens. Bioelectron., 1998, pp. 697–699.

[14] F. Lai and H. Huang, "Fabrication of high frequency and low-cost surface-acustic wave filters using near field phase shift photolitography," Microelectronic Engineering, 2006, pp. 1407–1409.

[15] L. Fan, H. Ge, S. Zhang, H. Zhang, and J. Zhu, "Optimization of sensitivity induced by surface conductivity and adsorbed mass in surface acoustic wave gas sensors," Sensor Actuat. B- Chem, 2012, pp. 114–123.

[16] M. D'Acunto and al., "Wize sniffer - a new portable device designed for selective olfaction," in International Conference on Health Informatics, 2014, pp. 577–582.

[17] D. Shier, J. Butler, and R. Lewis, Hole's Human Anatomy and Physiology. McGraw-Hill 11th Ed, 2007.

[18] P. Clifford and D. Tuma, "Characteristics of semiconductors gas sensors i. steady state gas response," Sensors and Actuators, vol. 3, 1983, pp. 233–254.

[19] R. Cannon, "Role of nitric oxide in cardiovascular disease: focus on the endothelium," Clinical Chemistry, vol. 44, 1998, pp. 1809–1819.

[20] J. Jones and S. Clarke, "Effect of expiratory flow rate on regional lung emptying," Clin. Sci., 1969, pp. 343–56.

[21] N. Anthonisen, P. Robertson, and W. Ross, "Gravity-dependent sequential emptying of lung regions," Journal of Appl. Physiol., 1970, pp. 589–95.

[22] F. DiFrancesco and al., "Implementation of fowler's method for end-tidal air sampling," Journal of Breath Research, 2008, p. 037009 (10pp).

[23] J. Jones, "The effect of pre-inspiratory lung volumes on the result of the single breath o_2 test," Respiratory Physiology, 1967, pp. 375–85.

[24] W. Miekisch, S. Kischkel, A. Sawacki, T. Lieban, M. Mieth, and J. Schubert, "Impact of sampling procedures on the result of breath analysis," 2008, p. 026007 (7pp).

SAT406M. Physiological Status Determination of a Wrist-Worn Personal Locator Beacon User: Preliminary Results

Alejandro de Miquel, Pere Molina, Ismael Colomina and Marta Blázquez

GeoNumerics S.L.
Castelldefels, 08860 Barcelona, Spain
Email: {alejandro.demiquel, pere.molina, ismael.colomina, marta.blazquez} @geonumerics.com

Daniel Katz and Ohad Barak

Mobit Telecom ltd.
Kiryat Ono, 55451 Israel
Email: dan@mobitcom.com
jo@traveling-jo.com

Michel Monnerat and Thibaud Calmettes

Thales Alenia Space France
Toulouse, 31100 France
Email: {michel.monnerat, thibaud.calmettes}
@thalesaleniaspace.com

***Abstract*—This paper presents the concept, developments and preliminary results of the Horizon 2020 project named SAT406M. The goal of this project is to develop an application based on a wrist-worn device, conceived to be a maritime application, and the use of European Global Navigation Satellite Systems, particularly the Galileo system. It provides an end-to-end solution based on the Galileo Search and Rescue service, using its unique Return-Link-Message function, improving the mobility and safety of citizens. In particular for this paper, we focus on the development and the first testing results of a physiological monitoring component included in the device. This component will provide the Search and Rescue services with additional information about the SAT406M user's physiological status once the distress alarm is triggered. The algorithm implemented uses some stochastic techniques to deduce the SAT406M user's physiological status, encoded in two bits, from sensor inputs. The results here presented, which are still preliminary results from an intermediate stage of the project, show a good accuracy in most of the cases, but not all of them yet. The proposed improvements, clear and easy to implement in the algorithm, make us conclude that it has the potential to end up determining the SAT406M user's physiological status with a significantly higher accuracy, improving this way the user's safety.**

Keywords-Galileo; Personal Locator Beacon; Search and rescue; IMU.

I. Introduction

Over the last few years, the market of the wearable smart devices, and in particular the smartwatches market, has experienced a huge growth. This has been possible, to a large extent, thanks to the development in sensor technology. Sensors are steadily becoming smaller, cheaper and more precise, driven in particular by the microelectromechanical systems (MEMS) technology. Inertial sensors, among others, have been miniaturized, resulting in small, wearable devices suitable for measuring the motion of its carrier. This has boosted research and development in various fields such as robotics [1], satellite technology [2], optics [3], human motion analysis [4], [5], [6], [7] and many more. Taking the market of smartwatches and smartbands as example, one can nowadays easily find wrist-worn devices that measure the user's heart rate [8], or track and analyse one's daily activity, [9].

One of the fields whose applications have the potential to take benefit from these technologies is Search and Rescue (SAR). In particular, the use of sensors in Personal Locator Beacons (PLB) can still be broadly enlarged. PLBs are devices carried by sailors, hikers and all kind of adventurers as a safety tool. If they are in a distress situation, the PLB can be activated, sending an alert via satellite communications. Once the alert is sent, the PLB provides periodically the user's position to a SAR team, whose goal is to rescue the person in distress as quickly and efficiently as possible. With the advent of the Galileo technology, some unique Global Navigation Satellite System (GNSS) features will be available for the use of PLBs, such as the Return-Link-Message (RLM) or the ability of sending some additional information, apart from the user's position.

Nowadays, PLBs are too expensive and bulky for mass market. Moreover, it is not easy to find a wearable PLB; the Breitling watches [10] are an example. Wearable PLBs do not only have the advantage to be attached to the user; they also have the possibility to include additional sensor technology. Therefore, there is a clear opportunity for the advent of smaller, wearable PLBs that may benefit from the miniaturization trend of technology. In addition, given the future multi-constellation GNSS panorama, PLBs are likely to feature world-wide coverage for positioning and distress message reporting. It is needless to say that this potential has a direct impact on the quality of SAR services and safety of distressed people.

In this paper, we present the SAT406M, a research and development project in progress that aims to develop a wrist-worn PLB. In particular, we focus on the PLB's physiological monitoring component. This component will consist of an algorithm deducing the PLB user's physiological status from Inertial Measurement Unit (IMU) and GNSS inputs. MEMS

IMUs have already been used to analyse human motion in many contexts, that range from pedestrian dead reckoning using one several sensors attached to the body [5], [7], to qualitative motion analysis with the IMU placed in a pocket [4], [6]. However, the approach of using of an IMU to deduce the physiological status of a wearable-PLB user is new.

To present this research, we firstly explain the project in Section II, providing insights on its foundations and key innovative features. Secondly, in Section III, we describe one of the innovative components of the proposed PLB, the Physiological Monitoring component. In this same section, we also present and interpret the preliminary results obtained at the current stage of the project. Finally, some conclusions are drawn in Section IV.

II. The SAT406M concept

SAT406M is a Horizon 2020 project that aims at developing a wrist-worn PLB, specially targeting at marine environments and users. This beacon will be a 406MHz Cospas-Sarsat [11] compatible one, and will integrate a Digital Selective Calling (DSC) transceiver compatible with marine Very High Frequency (VHF) radios. This H2020 project started in February 2015 and is expected to finish in February 2018.

The SAT406M concept is based in Mobit Telecom's SAT406 [12] (Figure 1), the world's first affordable wrist-worn PLB. It will make use of Thales Alenia Space MEOLUT technology for SAR satellite solutions [13]. Even though it is conceived to be used mainly by boaters and sailors, it can also be a life-saving tool for travellers, pilots and all kind of adventurers that run a constant risk and can, at some point, be in need of the SAR services. If a SAT406M user considers that he or she is in a critical situation, the PLB alarm can be triggered. The alarm triggering procedure is complex enough to avoid false alarms, but also easy enough to be executed in a distress situation. Once this has been done, the distress alarm is sent with an Ultra High Frequency (UHF) 406 MHz Cospas-Sarsat compatible transmitter and a VHF DSC transceiver.

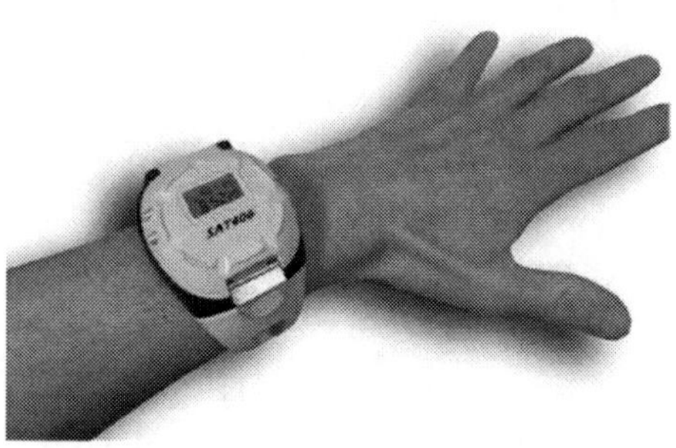

Figure 1. SAT406 PLB

Thanks to the VHF signal, the nearby boats will be aware of a potential distress situation notified by the user, providing them the means for assistance if necessary. Moreover, thanks to the UHF signal located on the 406MHz frequency for GNSS, such as Galileo, this alarm will be sent to the SAR services. Once received, a notification of acknowledgement will be sent to the PLB via the RLM service.

In the project, an innovative communication method is being developed that will enhance the standard communication between the PLB and the SAR/Galileo system, using an uplink solution compatible with the Cospas-Sarsat standards and the Galileo SAR downlink. In this way, the SAR data throughput between the beacon and the SAR/Galileo system will be increased.

One of the innovative features to be included in the upgraded PLB device is the capability of automatically interpret and notify distress situations. Since the PLB user may be in a situation in which no manual alarm triggering is possible (loss of consciousness, high stress, etc.), the goal of the physiological monitoring component is to autonomously provide information to the SAR services about the status of the person based on the PLB built-in sensors. This will be done automatically each five minutes once the alarm has been triggered for the first time.

III. Physiological monitoring

The physiological monitoring in SAT406M is based on motion and positioning sensor inputs. The current approach is to deduce the user's physiological status from IMU and GNSS data, and to encode it in a minimal data structure to be easily transmitted. The result of the physiological monitoring will be then reported to the SAR services, who can take profit of this additional information when executing the SAR operation. No other sensors are implemented due to design and power consumption limitations.

The selection of the physiological features to be monitored by the algorithm is one of the crucial steps. Many aspects define the potential distress of a person, ranging from vital signs or motion of the body, to environmental or weather conditions. Given the particular requirements gathered along the project, two status worlds are defined: the 'health status' and the 'qualitative positioning status'. These two categories set a clear distinction about the personal user condition and his/her whereabouts; in addition, many states can be defined for each of these categories. At this stage of the project development, we have defined two possible states for the 'health status', namely 'alive' and 'unknown', and two possible states for qualitative positioning, namely 'in water' and 'unknown'. Far from being exhaustive and complete for all the potential applications, this selection of states is derived from the SAT406M context and requirements. The definition of the health status world's states follows from trying to determine the probably most valuable information for the SAR services: knowing if the user is alive. Since the product is specifically thought to be a maritime application, it also makes sense to consider the states of the qualitative positioning status in the way proposed.

A. *Input/Output*

The input consists of IMU and GNSS measurements, acquired in a modality conditioned by the current PLB. During about 20 seconds each 5 minutes, these sensors will be turned on to collect measurements. The sensors cannot be constantly turned on because of the Cospas-Sarsat battery life requirements. Each 5 minutes, once the data has been collected by the sensors, they will be analysed by the physiological monitoring algorithm, and the user's physiological status will be deduced. This information will then be sent to the SAR services.

The specific IMU to be integrated in SAT406M is Bosch Sensortech's BMI160 [14]. Table I shows the specifications of this IMU. If some parameter accepts several options, only the one chosen for the project is specified. The measurements are collected at an output data rate of 25Hz from three accelerometers, measuring linear accelerations, and three gyroscopes, measuring angular velocities. Figures 2 and 3 show examples of accelerometer and gyroscope data respectively, collected by an IMU on different motion situations.

TABLE I. BIM160 specifications

	Accelerometer		Gyroscope	
Parameter	Value	Units	Value	Units
Resolution	16	bit	16	bit
Range	± 4	g	± 1000	°/s
Sensitivity	8192	LSB/g	32.8	LSB/°/s
Sens. temperature drift	± 0.03	%/K	± 0.02	%/K
Sens. change over voltage	± 0.01	%/V	± 0.01	%/V
Zero offset	± 150	mg	± 3	°/s
Nonlinearity	± 0.5	%FS	± 0.1	%FS
Output noise	180	$\mu g/\sqrt{Hz}$	0.007	$°/s/\sqrt{Hz}$

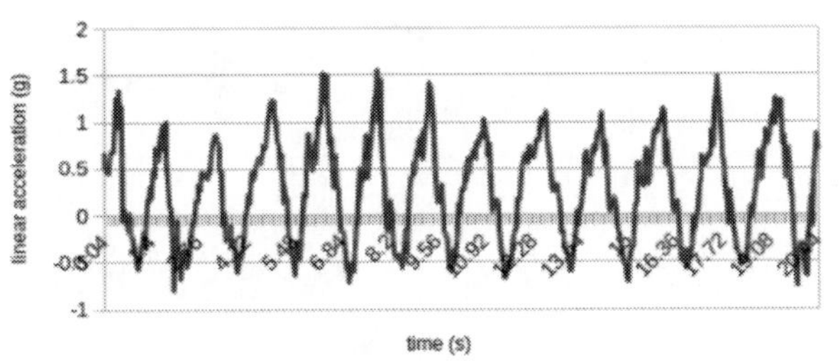

Figure 2. Accelerometer. User swimming

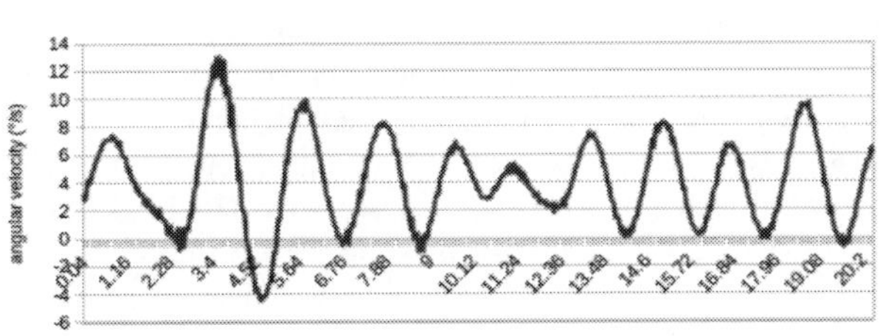

Figure 3. Gyroscope. IMU on a boat

Figure 2 corresponds to the measurements taken by an accelerometer placed on a person's wrist while swimming, breaststroke style. Figure 3 corresponds to the measurements taken by a gyroscope placed on a boat, while it was advancing at a speed of about 10 knots. In both cases, periodicity is a clear feature, but the signal's shape suggests that the periodicity is produced by different kinds of motion. With the information given by such features and other ones, also provided not only by an IMU but also a GNSS receiver, the goal is to determine the user's physiological status, in terms of the defined states.

Indeed, the IMU is the primary sensor used in SAT406M, and its measurements clearly provide meaningful information about the experienced motion. Parameters such as the magnitude of the measurements, the periodicity (if any) and its related frequency, or the amplitude of the observed signal, can be significantly distinct when acquired in various platforms (pedestrian, vehicle, etc.) and types of motion (standing, swimming, walking, etc.). Additionally, GNSS data might also be helpful to describe the context of the PLB user.

Regarding the output, it is a goal of the algorithm to generate a minimal data structure to express the target outputs describing the health and qualitative positioning status of the user. Actually, the amount of information given by the output is limited by the Cospas-Sarsat message standards, and it is only thanks to the innovative communication method developed by Mobit Telecom ltd. that we can send two bits encoding the user's physiological status. In line with this goal, the output of two bits encodes the states 'alive', 'unknown' and 'immersed in water', 'unknown'. This seems to be the most relevant information to be given to the SAR services about the user's status encoded in only two bits. One can easily deduce that there exist four possible outputs: 'Alive/In water' (A/W), 'Alive/Unknown' (A/?), 'Unknown/In water' (?/W) and 'Unknown/Unknown' (?/?).

In fact, since the number of defined states is finite, concretely set to four, one can think of the whole physiological status determination concept as a directed graph with four vertices. In this graph, each vertex represents one of the possible outputs, i.e. one of the states the user can be in. At each point in time, a probability is associated to each vertex, representing the probability of the user being in that state. The directed graph edges represent the possible transitions from a state to another one. This concept can be generalized to any number of states, and is known as "qualitative navigation" or "graph navigation".

B. *Algorithm*

The physiological monitoring algorithm's output is deduced from a set of four probabilities. In order to express this, a probability vector is defined:

$$v^t = \begin{pmatrix} v_1^t \\ v_2^t \\ v_3^t \\ v_4^t \end{pmatrix} = \begin{pmatrix} P_{A/W} \\ P_{A/?} \\ P_{?/W} \\ P_{?/?} \end{pmatrix}, \text{ where } \sum_i P_i = 1,\ P_i \geq 0. \quad (1)$$

Here, the t stands for a timestamp, meaning that this is the probability vector representing the user's state at time t. Hence, each element v_i^t represents the probability of the SAT406M user being in state i at time t.

In order to compute the final probability vector at time t, not only the sensors' data is considered, but also the user's state at time $t-1$. This is done by multiplying a stochastic transition matrix M^t by the probability vector at time $t-1$:

$$v^t = M^t v^{t-1} = \begin{pmatrix} \sum_{j=1}^4 m_{1j} v_j^{t-1} \\ \sum_{j=1}^4 m_{2j} v_j^{t-1} \\ \sum_{j=1}^4 m_{3j} v_j^{t-1} \\ \sum_{j=1}^4 m_{4j} v_j^{t-1} \end{pmatrix} = \begin{pmatrix} v_1^t \\ v_2^t \\ v_3^t \\ v_4^t \end{pmatrix}. \quad (2)$$

Here, the term 'stochastic matrix' refers to the fact that the conditions $\sum_{i=1}^4 m_{ij} = 1, \quad m_{ij} \geq 0$ hold for each j. It is apparent that each probability vector is conditioned by its estimation on a previous epoch, leading to an iterative process. Like the elements of the probability vector, the elements of the transition matrix also have a clear interpretation: the element m_{ij} represents the probability of transitioning from state j to state i.

The determination of each of these elements depends on a sensor-dependent contribution, determined by the values of the parameters deduced from the raw sensor data, and a sensor-independent contribution: a priori, if the user is in a given state, the probability of transitioning to a different (or the same) state may not be equal for each state.

This is expressed with the equation

$$m_{ij} = W\alpha_i + (1-W)\beta_{ij}. \quad (3)$$

In this equation,

- The α_i are the sensor-dependent coefficients. They change from time $t-1$ to time t, and represent the probability of the user being in state i according to the data acquired between these two times. Clearly, the equality $\sum_{i=1}^4 \alpha_i = 1$ must hold.
- The β_{ij} are the data-independent (and thus also time-independent) coefficients, and represent the probability of the user transitioning from state i to state j a priori. For these coefficients, the equality $\sum_{i=1}^4 \beta_{ij} = 1$ holds.
- W is a weight, a real number between 0 and 1, that allows to control the importance given to the information coming from the sensors' data.

C. Preliminary testing and results

Due to the restrictions related to the PLB's computational capacity, a light implementation of the algorithm described above has been written in C++. In the next stages of the project, this algorithm will be migrated to the final platform.

In order to validate this algorithm in realistic situations, some test cases have been performed involving a person in a marine environment and experiencing different situations. The platform used to acquire IMU measurements was an iPhone 6, which includes an InvenSense MP67B IMU. This IMU presents very similar specifications to the IMU to be integrated in the final version of SAT406M. A smartphone platform was selected due to the ease of use and the already available apps to acquire measurements from the built-in sensors. The smartphone was attached to the wrist of the person with a water-proof case.

We acquired data in a range of situations that basically include standing on a small boat and being immersed in water, either swimming, slightly moving or not moving at all. For the cases on the boat, we also collected data of the IMU not worn by the person, but steady on a table. With these tests, we target at the situations when the user is not wearing the device, is sleeping, dead or unconscious lying on the floor. Finally, we note that no GNSS data was considered at this stage of the project. Figure 4 shows a representative sample of the results obtained when running the algorithm with different sets of data. The green cells correspond to true positives, i.e. the output corresponds to the reality. For false positives, we highlight in red the algorithm output, and we use blue to indicate the truth. The initial probability vector has been set to (0.25, 0.25, 0.25, 0.25) in all cases here presented. These results correspond to one or more iterations of the algorithm considering IMU measurements during 20.48 seconds. Again, the algorithm will execute one iteration each 5 minutes.

	A/W	A/?	?/W	?/?
In water, moving arms to avoid sinking	0.144148	0.314897	0.122503	0.418452
Swimming breaststroke (it. 1)	0.359905	0.331564	0.064455	0.244076
(it. 2)	0.380773	0.343455	0.055093	0.22068
Swimming forward crawl	0.363996	0.337172	0.0740269	0.224805
In water, dead (it. 1)	0.130764	0.201391	[illegible]	0.413584
(it. 2)	0.0918138	0.171366	0.24674	[illegible]
IMU on a still boat (it. 1)	0.10358	0.143995	0.239326	[illegible]
(it. 2)	0.119274	0.13207	0.178376	0.540505
IMU on a moving boat (it. 1)	0.090588	0.159977	0.171894	0.562531
(it. 2)	0.0945691	0.134524	0.134815	0.606317
(it. 3)	0.0788965	0.125106	0.128332	0.623337
User standing on a moving boat (it. 1)	0.152387	0.233552	0.197714	0.401347
(it. 2)	0.209262	0.323019	0.116418	0.336302

Figure 4. Preliminary results

We start analysing the correct preliminary results obtained during these tests. Looking at the table, it can be seen that the software clearly relates the situation of the IMU being motionless on a boat (that is, not worn by the user) to the state (?/?), which is the desired output. The software also correctly detects if the user is swimming. Actually, the outputs (A/W) and (A/?) feature high, almost equal probability leading to potential false positives -yet, the software yields a correct and necessary information, which is the user being alive.

On the other hand, in three situations the software output is (?/?), while the real output should be another one. Firstly, in the case in which the user is just moving arms to avoid sinking, some activity is clearly detected, but since the user is moving the arms slowly and the sea was calm, it is not clear which kind of activity it is. Secondly, in the case where the user simulated to be dead on water, the algorithm tends to the (?/?) state. Yet, it must be noticed that the probability corresponding to (?/W) is significantly higher than in the other cases. And finally, in the case where the user was standing on a moving boat, the software detects some activity, if we compare it to the other cases. But since the user was almost not moving, this small activity is still not detected by the software as (A/?). As we can see, the current algorithm outputs tend to the states with '?' if the contrary is not clear.

It is also to be noted that, in general, in the cases where there are more than a single iteration, each iteration reinforces the output given by the algorithm.

It must be remarked that determining the SAT406M user's physiological status is a challenging task. In particular, if the user is hardly moving, being able to discern between situations in which the user is immersed in water and situations where the user is on some kind of boat or platform can be considerably difficult. This is basically due to the effect of the waves, whose range of different signals that can generate is very large, and depends mainly on the sea conditions.

IV. Further Research and Conclusions

We have introduced the SAT406M project, which is one of the first approaches to this kind of technology. It makes use of the whole constellation of SAR-ready GNSS, including the in the future full operational Galileo, that has the RLM as remarkably useful feature.

We have focused on the algorithm determining the user's physiological status, information that will be sent to the SAR services for them to act as efficiently as possible. This, in addition to the fact that the PLB is wrist-worn, is a clear advantage for improving the user's safety with respect to other PLBs. On the other hand, the small size of the PLB restricts the memory and the computing capacity. Also, the amount of information given to the SAR services is restricted due to communication standards.

The algorithm for the physiological monitoring has been designed following a rigorous mathematical approach based in stochastic theory and state estimation techniques. Additionally, its implementation is modular and extensible, enabling other sources of information i.e. new sensors to be also included in the process with low effort and minimal modifications.

The software's performance is acceptable considering that it is a prototype version, but it still tends excessively to the output 'unknown' if the contrary is not clear. This indicates the need for fine tuning based on multiple sets of data, with high repeatability of the simulated situations, and varying the test person and the sea conditions.

Also, GNSS data, which is still not considered in the software's current version, will be considered in the future. This kind of data will contribute mostly to the determination of the qualitative status world. For example, if the user is moving at high speed on a boat, he or she will probably be alive, which might not be clearly detectable only with the IMU data. All this will yield the identification of further parameters, and the improvement of the currently considered ones, contributing to the determination of the PLB user's physiological status and the robustness of the system.

Next steps of the project also include testing, working and obtaining results with the final platform. In addition, dissemination and commercial activities will be executed, to launch this product to the mass market.

In conclusion, the product under development in the SAT406M project has the potential to improve significantly the safety of the PLB users, and might open the door to the implementation of other new technologies in such devices.

V. Acknowledgments

The research leading to these results has been funded by the European Community Horizon 2020 Programme under grant agreement no. 640387 managed by the European GNSS Agency (GSA).

References

[1] L. Ferranti and F. Cuomo, "Nano-wireless communication for microrobotics: Bridging the gap," in Proceedings of the Second Annual International Conference on Nanoscale Computing and Communication, ser. NANOCOM' 15. New York, NY, USA: ACM, 2015, pp. 31:1–31:6. [Online]. Available: http://doi.acm.org/10.1145/2800795.2800803 [accessed: 2016-06-13]

[2] D. Tithi and D. Ravishankar, "Role of MEMS Technology in Improving the Satellite and Space Communication System: A Review," in Proceedings of the Manipal International Conference on Technology Management, MiCTM 2015 March 25–26, 2015, Dubai, UAE.

[3] F. Chollet, "Devices based on co-integrated mems actuators and optical waveguide: A review," Micromachines, vol. 7, no. 2, 2016, p. 18. [Online]. Available: http://www.mdpi.com/2072-666X/7/2/18 [accessed: 2016-06-13]

[4] P. Molina, I. Colomina, M. Troger, B. Hofmann-Wellenhof, and C. Aguilar, "Non-conventional INS/GNSS integration for qualitative motion analysis in caregiving applications," in ION GNSS 2010, Portland, Oregon, USA., Sep. 2010, pp. 542–555.

[5] Y. Qilong and C. I-Ming, "Localization and velocity tracking of human via 3 imu sensors," Sensors and Actuators A: Physical, vol. 212, 2014, pp. 25–33.

[6] E. Lockhart, R. Soangra, J. Zhang, and X. Wu, "Wavelet based automated postural event detection and activity classification with single imu (tempo)," Biomed Sci Instrum, vol. 49, 2013, pp. 224–233.

[7] A. R. Jimnez, F. Seco, C. Prieto, and J. A. Guevara, "A comparison of Pedestrian Dead-Reckoning algorithms using a low-cost MEMS IMU," in Proceedings of the Intelligent Signal Processing 2009, WISP 2009 26-28 August 2009 Budapest, Hungary, pp. 37–42.

[8] "Apple Watch," URL: http://www.apple.com/watch/ [accessed: 2016-06-13].

[9] "Fitbit," URL: http://www.fitbit.com/ [accessed: 2016-06-13].

[10] "Breitling," URL: http://www.breitling.com/en/ [accessed: 2016-06-13].

[11] "Cospas-Sarsat," URL: http://cospas-sarsat.int/en/ [accessed: 2016-06-13].

[12] "SAT406," URL: http://www.sat406.com/ [accessed: 2016-06-13].

[13] "TAS MEOLUT," URL: https://www.thalesgroup.com/en/worldwide/space/news/meolut-next-breakthrough-technology-search-rescue-satellite-solutions [accessed: 2016-06-13].

[14] "Inertial Measurement Unit BMI160," URL: https://www.bosch-sensortec.com/bst/products/all_products/bmi160 [accessed: 2016-06-13].

Rehabilitation Robot Based on Three-axis Force/Torque Sensor

Han-Sol Kim and Jae-Hyun Jung
Department of Control & Instrumentation Engineering
Gyeongsang National University
501 Jinjudae-ro, Jinju, Republic of Korea
e-mail: geck@gnu.ac.kr/ replayonion@gnu.ac.kr

Gab-Soon Kim
Department of Control & Instrumentation Engineering/ERI
Gyeongsang National University
501 Jinjudae-ro, Jinju, Republic of Korea
e-mail: gskim@gsnu.ac.kr

***Abstract*—We describe the ankle rehabilitation robot using a three-axis force/torque sensor. The manufactured three-axis force/torque sensor which can detect two directional force Fx, Fz and one directional torque Tz, was fabricated, and it was attached to an ankle rehabilitation robot. The robot was designed and manufactured to perform a ankle bending flexibility rehabilitation exercise. The results of a characteristics test for the developed ankle rehabilitation robot showed that it was safely operated while the ankle bending flexibility rehabilitation exercise was performed.**

Keywords-component; ankle rehabilitation robo;, rehabilitation exercise; three-axis force/torque sensor; rated output; interference error.

I. INTRODUCTION

The feet of severe stroke patients are generally not so available as that of normal. In order to use their feet in everyday life, their feet must receive rehabilitation exercises. An ankle-bending flexibility rehabilitation exercise is performed to make the patient's ankle flexible. The ankle-bending flexibility rehabilitation exercise rotates the ankle in a clockwise direction or counter-clockwise direction. It is very difficult to deal with a number of severe stroke patients and because of it, some of the severe stroke patients can't receive adequate rehabilitation exercise.

Developed ankle rehabilitation robot [1] was designed and manufactured for the unique neuromuscular facilitation of stroke patients. An ankle-bending rehabilitation exercise of patient's ankle was performed, and the results were good. A torque sensor was attached to the footrest and the main body of the robot to measure the rotational force of the ankle. Ankle rehabilitation robots [2] has been designed and manufactured to perform a virtual walking exercise using the haptic technology, and the ankle of the subject (normal) was tested by using the robot. The robot was operated smoothly, but the rotational force exerted on the ankle could not be measured. So, the robot can't get the same effect as a rehabilitation exercise conducted by specialized rehabilitation therapists. The ankle rehabilitation robots developed so far can't exert the same effect as a therapist, and can't detect the emergency signal and return to initial state during the emergency situation because the robots have not had the multi-axis force/torque sensor. Multi-axis force/torque sensor for ankle rehabilitation robots must measure the torque of the ankle and the forces or torques during the emergency situation. Previously developed multi-axis force/torque sensors are from two-axis to six-axis force/torque sensors [3][4], but their price are expensive, and they are not appropriate to adhere to the developed rehabilitation robot, and the rated capacity of each sensor is not fit. So the sensor should be newly designed and manufactured.

The rest of this paper is organized as follows. Section II describes the design and manufacture of three-axis force/torque sensor. Section III describes the design of ankle rehabilitation robot. The acknowledgement and conclusions close the article.

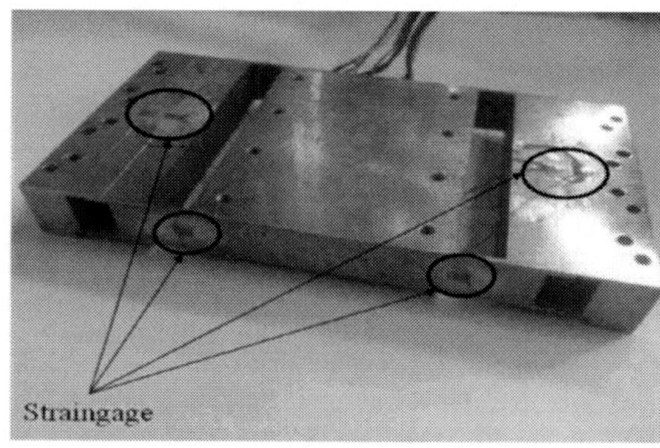

Figure 1. Manufactured three-axis force/torque sensor.

II. DESIGN AND MANUFACTURE OF THREE-AXIS FORCE/TORQUE SENSOR

The three-axis force/torque sensor was designed using by the finite element method (FEM). The rated outputs of the variables for designing the three-axis force/torque sensor are determined by the rated force and torque of each sensor of the three-axis force/torque sensor are Fx=300N, Fz=100N, Tz=15Nm, the size of the sensor is 136mm×74mm×17mm, and the rated strain at the attaching location of strain-gage is about 250 $\mu m/m$. The lengths l1', l1 and l2 are 5mm, 5mm and 10mm respectively, the widths b1 and b2 are 74mm and 14mm, and the thicknesses t1', t1 and t2 are 1.3mm, 0.7mm and 1.4mm respectively.

The three-axis force/torque sensor was fabricated by using the bond (M-200) and the strain gauges (N2A-13-S1452-350, made in Micro-Measurement Company, gauge constant 2.03, size 3×5.2mm), and constructed by Wheatstone bridge. Figure 1 shows the photograph of the manufactured three-axis force/torque sensor. The characteristics experiment of the three-axis force/torque sensor was performed with the multi-axis force/moment sensor calibration system developed by Kim [5] and the measuring device (DMP40). The maximum interference error of the three-axis force/torque sensor was less than 1.24%. And the maximum repeatability error and the maximum non-linearity error of each sensor were less than 0.03% and 0.02% respectively.

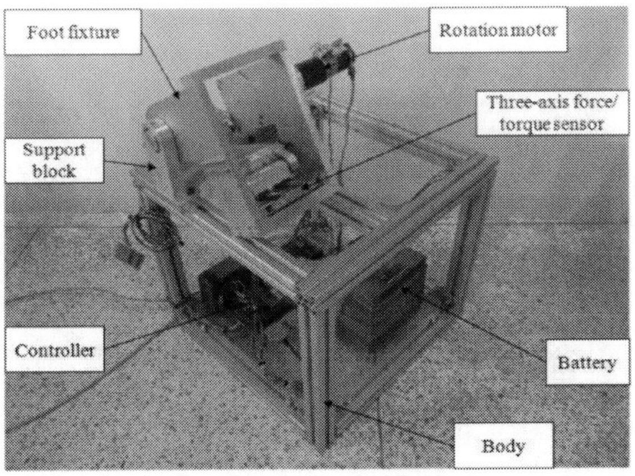

Figure 2. The manufactured ankle rehabilitation robot for the ankle-bending flexibility rehabilitation exercise.

III. Design of the Ankle Rehabilitation Robot

Figure 2 shows the manufactured ankle rehabilitation robot for the ankle-bending flexibility rehabilitation exercise. The developed ankle rehabilitation robot is composed of a body, a support block, a three-axis force/torque sensor, a rotation motor, a motor drive, a high-speed controller, a battery, and so on. The Fx force sensor of the three-axis force/torque sensor measures the rotational force of the ankle. Fz force sensor and Tz torque sensor detect the force and torque when the emergency state is generated during the ankle rehabilitation exercise. Figure 3 (a) shows the graphs of emergency characteristic experiment of the manufactured ankle rehabilitation robot. Fx is the graph measuring the rotational force of the ankle when the ankle rehabilitation robot rotates, and Fz is the force that occurs because of the soles of wheat up, and Tz is the torque generated in the case that a force applied on the sole of the big toe part. The emergency situation is generated that more than 10 Nm torque or more than 10N is changed suddenly, and the program was designed after emergency. The ankle rehabilitation robot developed in this paper can securely carry out the ankle-bending flexibility rehabilitation of the patient, because the robot has the ability to stop and return to the initial state when an emergency situation occurs.

Figure 3 (b) shows the graph of the characteristic experiment for the ankle-bending flexibility rehabilitation exercise using the ankle rehabilitation robot. The rotational force (force Fx) in the bending direction was -52.3N, and that in the spreading out direction was 12.1N. The force control in each reference rotational force was carried out with PI control (Kp: 0.79, Ki: 0.04), and the values of the reference rotational forces -52.3N and 12.1N in the bending direction and the spreading out direction were shaken, because the foot moves in each applied reference force status in the bending direction and the spreading out direction.

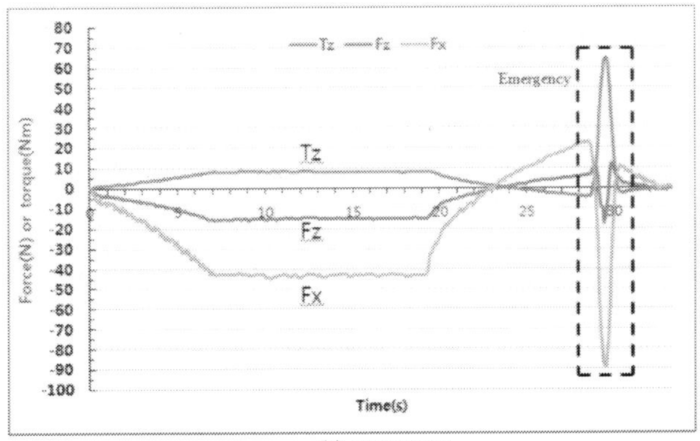

(a) emergency

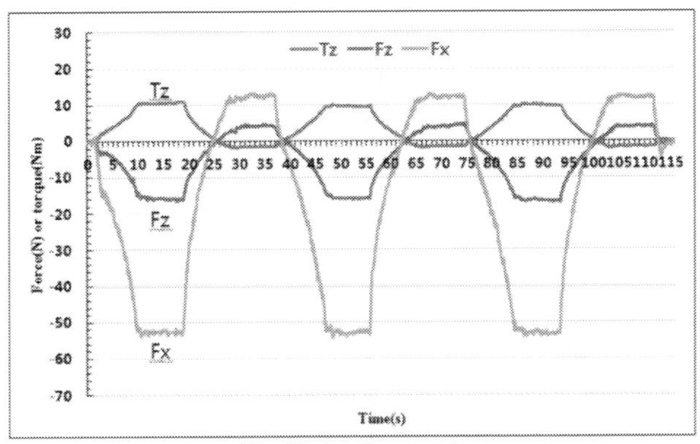

(b) ankle-bending exercise

Figure 3. Graphs of the characteristic experiment for the emergency and the ankle-bending flexibility rehabilitation exercise using the robot.

IV. Conclusions

The three-axis force/torque sensor was designed and fabricated for the ankle rehabilitation robot, and its interference error, a non-linear error and a repeatability error were less than 1.24%, 0.04% and 0.04% respectively. It was confirmed that the developed ankle rehabilitation robot was operated properly in the characteristic experiment for the ankle-bending flexibility rehabilitation exercise. Therefore, it is thought that the developed ankle rehabilitation robot can be applied to severe stroke patient for the ankle-bending flexibility rehabilitation exercise.

Acknowledgment

This research was supported by Basic Science Research Program through the National Research Foundation of Korea(NRF) funded by the Ministry of Science, ICT and Future Planning(No. 2015R1A2A2A01002952)

References

[1] Z. Zhoua, Y. Zhou, N. Wang, F. Gao, K. Wei, and Q. Wang, "A proprioceptive neuromuscular facilitation integrated robotic ankle-foot system for post stroke rehabilitation", Robotics and Autonomous Systems, vol. 73, 2015, pp. 111-122.

[2] K. J. Chisholm, K. Klumper, A. Mullins, and M. Ahmadi, "A task oriented haptic gait rehabilitation robot", Mechatronics, vol. 24, no. 8, 2014, pp. 1083-1091.

[3] G. S. Kim, "Development of a Six-Axis Force/Moment Sensor with Rectangular Taper Beams for an Intelligent Robot," International Journal of Control, Automation, and Systems, vol. 5, no. 4, 2007, pp. 419-428.

[4] K. J. Lee, and G. S. Kim, "Design of Structure of Four-Axis Force/Torque Sensor with Parallel Step Plate Beams," Journal of Institute of Control, Robotics and Systems, vol. 20 no. 11, 2014, pp. 1147-1152.

[5] G. S. Kim, and J. W. Yoon, "Development of calibration system for multi-axis force/moment sensor and its uncertainty evaluation," Korean Society Precision Engineering, vol. 24, no. 10, 2007, pp. 91-98.

White Light Interferometry: Correlogram Correlation for Surface Height Gauging

Noise stability

Ilia Kiselev and Michael Drexel
Breitmeier Messtechnik GmbH
NanoFocus AG
Ettlingen, Germany
email: {kiselev, drexel}@breitmeier.de

***Abstract*—Established methods to gauge the surface height by the white light interferometry do not use the full information contained in a correlogram. As the result, the envelope evaluation methods suffer from susceptibility to noise, whereas the phase methods are prone to the "2-pi ambiguity". In the approach of the present paper, the surface position is determined via the correlation of the local correlogram with a reference correlogram, thus benefiting from its complete information. Accuracy and tolerance to noise of this method is by more than one order of magnitude higher, than that of the envelope methods; the 2-pi ambiguity has not revealed itself so far. Another advantage of the suggested method is the immediate availability of a suitability criterion for a local correlogram – the correlation coefficient with the reference correlogram.**

Keywords-Interferometry; Surface Topology; Noise Immunity.

I. Introduction

Among sensor device technologies, the white light interferometry (WLI) is established as one of the most popular methods of surface topography evaluation. The challenging problem is false evaluations of the surface height, which are affected by different kinds of noise inevitably appearing during any measurement. On the one hand, there is a continuous search for data evaluation methods that are immune to noise, on the other hand, being aware of error inevitability, one is looking for a possibility to assess the confidence level of the surface height evaluation – on every pixel of the optical field - in order to sort out improper ones [1]. Although the assessment of the confidence level does not prevent appearance of false height estimations, yet it allows preventing false conclusions during a further surface topology analysis.

The WLI data are primarily represented by a set of correlograms from different pixels. There are two commonly recognized ways of correlogram processing to estimate the surface height: the method of the correlogram envelope maximum/centroid calculation and the method of correlogram phase tracking [1][2]. Both methods have their own advantages and shortcomings: the first is robust when applied to rough torn surfaces but shows higher variations caused by the data noise [3]; the second one, vice versa, is known providing low variations / high reproducibility but cannot be applied to rough surfaces being prone to the 2-pi ambiguity [2]. Disadvantages when applying these methods are actually to be expected - both make use only of a part of the information contained in the signal. The way to go is to involve the complete information in a single evaluation procedure. There are continuous attempts to combine both methods in order to profit from the advantages of both of them [4], yet both kinds of shortcomings remain.

The intention of the present study is to obtain a data evaluation procedure, which uses complete correlogram information, and to obtain improvement in both the noise tolerance and the confidence level assessment. It is suggested to find - in the measured intensity z-distribution – the interval which is most similar to the known reference correlogram of the interferometer. The position of the interval will give the position of the surface and the level of similarity would give the confidence level for this height estimation. This is exactly what is provided by the cross-correlation function between the measured intensity distribution and the reference correlogram: it gives both the position of maximal resemblance and the level of similarity. Note that this method uses the complete information contained in the correlogram signal: both phase and envelope information, since its complete form is involved in correlation analysis. Thus, the noise stability of the correlogram cross-correlation method is expected to be as good as with the phase method, and as in the envelope evaluation methods no phase ambiguity should appear.

In Section II, a short description of the method is given; the results of a testing of the method by correlogram and noise simulation are given in the subsection "A" of Section II; in subsection "B", the results of an application of the method to measurements on smooth surface are presented. In this way, the subsection "A" describes mainly the influence of measurement noise whereas the consideration of subsection "B" concerns both the instrumental noise and the surface reflection variations.

II. Realization of Correlogram Correlation Method and Testing of Its Stability Against Noise.

The cross-correlation function has been used as the gauge of the correlogram packet position and the level of similarity. The employed normalized cross-correlation function is given by

$$K = \int_{-\infty}^{\infty} I(z) I_0(z+\tau)dz \Bigg/ \sqrt{\int_{-\infty}^{\infty} I^2(z)dz \int_{-\infty}^{\infty} I_0^{\,2}(z)dz}\,, \qquad (1)$$

where I is a measured pixel-correlogram, I_0 is the reference correlogram, z is the interferometer scan coordinate. Of course, the cross-correlation has been calculated on the digitalization net, originally with the step of interferometer frame distance Δz. In fact, the MATLAB function *xcov* has been employed to calculate K. The position of absolute maximum of K has been interpreted as the local height of surface relative to that of reference surface which produces the correlogram I_0. The value $K_{max} < 1$ (= maximum correlation coefficient) gives the confidence level for the current pixel.

Certainly, the scan discretization interval of interferometer Δz produces a too rough net: the surface has to be localized much more accurately. Therefore, an interpolation of intermediate points has been performed producing a net 10 times denser. In this study, a proper interpolation has been performed to keep the spectrum of the function unchanged by the interpolation. Specifically, digital Fourier transform of the original function is performed; the present harmonics are kept unchanged, but supplemented with harmonics of higher frequencies and zero amplitude; finally the reverse transformation produces the function on the dense net. It can be proven that such an interpolation of the correlograms followed by the calculation of their cross-correlation gives the same result as the primary calculation of cross-correlation on the rough net followed by the interpolation. The latter variant lowers computation costs, and being much more effective, has been used in present study. Further accuracy elevation is achieved by the parabolic interpolation on the three points near the maximum of K.

A. Simulation

A simulation has been carried out in order to obtain the surface height assessment at different noise levels. The correlograms have been simulated on a digitalization net z_i just as the harmonic modulated with the Gaussian envelope:

$$I_i = A\exp\left\{-\log(2)\left[(z_i - z_0)/W_\lambda\right]^2\right\}\times \cos\left[(2\pi/\lambda_0)(z_i - z_0)\right] + \sigma_{noise} rand(i), \qquad (2)$$

where A is an arbitrary amplitude; z_0 is the position of the correlogram maximum, W_λ is half-width of the correlogram; λ_0 is its main wave length, σ_{noise} is the noise dispersion, *rand* is the function producing normally-distributed random values with zero mean value and the unit dispersion. Thus, white noise has been used, not in complete correspondence with the distortion noise produced by surface inhomogeneities which reveal themselves mainly in additional phase shifts [5], but representing well the instrumental noise.

Figure 1, (a)-(c) shows how the noise of different level distorts the correlograms. The correlogram corruption grows from a slight disturbance at the relative level of 0.01 to a very substantial packet spoiling at the 0.1-level and to complete correlogram distraction at the level 0.3. Following values have been used for the simulation: Δz = 40 nm; λ_0 = 300 nm; $W_\lambda = 2\lambda_0$. For the presented correlogram correlation (CC) method, the correlogram without noise ((2), σ_{noise} = 0) has been used as reference correlogram.

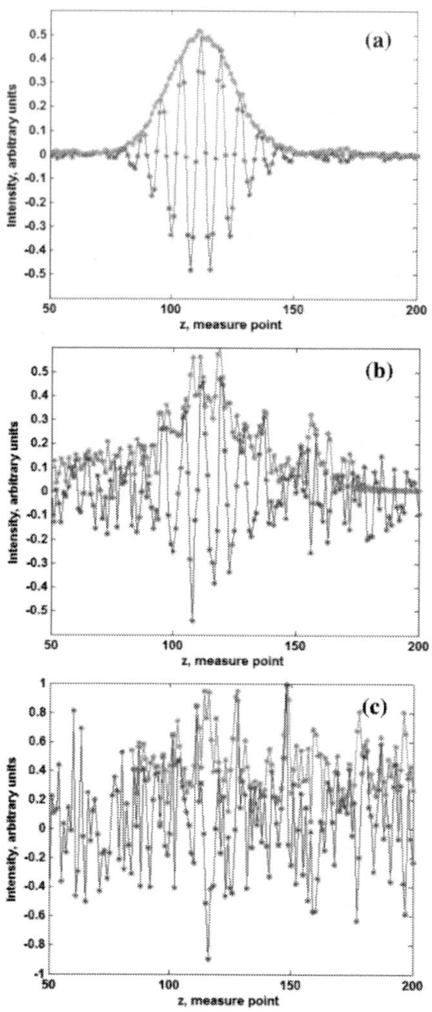

Figure 1. Correlogram corruption at different noise levels: (a) – noise dispersion σ_{noise} is 0.01 of the double correlogram amplitude; (b) σ_{noise} = 0.1; (c) σ_{noise} = 0.3. The red lines show the corresponding envelope.

For the comparison with the results of the correlogram correlation method, the signal envelopes have been calculated using the known formula of square summation of correlogram with its Hilbert transform [1]. The two most common methods to determine the correlogram position have been used: the parabolic approximation of half-height envelope followed by the determination of its maximum and the calculation of the half-height envelope centroid. No filtration of the envelope [5] has been applied relying on the averaging which is automatically provided by these two envelope position evaluation methods owing to usage of the complete half-height envelope.

As expected, the height determination has been exact at zero noise level by all the tested methods. The mean values of deviations of height estimation from the height z_0 specified in (2) have been calculated as the average over 1000 repetitions. These deviations appearing when using the correlogram correlation method and the two envelope evaluation methods are presented in Figure 2.

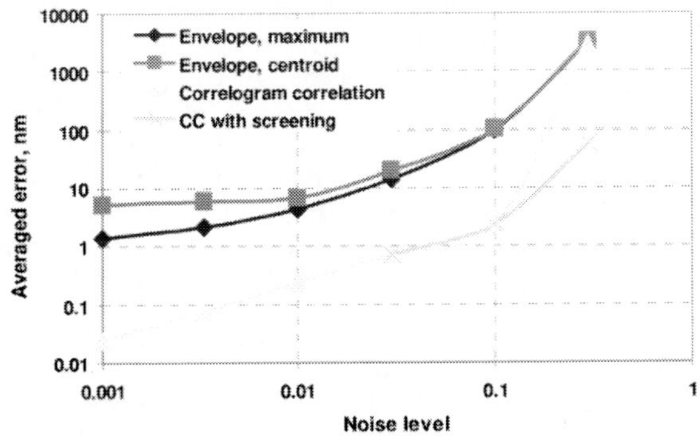

Figure 2. Mean deviation obtained by the two envelope methods and the correlogram correlation method.

Following conclusion can be drawn from the data of Figure 2:

a) For white noise, the deviation of the correlogram correlation method is approximately 1.5 orders of magnitude below the errors produced by the envelope methods.

b) In practice, the noise levels of about 0.1 are not rare. At these levels the errors of envelope methods are already inacceptable while that of CC are still just about 2-3 nm.

c) It is known that the deviations of the phase method are about 7 times smaller than that of envelope methods [1]. Here the inaccuracy of CC is still lower.

d) Within the CC method, the confidence estimation is readily available, and can be used to screen out the worst corrupted correlograms when calculating the mean value of surface height. Such a screening has been performed, and the result is given in Figure 2. The threshold maximal correlation coefficient with the reference correlogram here has been 0.5. All correlograms of lower correlation have been omitted. Moreover, the height deviation values produced by the remaining correlograms have been weighted for the averaging; the maximal correlation coefficients with the reference correlogram have been used to get the weights. Up to the noise level of 0.1, the error level is practically the same as that of pure CC, but at the noise level 0.3 the error is still moderate (56 nm) while other methods fail completely.

The deviations from unity of the averaged correlation coefficients obtained by the CC for the noise levels of 0.03, 0.10, 0.30, are correspondingly: 0.018, 0.16, 0.63. The values of coefficients at the lower noise level are practically indistinguishable from 1.

B. Measurement on a smooth surface

For a validation with experimental data, a measurement on polished Si wafer has been evaluated. The Mirau interferometer, Breitmeier Messtechnik GmbH, with the interferometer objective Nikon CF IC EPI of x10 magnification has been employed for this measurement. The frame area of the objective is 0.66x0.89 mm^2. The low camera resolution of 518x692 pixels has been chosen in order to keep data amounts reasonable. The diode light source has a spectrum energy distributed in the range of 490 - 740 nm. The sampling step size of 40 nm, minimal for the instrument, has been chosen. A typical correlogram is shown in Figure 3, on the top. On the bottom of the figure, the correlogram which has been chosen to be the reference one for the CC method is depicted. It has been just arbitrarily picked among the available correlagrams of the same data stack as one which seemingly contains low noise and form

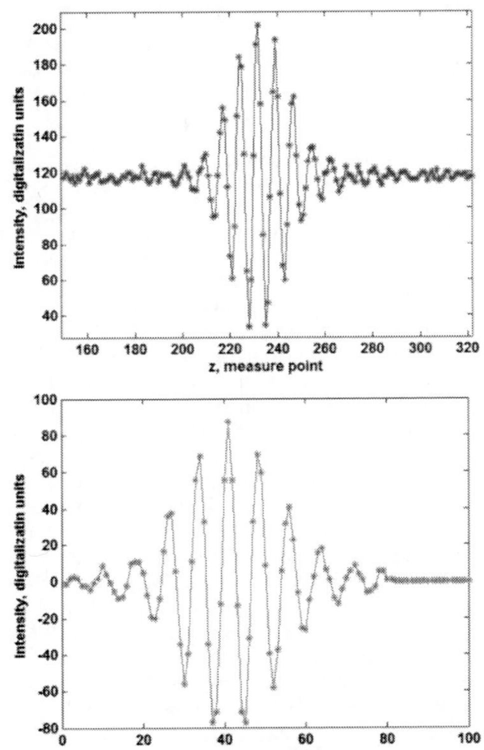

Figure 3. A typical correlogram measured on smooth surface (picture above) and the correlogram used as the reference correlogram (below).

distortions. The reference correlogram is already devoid of the mean level and slope and shortened in length, in order to exclude surplus noise. Comparing the correlogram pictures in Figure 3 with those of the simulation, the noise level can be roughly estimated to be about 0.02. The evaluated distributions of surface heights along a stretch of the optical field are illustrated in Figure 4.

The height dispersion provided by the envelope maximum estimation method is 5.6 nm, the dispertion provided by the envelope centroid method – 9.6 nm, and of the CC method it is 0.45 nm. Thus, the CC demonstrates an accuracy 12 times higher, than that of the envelope method. The dispersions found correspond well to the results of the simulation given in Figure 2, assuming the estimated noise level is in the vicinity of 0.02.

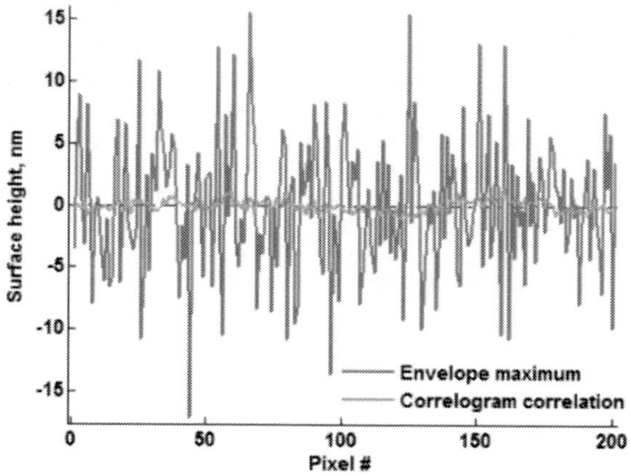

Figure 4. Surface heights obtained by envelope and correlogram correlation methods on a smooth Si surface along a line segment of the optical field.

The CC method is expected to have still higher superiority: its dispersion seemingly contains also a fraction of the real surface height variation. This part in the height dispersion by the envelope method is apparently negligible. Therefore, there is no correlation between the height profiles measured using both methods: their correlation coefficient amounts just to 0.08. Notice that the accuracy improvement by CC in relation to the envelope method again exceeds the accuracy gain commonly provided by the phase method as compared to the envelope method [1].

For a practical realization of the CC method, a reference correlogram is needed. Ideally, it should be measured on a smooth surface of the material in question and then properly averaged over a set of pixels. In this case, it contains also the particularities of surface reflection. Often it is sufficient to employ just one of the correlograms measured on the surface. Furthermore, because the form of a noiseless correlogram is mainly determined by the instrument itself, it is expected that an on mirror measured I_0 will work in the majority of situations. Thus, there is no problem to obtain the reference correlogram in the practice. Especially not in a standard industrial application, where many surfaces are routinely inspected and the same I_0 can be used unless the WLI needs a recalibration. A doubt could arise when thinking about using the CC method because of an allegedly high computation time for the cross-correlation function. But if done employing the very quick procedure of the fast Fourier transform (direct and reverse), it is, in fact, not time expansive. Moreover, the procedure can be further developed, say, resettled in the frequency domain in order to get a still quicker performance.

III. Conclusion and Future Work

The introduced correlogram correlation method uses the complete information contained in the correlogram and thus is supposed to have a noise immunity at least not lower, than that of the phase method. The noise immunity implies tolerance to both the measurement disturbances and imperfections of local surface reflection. At the same time, it is not supposed to exhibit a phase ambiguity. The first supposition is confirmed in the present study with the help of simulations and a measurement on a smooth surface: the accuracy of the CC method exceeds that of the envelope method by more than one order of magnitude. The confirmation of the absence of an ambiguity is a matter of further research, involving the evaluation of measurements on rough surfaces and possibly simulations.

It is demonstrated that the CC method can be used, when analyzing data with a noise level at which the employment of the envelope estimation methods is impossible.

Another advantage of the method is that it automatically provides a measure to be used for screening of inapt correlograms from further evaluations – the coefficient of correlation with a reference correlogram. This confidence parameter can be used for further surface structure evaluations. It is shown here that its application allows height evaluation even from very corrupted correlograms.

References

[1] P. de Groot, "Principles of interference microscopy for the measurement of surface topography," Advances in Optics and Photonics, vol. 7, 2015, pp. 1-65.

[2] P. de Groot, "Interference microscopy for surface structure analysis," in Handbook of Optical Metrology: Principles and Applications, T Yoshizawa, Ed., Boca Raton: CRC Press, 2015, pp. 797–809.

[3] T. Dresel, G. Häusler, and H. Venzke, "Three-dimensional sensing of rough surfaces by coherence radar," Appl. Opt., vol. 31, 1992, pp. 919–925.

[4] J. Schmit and A. G. Olszak, "Challenges in white-light phase-shifting interferometry," Proc. SPIE 4777 Interferometry XI: Techniques and Analysis, SPIE Press, June 2002, pp. 118–127, doi: 10.1117/12.472230.

[5] J. Seewig, T. Böttner, and D. Broschart, "Uncertainty of height information in coherence scanning interferometry," Proc. SPIE 8082, Optical Measurement Systems for Industrial Inspection VII, SPIE Press, May 2011, pp. V-1 - V-9, doi:10.1117/12.895006.

Crude Oil Detection using CMOS Image Sensor and UV LED

Sangwoo Oh, Moonjin Lee
Maritime Safety Research Division
Korea Research Institute of Ships and Ocean Engineering
Daejeon, Republic of Korea
swoh@kriso.re.kr, moonjin.lee@kriso.re.kr

Dongmin Seo, Kiyoung Ann, Sungkyu Seo†
Department of Electronics and Information Engineering
Korea University
Sejong, Republic of Korea
ehdals20907@korea.ac.kr, aky0902@korea.ac.kr, sseo@korea.ac.kr

***Abstract*—Crude oil detection in the sea is an important task for the prevention of oil spill and the oceanic environment management. To measure the crude oil which is dissolved in the seawater, a sensor based on the fluorescence spectroscopy is widely used, because it is made up of hydrocarbon compounds. However, most of these sensors use an ultraviolet mercury lamp, several optical filters, and the photomultiplier tube (PMT). These components make the sensing platform large and expensive. To address these issues, we have developed the fluorometer, which is composed of optical devices having cost effectiveness and compact size, such as complementary metal-oxide-semiconductor (CMOS) image sensor and ultraviolet (UV) light-emitting diode (LED). In this paper, we provide the sensing platform, the principal sensing mechanism and the test results, which were obtained by an experiment using two different crude oils. Through these results, we can show the sensing performance of our novel fluorometer for the detection of crude oil.**

Keywords-crude oil detection; fluorometer; in-situ sensor; CMOS image sensor; UV LEDs.

I. INTRODUCTION

Contamination evaluation of oil spilled in sea water is a critical step in the procedures of ocean recovery. To this end, a number of sensing systems have been developed to assess the degrees of the residual contaminants in the sea water [1][3][5][6][7]. Among those various sensing modalities, the fluorescence spectroscopy based system has been widely accepted because it can precisely quantify the concentration of total petroleum hydrocarbons (TPHs) which is a mixture of toxic chemicals originated from crude oil [2][4][8].

The main components of the fluorescence spectroscopy system are an ultraviolet (UV) light source, e.g., UV mercury lamp, the monochromator, multiple excitation/emission filters, and a photomultiplier tube (PMT) optical sensor. However, those key components of the fluorescence spectroscopy make the system often expensive and bulky, limiting the widespread use of the fluorescence sensing system especially for the sea water monitoring.

In this work, we introduce a compact and cost-effective fluorometer which is only composed of compact and low-cost optoelectronic components such as complementary metal-oxide-semiconductor (CMOS) image sensor, i.e., ~14 USD per chip, and UV light-emitting diode (LED), i.e., ~5 USD per chip.

In this paper, we will provide the design of our sensing platform, the principal sensing mechanism and the test results, which were obtained by an experiment using two different crude oils.

II. MATERIALS AND METHODS

To demonstrate the performance of this simple fluorometer, two different crude oils from Iraq and Russia were utilized. Figure 1 shows the schematic representation and experimental setup of our proposed compact and cost-effective fluorometer. The main characteristic of the proposed system is to employ the CMOS image sensor and UV LED for its sensor and light source. Since the CMOS image sensor has more than 5 mega pixels, corresponding to the same numbers of the sensors, variation of the fluorescence measurements was much smaller than that of the PMT, an expensive high-end single pixel photo-detector most widely accepted by oil spilled sea water detection systems commercially available.

III. RESULTS AND DISCUSSION

Figure 2 shows the oil detection performance of the proposed system. To determine the limit of detection (LOD) of the proposed system, each oil sample was diluted by hexane solutions ranging from 1,000 ppm to 100 ppb and the measurements were triplicated at each concentration. In Figure 2, the averaged pixel intensity at each concentration has been calculated to plot the sensorgram. Figure 3 shows the raw digital images of the fluorescence emission from the various concentrations of the crude oils, captured by the CMOS image sensor.

With this result, we can draw the dynamic detection range of the proposed sensing platform. In the case of Russian crude oil, it has a linear detection range from 1 ppm to 1000 ppm, whereas, in the case of Iraqi crude oil, the light intensity acquired by CMOS image sensor was saturated between 100 ppm and 1000 ppm. Thus, the dynamic detection range of that case is from 1 ppm to 100 ppm. Through these two experiments, we can see that the amount of TPHs in Iraqi crude oil is more than that in Russian crude oil.

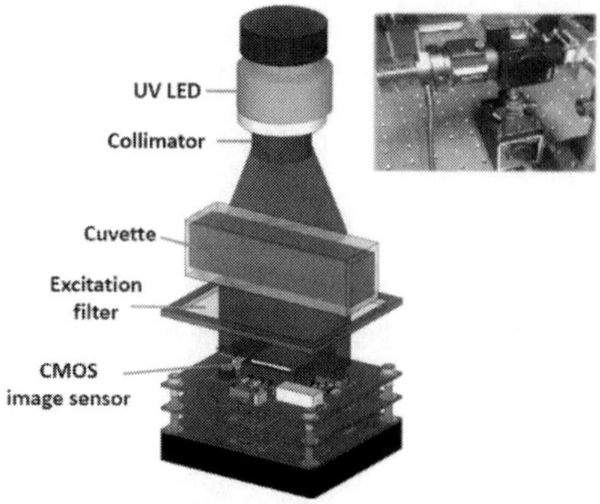

Figure 1. Schematic diagram and experimental setup of the proposed compact and cost-effective fluorometer.

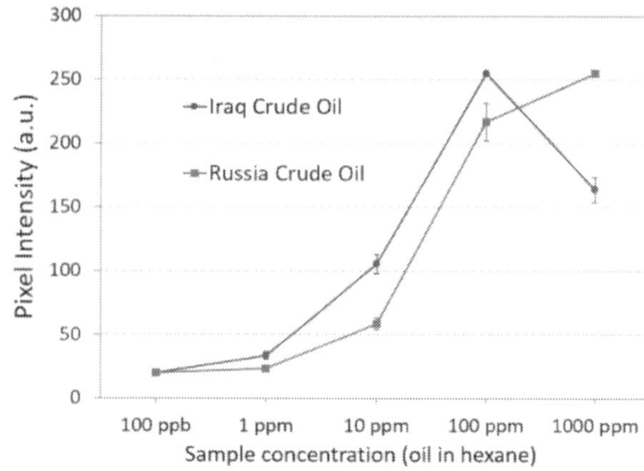

Figure 2. Fluorescence based oil detection results of the proposed system for crude oils from Iraq and Russia.

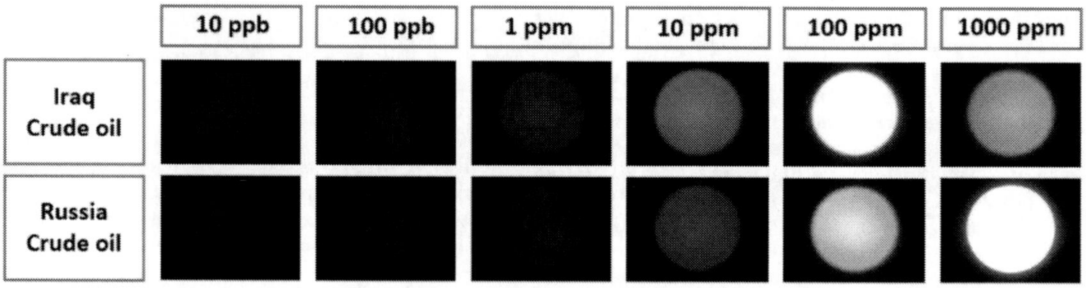

Figure 3. Raw CMOS images of the fluorescence emission from the various concentrations of the crude oils.

IV. Conclusions

In summary, a compact and cost-effective fluorometer using UV LED and CMOS image sensor for crude oil detection was proposed and demonstrated. According to the experimental results, the LOD of the proposed simple system was ranging from 1 ppm to 100 ppm or 1,000 ppm, which is comparable to that of a commercial fluorescence spectroscopy system, i.e., TD-500D (Turner Designs Hydrocarbon Instruments, USA). In this presentation, we will also discuss another experimental protocol that can push the LOD of the proposed system down to ~10 ppb.

Acknowledgment

This work was supported by the Korea Research Institute of Ships and Ocean Engineering (KRISO) Endowment-Grant (PES2240).

References

[1] A. MacLean, C. Moran, W. Johnstone, B. Culshaw, D. Marsh and P. Parker, "Detection of hydrocarbon fuel spills using a distributed fibre optic sensor," Sensors and Actuators A, vol. 109, pp. 60–67, 2003.

[2] C. Chase, S. Bibber and T. Muniz, "Development of a Non contact Oil Spill Detection System," Proceedings of MTS/IEEE Oceans, vol. 2, pp. 1352-1357, 2005.

[3] H. Denkilkian, A. Koulakezian, R. Ohannessian, M. Joujou, A. Chehab and I. Elhajj, "Wireless Sensor for Continuous Real-Time Oil Spill Thickness and Location Measurement," IEEE Transaction on Instrumentation and Measurement, vol. 58, pp. 4001-4011, 2009.

[4] S. Jocis, and A. Vuorenkoski, "Spectral Fluorescence Characteristics of Commercially Available Hydrocarbon Sensors," Proceedings of the National Conference on Undergraduate Research (NCUR), pp. 231-241, 2014.

[5] S. Oh, M. Lee and H. Choi, "Development of Hydrocarbon Oil Detection Sensor using the Swelling Property of Silicone Rubber," Journal of the Korean Society for Marine Environmental Engineering, vol. 14, pp. 280-286, 2011.

[6] S. Oh and M. Lee, "Oil Spill Detection Mechanism using Single-wavelength LED and CCD," Journal of the Korean Society for Marine Environmental Engineering, Vol. 15, pp. 323-329, 2012.

[7] S. Oh and M. Lee, "Oil Thickness Measurement by Light Absorption Analysis," Journal of the Korean Society for Marine Environment and Energy, Vol. 16, pp. 263-267, 2013.

[8] V. Malkov and D. Sievert, "Oil-in-Water Fluorescence Sensor in Wastewater and Other Industrial Applications," Power Plant Chemistry, vol. 12, pp. 144-154, 2010.

Response Time Investigation Based on GaAs Position Sensitive Detector

Tzu-Hsuan Huang, Meng-Chyi Wu
Institute of Electronics Engineering
National Tsing Hua University
Hsinchu, Taiwan
e-mail: s9863809@m98.nthu.edu.tw
e-mail: mcwu@ee.nthu.edu.tw
Chieh Lo
Graduate Institute of Electrical Engineering
National Taiwan University
Taipei, Taiwan
e-mail: a0937869023@gmail.com

Hao Lo
Interdisciplinary Program of Engineering
National Tsing Hua University
Hsinchu, Taiwan
e-mail: hao29147535@gmail.com
Wen-Shiung Lour
Department of Electrical Engineering
National Taiwan Ocean University
Keelung, Taiwan
e-mail: wslo@mail.ntou.edu.tw

Abstract—**This work reports on response times of a GaAs-based p-i-n Position-Sensitive Detector (PSD) operated in lateral and transverse photovoltaic modes. Visible light spots with wavelength values of 405, 532, and 638 nm were employed for measuring both static and dynamic properties of the proposed p-i-n PSD. The extracted sensitivity is 4.1 mV/mm for the 405 nm light with a power of 3 mW while it was 14.3 mV/mm for the 638 nm light. The measured nonlinearities were 1.0%~1.9%, 1.7%~2.25%, and 0.25%~1.25% for 405, 532, and 638 nm lights, respectively, with a power of 1 to 3 mW. Experimental results reveal that the shortest response time is available for the PSD tested with the 532 nm light.**

Keywords-GaAs HBT; p-i-n; photovoltaic; position sensitive detector; response time

I. INTRODUCTION

After finding of Lateral Photovoltaic Effect (LPE) [1], an important Position-Sensitive Detector (PSD) that has its output of Lateral Photovoltaic Voltage (LPV) changed linearly with light-spot position has been widely investigated by using various structures [2][8]. Effects of the LPE on Metal-Semiconductor (MS) structures have been reported to show PSD's sensitivities ranged from 12.4 to 28.8 mV/mm [2][4]. Currently, Si-based structures are preferred for low-cost infra-red PSDs. However, there has been little research about PSDs based on GaAs-based p-i-n structures [5][7] which are appropriate for visible-light positioning. In this work, a GaAs p-i-n structure being layer-compatible to the base-collector junction of an InGaP-GaAs Heterojunction Bipolar Transistor (HBT) was utilized to fabricate a visible-light PSD. Thus, it is possible to integrate a PSD with an HBT amplifier and hence to design a PSD circuit. In addition to wavelength and power dependences of sensing properties of the proposed GaAs p-i-n PSD, response times reflecting light-on and light-off were also addressed. Experiments and measurements about the proposed PSD are described in following section. In Section III, experimental results including key merits, such as sensitivity, linearity, and response time, are reported with theoretical discussion. Finally, conclusions are drawn.

II. EXPERIMENTS

Fig. 1 shows a cross-sectional view of the p-i-n structure used to fabricate a visible-light PSD. It was grown on a (100)-oriented semi-insulating GaAs substrate by a Metal-Organic Chemical Vapor Deposition (MOCVD) system and consisted of a n^+-GaAs layer (600 nm, $n^+=5\times10^{18}$ cm^{-3}), a n^--GaAs layer (600 nm, $n^-=1\times10^{16}$ cm^{-3}), and a p^+-GaAs layer (80 nm, $p^+=3\times10^{19}$ cm^{-3}) in sequence. Actually, it is layer-compatible with the base-collector-subcollector structure of a conventional InGaP-GaAs HBT. After defining an active region, AuGeNi was deposited as a common electrode (C) upon the exposed n^+-GaAs layer. Finally, AuZn was deposited to form two electrodes (A and B) upon the p^+-GaAs layer. A spacing between electrodes A and B is as long as 14 mm. Point O, the center between the electrodes A and B, is defined as origin of light-spot position (x=0). The light-spot position is positive (x>0) when the light spot is on the right side of point O. A voltage appearing between the electrodes A and B was measured as the LPV value while that between the electrodes A and C (or B and C) was measured as the Transverse Photovoltaic Voltage (TPV).

III. RESULTS AND DISCUSSION

Shown in Fig. 2(a) are the LPV values as a function of light-spot position for the p-i-n PSD tested with 405, 532, and 638 nm lights with a power of 3 mW. Common

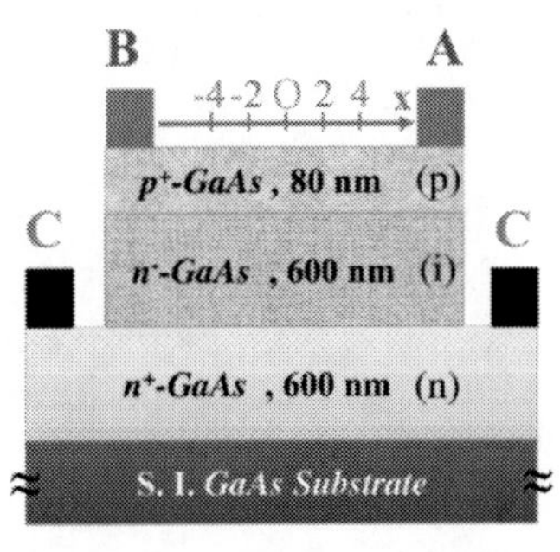

Figure 1. Cross-sectional view of a fabricated GaAs p-i-n PSD.

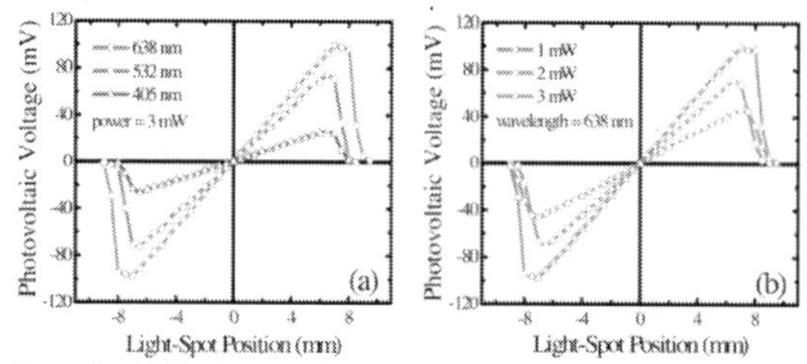

Figure 2. LPV values as a function of light-spot position for a PSD: (a) tested by 405, 532, and 638 nm lights with a power of 3 mW and (b) tested by a 638 nm light with a power of 1, 2, and 3 mW.

properties include: the LPV values are close to zero when the light spot is located at point O; if the light spot scans positively, LPV values also positively increase. On the contrary, they are negative when $x < 0$; maximum of the absolute LPV appears at $x \approx \pm 7$ mm; and moving the light spot beyond either the electrode A or the electrode B leads to abrupt decrease in the LPV. Two of the most important features associated with PSD's static sensing properties are sensitivity (S) and linearity. We find that the PSD tested by a 638 nm light has the highest S of 14.3 mV/mm as compared to those of 4.1 and 11.6 mV/mm by 405 and 532 nm lights. All nonlinearities obtained are below 2.5%, showing an excellent linear relationship with the light-spot position. Fig. 2(b) shows LPV values as a function of light-spot position for the p-i-n PSD tested by a 638 nm light with a power of 1, 2, and 3 mW. In addition to good linearity (> 98%), the sensitivity is enhanced from 6.7 mV/mm at 1 mW to 11.1 mV/mm at 2 mW and finally to 14.3 mV/mm at 3 mW. It is noticed that S is dependent on a number density of the initial electron-hole pairs. Thus, it is reasonable that (1) at the same power, the 405 nm light has the smallest S due to its least photons and (2) the larger power with more photons will lead to more initial electron-hole pairs. Experimental results are in good agreement with theoretical ones reported previously.

Fig. 3 shows wavelength dependence of response times of the GaAs p-i-n PSD in a lateral photovoltaic mode. The

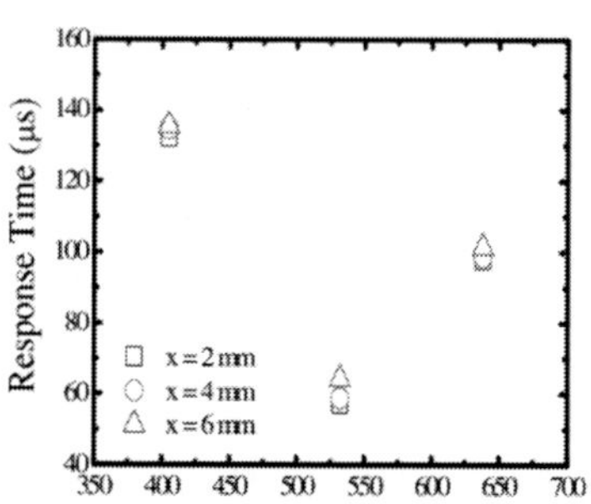

Figure 3. Wavelength dependence of response times of the PSD in a lateral photovoltaic mode.

parameter used is the light-spot position. It is found that the shortest response time is available for our PSD tested by a 532 nm light. Besides, we find that the light-spot position has no relevant effect on the response time. Thus, the swept time for holes and electrons reaching to p^+- and n^+-side layers, respectively, is considered to mainly determine the response time. When the 405 nm light spot is used, the swept time is dominated by electrons generated within the p^+- to i-GaAs region. On the contrary, it is dominated by holes generated in the deep i-GaAs region for the 638 nm light. Thus, a response time of 60 ± 4 μs for the 532 nm light is the shortest time as compared to those of 134 ± 2 and 99 ± 2 μs for the 405 and 638 nm lights. Although response times of TPV values are not shown here, comparisons to those of LPV ones will also be addressed in this presentation.

IV. CONCLUSIONS

GaAs-based p-i-n PSDs have been fabricated for visible-light positioning. A PSD tested by a 3 mW 638 nm light shows a sensitivity of 14.3 mV/mm, resulting in a sensitivity-distance product of ≈200 mV. Nonlinearities obtained from the present PSD are smaller than 2.5%. Response times of the LPV values are 99 ± 2, 60 ± 4, and 134 ± 2 μs when 638, 532, and 405 nm lights were used, respectively, that will be compared to those of TPV ones.

ACKNOWLEDGMENT

This work was financially supported by the Ministry of Science and Technology under contract no. MOST 104-2221-E-019-021-MY2.

REFERENCES

[1] J. T. Wallmark, "A New Semiconductor Photocell Using Lateral Photoeffect," Proc. IRE., vol. 45, 1957, pp. 474-483.

[2] C. Q. Yu, H. Wang, and Y. X. Xia, "Enhance Lateral Photovoltaic Effect in an Improved Oxide-Metal-Semiconductor Structure of TiO_2/Ti/Si," Appl. Phys. Lett., vol. 95, 2009, pp. 263506-1-263506-3.

[3] S. Liu, X. Xie, and H. Wang, "Lateral Photovoltaic Effect and Electron Transport Observed in Cr Nano-Film," Opt. Express, vol. 22, 2014, pp. 11627-11632.

[4] J. Henry and J. Livingstone, "Optimizing the Response of Schottky Barrier Position Sensitive Detectors," J. Phys. D: Appl. Phys., vol. 37, 2004, pp. 3180-3184.

[5] H. Águas, L. Pereira, D. Costa, E. Fortunato, and R. Martins, "Linearity and Sensitivity of MIS Position Sensitive Detectors," J. Mater. Sci., vol. 40, 2005, pp. 1377-1381.

[6] E. Fortunato and R. Martins, "Role of the Collecting Resistive Layer on the Static Characteristics of a 1D a-Si:H Thin Film Position Sensitive Detector," Rev. Sci. Instrum., vol. 67, 1996, pp. 2702-2707.

[7] E. Fortunato, G. Lavareda, R. Martins, F. Soares, and L. Fernandes, "Large-Area 1D Thin-Film Position-Sensitive Detector with High Detection Resolution," Sens. Actuator A-Phys., vol. 51, 1996, pp. 135-142.

[8] N. Tabatabaie, M. H. Meynadier, R. E. Nahory, J.P. Harbison, and L.T. Florez, "Large Lateral Photovoltaic Effect in Modulation-Doped AlGaAs/GaAs Heterostructures," Appl. Phys. Lett., vol. 55, 1989, pp. 792-794.

International Academy, Research, and Industry Association (IARIA)
412 Derby Way
Wilmington, DE 19810

ISBN 978-1-5108-2692-2

CURRAN ASSOCIATES INC.
proceedings
.com

Fourth International Conference on Cyber-Technologies and Cyber-Systems (CYBER 2019)

Held at NexTech 2019

Porto, Portugal
22 – 26 September 2019

IARIA